# SIMUL 2021

The Thirteenth International Conference on Advances in System Simulation

October 3 -7, 2021

Barcelona, Spain

**SIMUL 2021 Editors**

Frank Herrmann, OTH Regensburg, Germany

Manuela Popescu, IARA, USA/EU

Michel A. Audette, Old Dominion University - Norfolk, USA

**Printed from e-media with permission by:**

Curran Associates, Inc.
57 Morehouse Lane
Red Hook, NY 12571

**Some format issues inherent in the e-media version may also appear in this print version.**



Printed with permission by Curran Associates, Inc. (2023)

International Academy, Research, and Industry Association (IARIA)
412 Derby Way
Wilmington, DE 19810

Phone: (408) 893-6407
Fax: (408) 527-6351

petre@iaria.org

**Additional copies of this publication are available from:**

Curran Associates, Inc.
57 Morehouse Lane
Red Hook, NY 12571 USA
Phone: 845-758-0400
Fax: 845-758-2633
Email: curran@proceedings.com
Web: www.proceedings.com

## Table of Contents

# SIMUL 2021

# Forward

The Thirteenth International Conference on Advances in System Simulation (SIMUL 2021), held on October 3 - 7, 2021 in Barcelona, Spain, continued a series of events focusing on advances in simulation techniques and systems providing new simulation capabilities.

While different simulation events are already scheduled for years, SIMUL 2021 identified specific needs for ontology of models, mechanisms, and methodologies in order to make easy an appropriate tool selection. With the advent of Web Services and WEB 3.0 social simulation and human-in simulations bring new challenging situations along with more classical process simulations and distributed and parallel simulations. An update on the simulation tool considering these new simulation flavors was aimed at, too.

The conference provided a forum where researchers were able to present recent research results and new research problems and directions related to them. The conference sought contributions to stress-out large challenges in scale system simulation and advanced mechanisms and methodologies to deal with them. The accepted papers covered topics on social simulation, transport simulation, simulation tools and platforms, simulation methodologies and models, and distributed simulation.

We welcomed technical papers presenting research and practical results, position papers addressing the pros and cons of specific proposals, such as those being discussed in the standard forums or in industry consortiums, survey papers addressing the key problems and solutions on any of the above topics, short papers on work in progress, and panel proposals.

We take here the opportunity to warmly thank all the members of the SIMUL 2021 technical program committee as well as the numerous reviewers. The creation of such a broad and high quality conference program would not have been possible without their involvement. We also kindly thank all the authors that dedicated much of their time and efforts to contribute to the SIMUL 2021. We truly believe that thanks to all these efforts, the final conference program consists of top quality contributions.

This event could also not have been a reality without the support of many individuals, organizations and sponsors. We also gratefully thank the members of the SIMUL 2021 organizing committee for their help in handling the logistics and for their work that is making this professional meeting a success. We gratefully appreciate to the technical program committee co-chairs that contributed to identify the appropriate groups to submit contributions.

We hope the SIMUL 2021 was a successful international forum for the exchange of ideas and results between academia and industry and to promote further progress in simulation research.

**SIMUL 2021 Steering Committee**

Carlo Simon, Hochschule Worms - University of Applied Sciences, Germany
Frank Herrmann, University of Applied Sciences Regensburg, Germany

**SIMUL 2021 Publicity Chair**
José Miguel Jiménez, Universitat Politecnica de Valencia, Spain
Lorena Parra, Universitat Politecnica de Valencia, Spain

# SIMUL 2021

## Committee

### SIMUL 2021 Steering Committee

Carlo Simon, Hochschule Worms - University of Applied Sciences, Germany
Frank Herrmann, University of Applied Sciences Regensburg, Germany

### SIMUL 2021 Publicity Chair

José Miguel Jiménez, Universitat Politecnica de Valencia, Spain
Lorena Parra, Universitat Politecnica de Valencia, Spain

### SIMUL 2021 Technical Program Committee

Ahmed M. Abdulkhaleq, SARAS Technology/ University of Bradford, UK
Petra Ahrweiler, Johannes Gutenberg University Mainz, Germany
Chrissanthi Angeli, University of West Attica, Greece
Alfonso Ariza Quintana, University of Malaga, Spain
Natesh B. Arunachalam, The University of Texas at Austin, USA
Michel Audette, Old Dominion University, USA
Ana Paula Barbosa Póvoa, Universidade de Lisboa, Portugal
Marek Bauer, Politechnika Krakowska, Poland
John Betts, Monash University, Australia
Patrick Biemelt, University of Paderborn, Germany
Maria Julia Blas, Instituto de Desarrollo y Diseño (INGAR) | UTN-CONICET, Argentina
Paolo Bocciarelli, University of Rome Tor Vergata, Italy
Jalil Boudjadar, Aarhus University, Denmark
Christos Bouras, University of Patras, Greece
Lelio Campanile, Università degli Studi della Campania "L. Vanvitelli", Italy
Enrique Chirivella, University of the West of Scotland, UK
Franco Cicirelli, ICAR-CNR, Italy
Fábio Coelho, CEG-IST Instituto Superior Técnico | University of Lisbon, Portugal
Federico Concone, University of Palermo, Italy
Duilio Curcio, University of Calabria, Italy
Andrea D'Ambrogio, University of Roma TorVergata, Italy
Gabriele D'Angelo, University of Bologna, Italy
Luis Antonio de Santa-Eulalia, Business School | Université de Sherbrooke, Canada
Daniel Delahaye, ENAC LAB, Toulouse, France
Alexander Ditter, Friedrich-Alexander University Erlangen-Nürnberg (FAU), Germany
Anatoli Djanatliev, University of Erlangen-Nuremberg, Germany
Julie Dugdale, University Grenoble Alps, France
Mahmoud Elbattah, Université de Picardie Jules Verne, France
Sabeur Elkosantini, University of Carthage, Tunisia

Amr Eltawil, School of Innovative Design Engineering / Japan University of Science and Technology, Egypt
Diego Encinas, Informatics Research Institute LIDI - CIC - UNLP, Argentina
Fouad Erchiqui, Université du Québec en Abitibi-Témiscamingue, Canada
Zuhal Erden, Atilim University, Turkey
Mourad Fakhfakh, University of Sfax, Tunisia
Javier Faulin, Public University of Navarra, Spain
Sibylle Fröschle, University of Oldenburg, Germany
José Manuel Galán, Universidad de Burgos, Spain
Simon Genser, Virtual Vehicle Research GmbH, Graz, Austria
Katja Gilly de la Sierra-Llamazares, Universidad Miguel Hernández, Spain
Apostolos Gkamas, University Ecclesiastical Academy of Vella of Ioannina, Greece
Denis Gracanin, Virginia Tech, USA
Antoni Grau, Technical University of Catalonia, Barcelona, Spain
Andrew Greasley, Aston University, Birmingham, UK
Feng Gu, The College of Staten Island, CUNY, USA
Stefan Haag, University of Applied Sciences Worms, Germany
Magdalena Hańderek, Cracow University of Technology, Poland
Thomas Hanne, University of Applied Sciences and Arts Northwestern Switzerland / Institute for Information Systems, Switzerland
Eduardo Hargreaves, Petrobras, Brazil
Frank Herrmann, University of Applied Sciences Regensburg, Germany
Tsan-sheng Hsu, Institute of Information Science | Academia Sinica, Taiwan
Xiaolin Hu, Georgia State University, Atlanta, USA
Marc-Philippe Huget, Polytech Annecy-Chambery-LISTIC | University of Savoie, France
Mauro Iacono, Università degli Studi della Campania "Luigi Vanvitelli", Italy
Lisa Jackson, Loughborough University, UK
Maria João Viamonte, Institute of Engineering (ISEP) - Polytechnic Institute of Porto (IPP), Portugal
Matthieu Jonckheere, Universidad de Buenos Aires, Argentina
Peter Kemper, William & Mary, USA
Roozbeh Ketabi, University of Florida, USA
Youngjae Kim, Sogang University, Seoul, Korea
Hildegarde Koen, Council for Scientific and Industrial Research (CSIR), South Africa
Dmitry G. Korzun, Petrozavodsk State University | Institute of Mathematics and Information Technology, Russia
Anatoly Kurkovsky, Georgia Gwinnett College - Greater Atlanta University System of Georgia, USA
Massimo La Scala, Politecnico di Bari, Italy
Ettore Lanzarone, University of Bergamo, Italy
Herman Le Roux, Council for Scientific and Industrial Research (CSIR), South Africa
Fedor Lehocki, Slovak University of Technology in Bratislava, Slovakia
Laurent Lemarchand, University of Brest (UBO), France
Huiye Liu, Georgia Institute of Technology, USA
António M. Lopes, University of Porto, Portugal
Fabian Lorig, Malmö University | IoTaP, Sweden
Emilio Luque, University Autonoma of Barcelona (UAB), Spain
Johannes Lüthi, University of Applied Sciences - Fachhochschule Kufstein Tirol, Austria
Imran Mahmood, Brunel University London, UK
Fahad Maqbool, University of Sargodha, Pakistan

Eda Marchetti, ISTI-CNR, Pisa, Italy
Romolo Marotta, University of Rome "Sapienza", Italy
Niels Martin, Research Foundation Flanders (FWO) - Hasselt University, Belgium
Omar Masmali, The University of Texas, El Paso, USA
Michele Mastroianni, Università degli Studi della Campania "Luigi Vanvitelli", Italy
Andrea Matta, Politecnico di Milano, Italy
Roger McHaney, Kansas State University, USA
Nuno Melão, Polytechnic Institute of Viseu, Portugal
Roderick Melnik, MS2Discovery Interdisciplinary Research Institute | Wilfrid *Laurier* University, Canada
Adel Mhamdi, RWTH Aachen University, Germany
Owen Molloy, National University of Ireland, Galway, Ireland
Sébastien Monnet, LISTIC / Savoie Mont Blanc University, France
Federico Montori, University of Bologna, Italy
Jérôme Morio, ONERA (the French Aerospace Lab), France
Paulo Moura Oliveira, Universidade de Trás-os-Montes e Alto Douro (UTAD) / INESC-TEC Porto, Portugal
Nazmun Nahar, University of Jyvaskyla, Finland
Luis Gustavo Nardin, National College of Ireland, Ireland
Alessandro Pellegrini, Sapienza University of Rome, Italy
Tomas Potuzak, University of West Bohemia, Czech Republic
Dipak Pudasaini, Tribhuvan University, Nepal / Ryerson University, Canada
Francesco Quaglia, University of Rome Tor Vergata, Italy
Patrick Reinwald, University of Klagenfurt, Austria
Marco Remondino, University of Genova, Italy
Dupas Rémy, University of Bordeaux, France
Oscar Rodríguez Polo, University of Alcala, Spain
Kristin Yvonne Rozier, Iowa State University, USA
Julio Sahuquillo, Universitat Politecnica de Valencia, Spain
Ignacio Sanchez-Navarro, University of the West of Scotland, UK
Nandakishore Santhi, Los Alamos National Laboratory, USA
Victorino Sanz, ETSI Informática | UNED, Spain
Paulo Jorge Sequeira Goncalves, Instituto Politecnico de Castelo Branco, Portugal
Li Shi, Snap Inc., USA
Alireza Shojaei, Mississippi State University, USA
Patrick Siarry, Université Paris-Est Créteil (UPEC), France
Carlo Simon, Hochschule Worms - University of Applied Sciences, Germany
Leszek Siwik, AGH-UST University of Science and Technology, Krakow, Poland
Yuri N. Skiba, Universidad Nacional Autónoma de México, Mexico
Azeddien M. Sllame, University of Tripoli, Libya
Fabian Speicher, RWTH Aachen University, Germany
Giandomenico Spezzano, CNR-ICAR, Italy
Sven Spieckermann, SimPlan AG, Germany
Renata Spolon Lobato, UNESP - São Paulo State University, Brazil
Mu-Chun Su, National Central University, Taiwan
Grażyna Suchacka, University of Opole, Poland
Violet R. Syrotiuk, Arizona State University, USA
János Száz, Corvinus University, Hungary
Ingo J. Timm, Trier University, Germany
Klaus G. Troitzsch, Universität Koblenz-Landau, Germany

**Copyright Information**

# Toward an Interactive, Patient-specific, VR-based Obstetrics Simulator

Special track along with Thirteenth International Conference on Advances in System Simulation
October 03 - 07, 2021 - Barcelona, Spain

MA Audette, M Scerbo, L Tabacu,
Computational Modeling & Simulation Engineering, Psychology, and Mathematics & Statistics,
Old Dominion Univ, Norfolk, VA
{maudette, mscerbo, ltabacu}@odu.edu

AZ Abuhamad,
Obstetrics and Gynecology,
Eastern Virginia Medical School,
Norfolk, VA, USA,
abuhamaz@evms.edu

J Conery,
Radiology, Children's Hospital of The King's Daughters, Norfolk, VA, USA,
john.conery@chkd.org

C MacGowan,
Research MRI Core, Hospital for Sick Children, Toronto, Canada,
christopher.macgowan@sickkids.ca

VS Arikatla,
Kitware Inc, Carrboro, NC, USA
sreekanth.arikatla@kitware.com

RS Kakar,
Health Sciences,
Oakland University,
kakar@oakland.edu

M Parente, D Oliveira, RN Jorge,
Mechanical Engineering, Univ. Porto,
Porto, Portugal
{mparente, doliveira, rnatal}@fe.up.pt,

*Abstract*—**This paper presents a nascent collaborative effort to achieve a Virtual Reality (VR)-based, real-time, haptics-driven patient-specific obstetrics simulator. The high-level architecture and preliminary results are presented here; the latter are based on offline birthing simulation developed by team in conjunction with open-source visualization tools. The cornerstones of this simulator will be high-fidelity generic offline birthing simulation, an anatomy-to-image nonrigid registration pipeline exploiting fetal MRI, the open-source interactive medical simulation toolkit IMSTK augmented by high-throughput deep learning-based soft tissue deformation, open-source musculoskeletal dynamics simulation platform SimTk for representing fetal motion.**

***Keywords- birthing simulation; obstetrics; virtual reality; bimanual haptics.***

## I. INTRODUCTION

There is *high variability in obstetrics performance* within the United States, as well as *an egregious underperformance of the US* against developed countries and *of developing countries* against developed countries, all of which suggest that the current approach to obstetrics training could be improved. Specifically, Glance et al found that 13 percent of the four million US women giving birth annually experience one or more major complications [1]; they used multivariable logistic regression to assess the variation in obstetric complication outcomes across US hospitals (based on 750,000+ deliveries) and found an alarming disparity between high and low-performing hospitals. Lower-graded hospitals had *complication rates double those of better hospitals in vaginal deliveries*, at 22.55% and 10.42% respectively, as well as *five times those of better hospitals in cesarian deliveries*: 20.93% vs. 4.37%. In addition, a comparison study *found the US to be the worst-performing in maternal mortality in a group of 11 developed countries* [2]: in 2018, there were 17 maternal deaths for every 100,000 births in the US, a ratio more than double that of most other high-income countries [2]. Furthermore, *obstetric complications in developing countries are also distressing*, with 530,000 women worldwide dying annually and 95% of these deaths occurring in Africa and Asia [3].

An important risk factor in labor is *shoulder dystocia*, depicted in Figure 1, a difficulty in the delivery of the fetal shoulders after delivery of the head. Shoulder dystocia is characterized by approximate incidences of 1% for babies under 4 kg [4][5], 5% for babies between 4 and 4.5 kg, and 10% for babies heavier than 4.5 kg [5] respectively. Neonatal complications include death and cerebral palsy due to loss of oxygen to the baby's brain, from the dystocia itself, and brachial plexus injury complications such as Klumpke's paralysis and Erb's palsy caused by the action of the obstetrician. Maternal complications include vaginal and cervical lacerations as well as post-partum hemorrhage [6].

The current emphasis in simulation-based obstetrics training is on *mannequins* [7][8], as seen in Figure 2. These trainers are limited by the *paucity of clinically relevant complication*

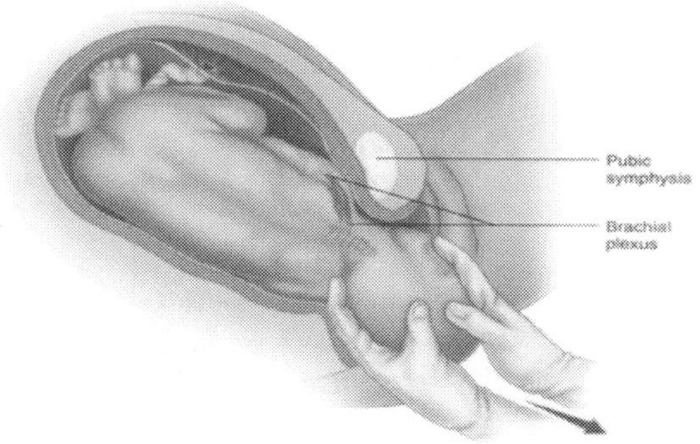


Figure 1. Shoulder dystocia. Mechanism of shoulder dystocia – retention of the anterior shoulder of the neonate above the pubic symphysis. Reproduced with permission from Obgynkey.com [10].

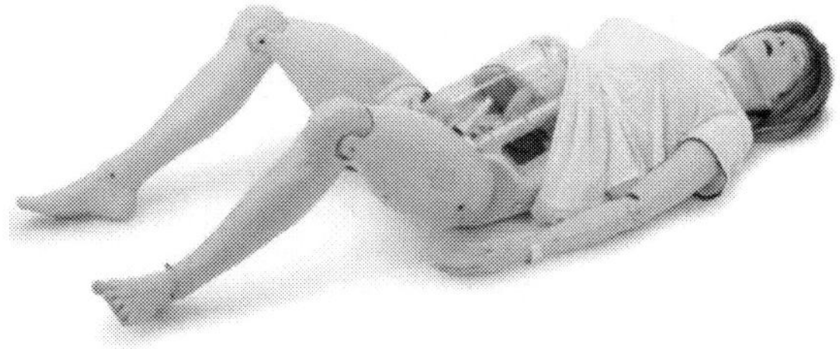

Figure 2. Birthing mannequin simulators. Leardal's SimMom reproduced with permission [7].

*models*, their *inextensibility to specific patients*, and *prohibitive costs precluding third world applications*. A seasoned obstetrician confronted with shoulder dystocia can draw from a set of appropriate corrective procedure such as the McRoberts maneuver, suprapubic pressure, delivery of the posterior arm, and a corkscrew maneuver, just to name four. Mannequins often enable only one correct procedure that can be invoked, which restricts the instruction. In contrast, VR simulation flexibly accommodates an inventory of solutions, predictive of the expert's approach. *The consideration of competing treatment options is readily supported in a suitable VR setting; it is infeasible on a mannequin*. VR simulation can be *personalized by warping multi-surface anatomies to a fetal medical image*, enabling practice on a patient of particular interest. One can retroactively warp a set of fetal and maternal anatomies to MRI datasets associated with complications [9], accounting for risk factors like maternal obesity and twin or premature pregnancies, *systematically preparing obstetricians for worse-case scenarios*. Fast-forwarding a few years, this project could potentiate midwives worldwide, namely in developing countries, through a suite of complication-embedding patient-specific simulations running on a tablet or cellphone, and personalized simulation of their patient of interest, imaged with a portable ultrasound scanner [11], feasible via *Anatomy Transfer (AT)* [12].

## II. MATERIALS AND METHODS

### A. *Building on Medical Ontologies and on a Descriptive Offline Birthing Simulation*

This paper will sketch a high-level picture of the nascent project and preliminary design objectives, while also alluding to resources available either through project members or open-source tools. The starting point for this planned interactive simulation is the work of Parente, Natal Jorge et al., [13], the offline birthing simulation represented in Figure 3, along with the biomechanical finite elements simulation of the maternal pelvic floor, during a simulated birth. The main components of the simulation are intended with practical clinical requirements in mind. In general, we advocate designing a medical simulation based on rigorous constraints founded on medical ontologies [14], which describe the intervention of the physician in terms of a sequence of discrete steps, within an algorithmic workflow. To this end, it is useful to exploit as a starting point a typical

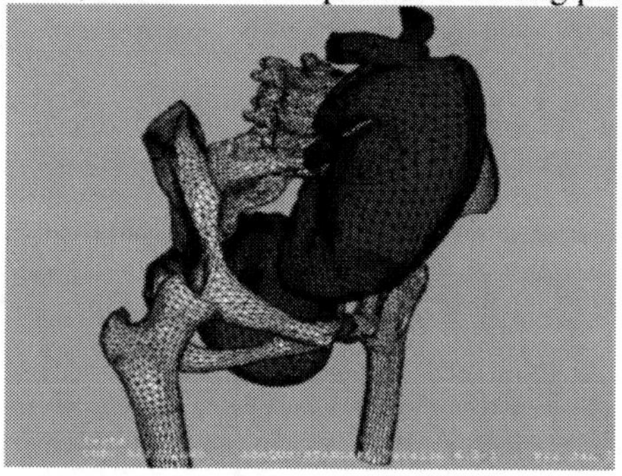

Figure 3. Prior results of Parente, Natal Jorge et al. [13] demonstrating birthing simulation under occipito-anterior neonate position and the biomechanical impact of these scenarios as pelvic floor stresses.

workflow that governs the actions of an obstetrician confronted with a shoulder dystocia case. In general, to make the simulator extensible in the future as well as representative of other complications, such as perinatal asphyxia uterine rupture, or excessive bleeding, this ontological workflow has to embed the typical response, such as found in a textbook or paper, to common complications. As shoulder dystocia is concerned, the workflow depicted in Figure 4 is considered typical [15] and can serve as a basis for our clinical requirements. In particular, the clinical response emphasizes the gradual application of maneuvers of increasing severity from the repositioning of the mother and suprapubic pressure, to the Corkscrew Maneuver, to Posterior Arm Delivery, to the Zavelli Maneuver and cesarean delivery, just to mention these few. The decision to transition to the next option, more drastic than the current technique, depends on the response of the fetus, as to whether or not it advances successfully. The implication of such a flexible, responsive approach on the part of the expert obstetrician, as a desirable training outcome, argues in favor of a VR-based interactive simulation, given the relative inflexibility of mannequin-based training, which tends to emphasize a single solution or maneuver. Our expert clinician (AA) argues that the Posterior Arm Delivery and corkscrew maneuvers must be emphasized in particular by the simulation.

### B. Preliminary Work in Predictive Simulation

In the prior work of Parente, Natal Jorge et al., [13][16], the fetus was considered has having a high stiffness, being controlled trough the usage of four control points. The fetus movements were optimized and defined in order to present the birth canal, the smallest possible fetus head diameter. After this manual optimization process, the final childbirth simulation was obtained, which included the deformation of the pelvic floor muscles. For these muscles a hyperelastic, transversely isotropic, constitutive model was used, which included the muscles fibers. Therefore, although being an advancement in term of childbirth simulation, this initial work contained several limitations and shortcomings, that we intend to improve upon.

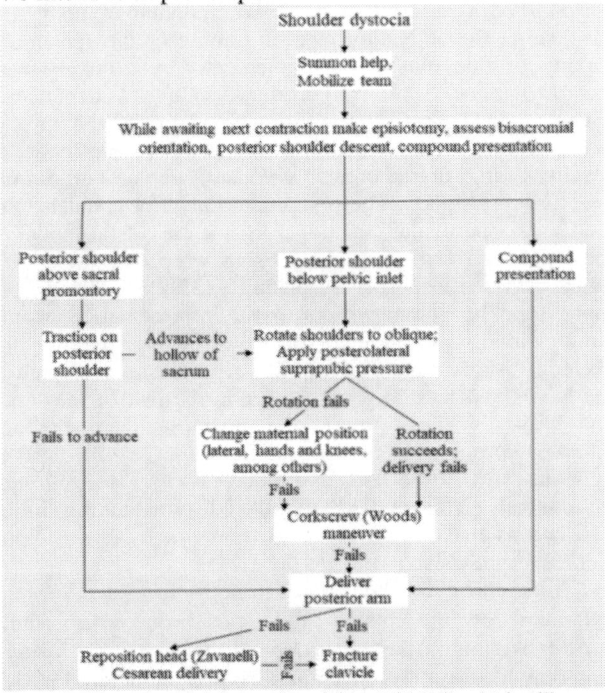


Figure 4. Obstetrics workflow, adapted from Hill [15], which will serve as ontological basis for the simulation.

### C. Overview of Design Approach and High-level Features

One of the immediate implications of the clinical requirements alluded to above is that the anatomical model of the fetus used in the VR simulation must be as faithful as possible to the biomechanics of the live neonate, in manner consistent with a real-time application, in order to enable some of the maneuvers encoded in this ontological workflow depicted in Figure 4. In particular, while the finite elements-based birthing simulation of Parente [13] corresponds to the state-of-the-art so far, despite a simple four-segment fetal model with folded arms as in Figure 3b, the interactive obstetrics simulator underway must have a fetus with fully animated limbs, especially biomechanically faithful arms, to enable training on the Posterior Arm Delivery. If the ObGyn resident were to reach for the posterior arm and manage to grip it, the arm must be movable and responsive to the intended maneuver. The anatomy of the fetus must also realistically respond to being nudged outward by the arm. As a result, it is apparent that one of the cornerstones of the simulator must consist of a dynamic piecewise-rigid simulation of the skeleton, in the style of Stanford University's OpenSim [18], with a haptic response provided by a pair of gloves such as Haptx [19].

Moreover, the original simulation of Parente took several hours to run [16], while we must strive to use every efficiency possible in order to achieve a real-time response, i.e. at least several times a second, with interpolative tricks to maintain visual and haptic feedback at suitable rates (30Hz, 200 Hz). This real-time requirement leads to several

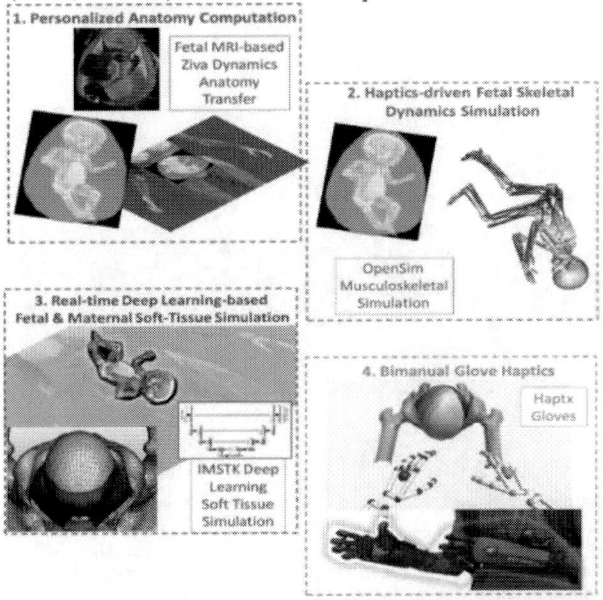


Figure 5. Main design features. From top to bottom: 1) patient-specific anatomical modeling, via Ziva Dynamics Anatomy Transfer, emphasizing a whole-body fetal model and a portion of the maternal anatomy; 2) haptics-driven fetal skeletal dynamics based on OpenSim [17]; 3) Deep Learning-based simulation of soft-tissue biomechanics based on IMSTK; 4) bimanual haptics via Haptx gloves.

important design choices, which are made explicit in Figure 5, which describes the high-level architecture and design features. First, this real-time consideration justifies a highly efficient approach to skeletal mechanics of the fetus, based on OpenSim [18]. One of the main challenges to this project will be to integrate OpenSim musculoskeletal simulation with haptics, even simple 6 degree-of-freedom haptics, to which end we will first integrate OpenSim with a real-time biomechanics simulation platform that also supports haptics: the Interactive Medical Simulation Toolkit (IMSTK) [20]. Second, and perhaps more critical given the likely soft-tissue bottleneck, real-time constraints presuppose that we adopt the fastest soft-tissue simulation techniques available, in conjunction with IMSTK, without which this project would be an exercise in futility. To this end, we will be exploiting a Deep Learning approach to soft tissue finite elements analysis, in the manner pioneered by Mendizabal, Cotin et al recently [21], which runs on a comparable real-time biomechanics platform SOFA. They were able to demonstrate *two orders of magnitude acceleration over comparable finite elements engines*: a volumetric beam simulation that would typically iterate at 0.5 second on SOFA ran at roughly at 4 ms based on Mendizabal's deep neural network implementation. While the SOFA deep learning FE synthesis is not yet available in open source, there are several DL-based finite elements simulation implementations available on GitHub, which could serve as a template for IMSTK's DL approach to finite elements analysis, whose implementation details are also published, such as Ononenko's MLFEM in 3D [22][23] and Xu's

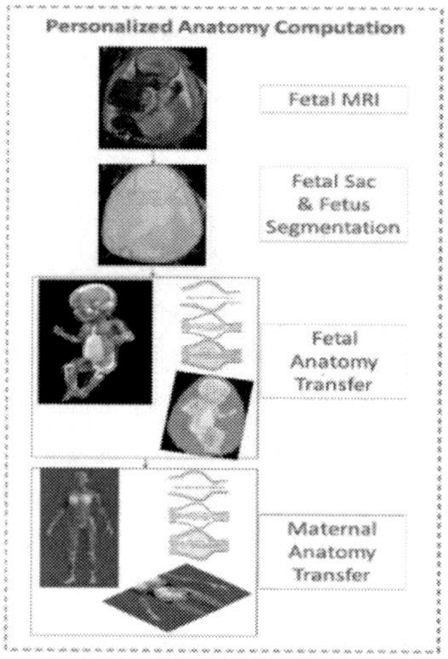


Figure 6. High-level approach to personalized anatomy computation: beginning with a fetal MRI volume, segment the fetal sac and the fetus, using a DL approach, trained with a deformable surface model [27] [28], use Anatomy Transfer to identify the fetus' skin surface, register bones in a piecewise-affine manner, warp soft tissues to the layer between bone and skin, and proceed likewise with maternal anatomy visible in the MRI.

NNFEM in 2D [24][25]. Briefly, the Mendizabal method, termed U-Mesh, and the competing techniques also cited here all apply a U-Net architecture [26] to estimating deformations from a mesh coinciding with the elastic solid of interest, based on training achieved by finite elements simulations. The original U-Mesh is a parameterized function that accepts a $\{3 \times n_x \times n_y \times n_z\}$ force tensor $\mathbf{f}$ as input and produces a displacement tensor $\mathbf{u}$ of the same size as output. Training data for U-Mesh are generated by solving a discretized *boundary value problem* (BVP) with the FE method. U-Mesh computations ran over 100 times faster than comparable FE simulations also designed for interactive processing, typically under 0.01 seconds, with graphical processor unit hardware [21]. The difference with this application, compared to any other DL elastic response simulation that preceded it, is that the fetal soft-tissue "envelope" must track the piecewise-rigid motion of the limbs: the estimation of the elastic tissue response would be intractable without first modeling the skeletal piecewise-rigid transform, which justifies the use of OpenSim. Ideally a detailed representation of muscles of the fetus and their activation should serve as the basis for the DL training. However, it may in fact be computationally onerous to model every muscle in such a detailed manner; an alternate solution may lie in an anatomically terse soft tissue layer, based on thick shell elements, which wraps over the bone scaffold and tracks the motion of the skeleton, in a manner first proposed by Parente.

### D. *Anatomical modeling and musculoskeletal simulation*

A detailed approach to modeling the musculoskeletal anatomy and its corresponding function could involve the warping of a descriptive model of the human body and associating the activation of each muscle with a tensing or flexing of that muscle, as implemented respectively with Ziva Dynamics' Anatomy Transfer technique, as depicted in Figures 6 and 7, and Muscle Firing simulation [29]. Our plan is to purchase an anatomist-drawn musculoskeletal model of a baby, from a digital content company such as TurboSquid or CGHero [30][31]. The first author has prior contacts with CGHero in particular, such as a ligamentoskeletal model of the spine and torso, which is being warped to target CT images for scoliosis surgery planning [32][33]. A naïve but more quickly computed soft-tissue representation would simply involve a simple soft-tissue layer covering the skeleton, whose thickness would vary anatomically: thin at the hands and feet, slightly thicker in the rest of the limbs and head, thickness around the torso. Such an approach could be computed as a distance map from the MRI-derived bone anatomy of the fetus and modeled with a collection of thick shell elements. IMSTK would produce the initial simulations that would serve to train the DL-based finite elements synthesis.

In addition to the above strategy for modeling the dynamics of the bones and soft tissue, the actual personalization of the fetal model will require some form of Anatomy Transfer (AT) technique, based on the original AT pioneered by Dicko et al., [12], and implemented by Ziva Dynamics, as shown in Figure 7.

The AT technique consists of an image analysis pipeline that uses as inputs a multi-surface musculoskeletal atlas and a putative skin surface of the subject, erodes the contained volume to model a fat layer, then applies a piecewise-affine registration followed by a relatively stiff elastic transformation to map a skeletal model within that inner layer, followed by an adjustment of the bone model based on a constrained, shape-preserving constrained registration and a final soft-tissue interpolation to scale and position the soft-tissue (muscle) layer within the fat layer.

This technique will be refined further over time based on two research tangents: i) accuracy improvements based on multi-surface deformable models developed by the author, which will imbed shape and pose statistics derived from fetal MRI and expert correction, and ii) surface mesh-based neural network-mediated automation, founded on a platform such as MeshCNN [35], which will obviate user supervision for the AT approach.

### *E. OpenSim-based Musculoskeletal Simulation*

Stanford's OpenSim is the leading open-source dynamic musculoskeletal simulation platform (Figure 8). An OpenSim Model is a codified description of a musculoskeletal system and its dynamics, and represents a topological graph of interconnected components [36]. Each component represents a self-contained module (biological structure, mechatronic device, etc.) comprising the Model, and contributes to building the computational system. The computational system consists of two parts: (1) the system of equations ("System"), which includes constant physical

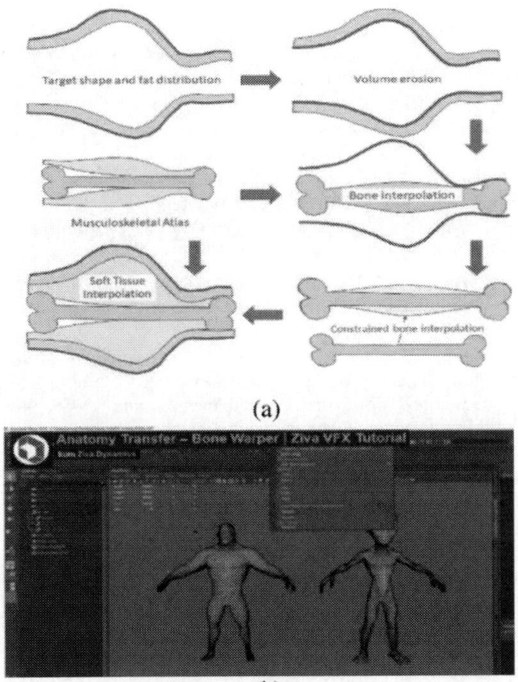


Figure 7. Anatomy Transfer. (a) High-level representation of the AT image analysis pipeline, adapted by the first author from Dicko [12]. (b) AT software available commercially from Ziva Dynamics [34].

parameters (mass, dimensions, etc.); and (2) the State, which includes all variables in the System that vary over time (e.g. joint angles). The developer designs an OpenSim Model that represents the physical system; OpenSim constructs the computational system of differential and algebraic equations that describe Model dynamics. This infrastructure will enable us to simulate the piecewise-rigid motion of the fetal and maternal skeletons, which will then determine deformations undergone by their respective soft tissues.

### *F. Virtual Reality-based Viewing and Bimanual Kinematics Integration with Leap Motion*

Virtual Reality-based viewing and integration with bimanual kinematics tracking based on Leap Motion were recently proposed in a thesis at University of Porto (M.P). This VR application leverages the generic anatomy of the mother's pelvis and the fetal anatomy developed by Parente, Natal Jorge and their collaborators. It is described next.

## III. Results and Discussion

The current VR application emphasizes surface rendering of the boundaries of the fetal and maternal finite elements model, based on a series of multi-surface snapshots, or static visualization models, obtained from the finite elements volumetric simulation, in conjunction with the Unity engine and a suitable colormap for visualizing biomechanical

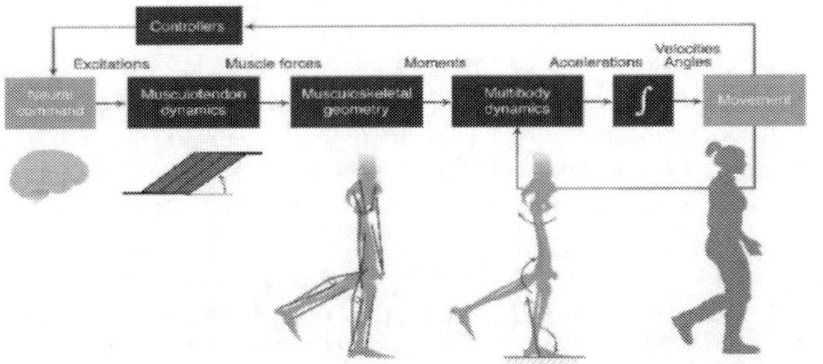


Figure 8. Musculoskeletal (MS) simulation in OpenSim [36]. Movement arises from an orchestration of the neural, muscular, skeletal, and sensory systems [36][37]. (Reproduced from PLOS One, with CCBY License.)

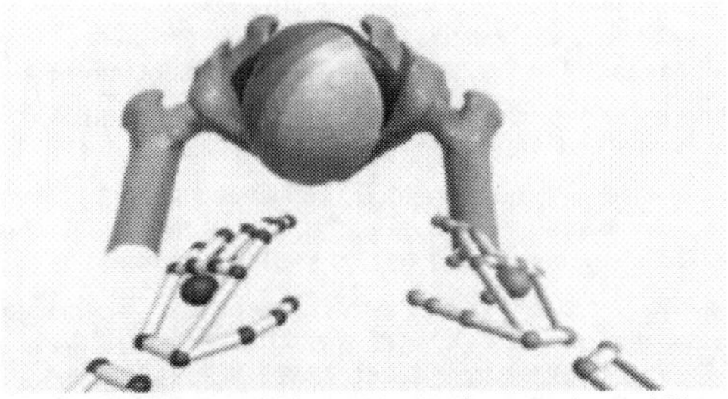

Figure 9. VR and bimanual kinematics implementations of Pinto [4], which will serve as template for the bimanual haptics-driven implementation on IMSTK. Real-time bimanual kinematics in the same 3D workspace as the fetus and mother's anatomy, tracked through Leap Motion's range-sensing analysis [38].

quantities such as stress magnitude [39]. This group also recently developed a template for our future bimanual simulation, based on Leap Motion tracking of the users hands, as shown in Figure 9 [38][39]. Obviously, the LeapMotion only keys on kinematics but does not imbed force feedback, which will be a requirement that is provided by the Haptx gloves, which will be supported in our final implementation [38]. IMSTK supports Unity-based 3D graphics as well as a variety of haptic devices [20].

## IV. Conclusions and Future Work

This paper centered on the nascent development of an interactive, patient-specific obstetrics simulator, based on substantial clinical justification. The foundation of this effort is the work of the Porto-based senior author's on predictive birthing simulation, featuring generic models of the fetus and of the mother. A second cornerstone that now makes this project feasible is the advent of deep learning-based approaches to simulating biomechanical finite elements, some of which is publicly available on GitHub. In addition, leveraging leading simulation toolkits, namely IMSTK and OpenSim, also is essential to achieving success. The bulk of the future work will center on the challenge of this integration between skeletal motion and soft-tissue layers surrounding this motion. Lastly, the application of a medical image analysis pipeline for personalizing these anatomical models, including the use of Ziva Dynamics' Anatomy Transfer software, as well as tools like SLICER and Insight Toolkit for medical image analysis, is also essential to achieving clinical relevance. The advantage of proceeding this way, while determining the requirements of the simulation based on medical ontologies, is that worst-case scenarios can be effectively synthesized, by artificially worsening cases of shoulder dystocia (increasing the size of the fetus' head for example) or making the umbilical cord take an inopportune path. Downstream of this simulation implementation, it will also be feasible to exploit portable ultrasound scanners, while potentiating the work of midwives in countries with limited access to obstetricians.

## References


[1] Glance LG, Dick AW, Glantz JC, Wissler RN, Qian F, Marroquin BM, Mukamel DB, Kellermann AL. Rates of major obstetrical complications vary almost fivefold among US hospitals. 2014 Aug, Health Aff (Millwood)., pp. 33(8):1330-6. doi: 10.1377/hlthaff.2013.1359. PMI.

[2] Roosa Tikkanen et al. Maternal Mortality and Maternity Care in the United States Compared to 10 Other Developed Countries, Commonwealth Fund, , 2020, https://doi.org/10.26099/411v-9255.

[3] Organization, World Health. The world health report 2005—make every mother and child count,". Geneva: Tech. Rep., WHO, , 2005.

[4] Ouzounian JG. Shoulder Dystocia: Incidence and Risk Factors. . Clin Obstet Gynecol. , 2016 Dec 8, Vols. 59(4):791-794. doi: 10.1097/GRF.0000000000000227. PMID: 27662540.

[5] Menticoglou S., Shoulder dystocia: incidence, mechanisms, and management strategies. Int J Womens Health. , 2018, Vols. 10:723-732. Published 2018 Nov 9. doi:10.2147/IJWH.S175088.

[6] Dajani NK, Magann EF. Complications of shoulder dystocia. 2014 Jun, Semin Perinatol. , pp. 38(4):201-4. doi: 10.1053/j.semperi.2014.04.005. PMID: 24863025.

[7] Leardal. Obstetric Solution SimMom® and MamaBirthie8. [Online] https://laerdal.com/us/products/simulation-training/obstetrics-pediatrics/obstetric-solution-simmom-and-mamabirthie/.

[8] Gaumard Inc. Meet Victoria, Model S2200. [Online] www.gaumard.com/s2200-victoria-childbirth-simulator#intro.

[9] Naeye RL., Maternal age, obstetric complications, and the outcome of pregnancy. Obstet Gynecol., 1983 Feb, Vols. 61(2):210-6.

[10] Obgynkey. Shoulder Dystocia - 3.1 Definition, Incidence and Main Risk Factors. [Online] https://obgynkey.com/shoulder-dystocia-6/.

[11] Butterfly, . Butterfly iQ+. [Online] store.butterflynetwork.com/us/en/product/butterfly-iq/pro/.

[12] Dicko AH, Liu T, Gilles B, Kavan L, Faure F, Palombi O, Cani MP,. Anatomy Transfer., ACM Transaction on Graphics 32(6) [Proceedings of SIGGRAPH Asia]. , 2013.

[13] Parente MP, Jorge RM, Mascarenhas T, Fernandes AA, Martins JA. The influence of an occipito-posterior malposition on the biomechanical behavior of the pelvic floor, 2009 May, Eur J Obstet Gynecol Reprod Biol. , pp. 144 Suppl 1:S166-9. doi: 10.1016/j.ejogrb.2009.

[14] Tapp A, Audette M, "Surgical GPS" proof of concept for scoliosis surgery. San Diego, CA, USA : Proceedings of Spring Simulation Conference , Article 58, 1–12., 2020.

[15] Hill MG, Cohen WR., Shoulder dystocia: prediction and management., Womens Health (Lond)., 2016, Vols. 12(2):251-61. doi: 10.2217/whe.15.103. Epub 2016 Feb 22.

[16] Parente MP, Jorge RM, Mascarenhas T, Fernandes AA, Martins JA. Deformation of the pelvic floor muscles during a vaginal delivery, Int Urogynecol J Pelvic Floor Dysfunct. , 2008 Jan, Vols. 19(1):65-71. doi: 10.1007/s00192-007-0388-7.

[17] Dixit NN, McFarland DC, Fisher MB, Cole JH, Saul KR., Integrated iterative musculoskeletal modeling predicts bone morphology following brachial plexus birth injury (BPBI), J Biomech. 103:109658. doi: 10.1016/j.jbiomech.2020.109658. , 2020 Apr 16.

[18] SimTk OpenSim. [Online] simtk.org/projects/opensim.

[19] Haptx . HAPTX GLOVES DK2 . True-contact haptics for VR + robotics. [Online] https://haptx.com/.

[20] Arikantla S, et al. Interactive Medical Simulation Toolkit. [Online] https://www.imstk.org/.

[21] Mendizabal A, Márquez-Neila P, Cotin S,., Simulation of hyperelastic materials in real-time using deep learning. 2020, Medical Image Analysis, Vols. Volume 59, doi.org/10.1016/j.media.2019.101569.

[22] Kononenko O, Kononenko I., Machine Learning and Finite Element Method for Physical Systems Modeling. arXiv:1801.07337 2018.

[23] Kononenko O, . oleksiyskononenko/mlfem. [Online] https://github.com/oleksiyskononenko/mlfem.

[24] Xu K, . kailaix/NNFEM Github. [Online] https://github.com/kailaix/NNFEM.jl.

[25] Xu K, Huang DZ, Darve E. Learning Constitutive Relations using Symmetric Positive Definite Neural Networks, arXiv, 2020, Vol. 2004.

[26] Ronneberger O, Fischer P, Brox T. U-Net: Convolutional Networks for Biomedical Image Segmentation, 2015. Medical Image Computing and Computer-Assisted Intervention, LNCS, Vol.9351: 234--241, .

[27] Audette M, Delingette H, Fuchs A, Astley O, Chinzei K, A Topologically Faithful, Tissue-guided, Spatially Varying Meshing Strategy for Computing Patient-specific Head Models for Endoscopic Pituitary Surgery Simulation, Int. J. Comput. Vision , August 1999, Vols. 32, 2 , 111-146. DOI: doi.org/10.1023/A:1008157432188.

[28] Haq R, Schmid J, Borgie R, Cates J, Audette MA. Deformable Multi-surface Segmentation of the Spine for Orthopedic Surgery Planning and Simulation, 2019, SPIE J. Medical Imaging, pp. 10 (1), 45-54.

[29] Ziva VFX 1.9 - ZIVA MUSCLES & FIRING. Ziva Dynamics Inc, . https://zivadynamics.com/resources/automatic-muscle-firing.

[30] CGHero. Fast, Flexible, and Cost Effective Art Production. [Online] https://cghero.com/.

[31] TurboSquid. 3D Models for Professionals. [Online] https://www.turbosquid.com/.

[32] Tapp A, Payer C, Schmid J, Bennett J, Audette MA. Automatic Generation and Novel Validation of PatientSpecific, Soft-Tissue Inclusive Spine Models from CT, Strasbourg, France, 2021. Medical Image Computing and Computer Assisted Intervention MICCAI CLIP.

[33] Audette MA, Schmid J, Goodmurphy C, Polanco M, Bawab, Tapp A, St-Clair HS Towards a Deformable Multi-surface Approach to Ligamentous Spine Models for Predictive Simulation-Based Scoliosis

Surgery Planning, Zheng G., Belavy D., Cai Y., Li S. (eds) Computational Methods and Clinical Applications for Spine Imaging. Lecture Notes in Computer Science, vol 11397. Springer, Cham. https://doi.org/10.1007/978-3-030-13736-6_8, 2018.

[34] Ziva Dynamics Inc,. Ziva VFX 1.9 ANATOMY TRANSFER . [Online] https://zivadynamics.com/resources/anatomy-transfer.

[35] Hanocka R, Hertz A, Fish N, Giryes R, Fleishman S, Cohen-Or D,. MeshCNN: A Network with an Edge, ACM Trans. Graph. 38, 4, Article 90 (July 2019), 12 pages. DOI:https://doi.org/10.1145/3306346.3322959, 2019.

[36] Seth A, Hicks JL, Uchida TK, Habib A, Dembia CL, et al. OpenSim: Simulating musculoskeletal dynamics and neuromuscular control to study human and animal movement, 2018, PLOS Computational Biology , Vol. 14(7): e1006223. https://doi.org/10.1371/journal.pcbi.1006223.

[37] Delp SL, Anderson FC, Arnold AS, Loan P, Habib A, John CT, Guendelman E, Thelen DG, OpenSim: open-source software to create and analyze dynamic simulations of movement, IEEE Trans Biomed Eng., 2007 Nov, Vols. 54(11):1940-50

[38] Ultraleap. Digital worlds that feel human. [Online] https://www.ultraleap.com/.

[39] Pinto SLA. Aplicação de Técnicas de Realidade Virtual na Simulação do Parto. s.l. : University of Porto, 2017.

# In Silico Investigation of Cardiac Arrhythmia Susceptibility in Long QT Phenotype

Anthony Owusu-Mensah
Biomedical Engineering
Old Dominion University (ODU)
Norfolk, USA
email: aowus003@odu.edu

Vicky Lam
Biomedical Engineering
Old Dominion University (ODU)
Norfolk, USA
email: vlam009@odu.edu

Bright Tsevi
Department of Engineering
Norfolk State University (NSU)
Norfolk, USA
email: b.tsevi@spartans.nsu.edu

Michel Audette
Computational Modeling and Simulation Engineering
Old Dominion University (ODU)
Norfolk, USA
email: maudette@odu.edu

Makarand Deo
Department of Engineering
Norfolk State University (NSU)
Norfolk, USA
email: mdeo@nsu.edu

*Abstract*— **Long QT Syndrome (LQTS) is associated with cardiac arrhythmia and sudden cardiac death. The Long QT Type 2 (LQT2) phenotype, which accounts for 35–40 % of all LQTS patients, is caused by mutations in HERG gene. The mechanisms of arrhythmia in presence of LQT2 conditions are not fully understood. We utilized anatomically and electrophysiologically realistic numerical simulations to elucidate the mechanisms of arrhythmia initiation in presence of blockade in rapid component of delayed rectifier potassium current, $I_{Kr}$. We utilized a 3D finite element model of rabbit ventricles integrated with His-purkinje network to simulate whole heart response to LQT2 conditions. We observed that the loss of $I_{Kr}$ function produced more severe phenotype in cardiac Purkinje cells than that in ventricular myocytes. Our simulations also revealed that arrhythmia susceptibility is increased when there is a loss of $I_{Kr}$ functionality. Our multi-scale computer modeling results provide useful insights into the potential mechanisms of arrhythmia in LQT2 conditions.**

***Keywords-Long QT Syndrome(LQTS); Cardiac modeling; Arrhythmia; Reentry;Purkinje fibers.***

## I. INTRODUCTION

The Long QT syndrome (LQTS) is an acquired or congenital cardiac electrical disorder characterized by the prolongation of the QT interval on an ECG, which is associated with life-threatening ventricular arrhythmias and sudden cardiac death [1]–[3]. Gene mutations in KCNQ1 (the gene that encodes slow delayed rectifier potassium current, IKs), HERG (the gene that encodes rapid delayed rectifier potassium current, $I_{Kr}$), and SCN5A (the gene that encodes fast inward sodium current, $I_{Na}$) are responsible for LQT1, LQT2, and LQT3 respectively, which account for 95% of the congenital LQTS in patients [3]–[5]. In LQT2, mutations in HERG cause partial or complete blockade of $I_{Kr}$ which delays the repolarization process causing action potential (AP) prolongation and subsequent prolonged QT interval in ECG. A myriad of $I_{Kr}$-blocking drugs, such as E-4031 (benzenesulfonamide), dofetilide or D-sotalol, may also lead to drug-induced LQTS [2]. Arrhythmia occurrence has been well documented in LQT2 patients, but exact mechanisms are still poorly understood.

Numerical biophysical models with high fidelity can offer the missing mechanistic link between experimental or clinical findings and their therapeutic implications. Fortunately, very advanced biophysical computer models, numerical techniques and computing facilities are available today to conduct realistic "numerical experiments". We have used detailed computer modeling to study the functional effects of various cardiac mutations [6]–[8] as well as to investigate complex arrhythmia mechanisms [9][10]. Iyer et al. used computer models of Purkinje Cell (PC) and Ventricular Myocyte (VM) to study alterations in channel functions in different LQT phenotypes and concluded that the His-Purkinje system (PS) may represent an important therapeutic target for heritable channelopathies [11].

Seemann et al. [12] used a heterogeneous and anisotropic three-dimensional computational model of the human ventricles to study LQT1, LQT2, and LQT3. Recently, patient-specific numerical models of LQTS using human induced pluripotent stem cell derived cardiomyocytes (hiPSC-CMs) have been used to investigate the loss of repolarizing currents on AP abnormalities [3][13][14]. The high incidence of LQT2 compared to other LQTS types except for LQT1 [15] and the significant consideration of the blockade of HERG channels in the developmental process for new drugs makes it more imperative to have a complete understanding of the mechanisms of LQT2 [16].

In this paper, we present a multiscale computer modeling approach to investigate the effects of complete or partial $I_{Kr}$ blockade at single cell and 3D ventricular anatomy levels in rabbit heart. The effects of $I_{Kr}$ block on AP morphology in two cell types: ventricular myocytes (VM) and cardiac Purkinje cells (PCs), and implications on reentry initiation in ventricles were studied systematically.

This paper is composed of four main sections. In section 1, which is the introduction, gives an overview of LQTS. A literature review on how LQTS has been studied both in simulation and experimentation. It then follows up with a justification for studying LQT2 syndrome and the approach we used for the studies. Section 2 describes how we performed single cell biophysical and 3D anatomical simulations respectively. We further explained how reentry was initiated in the 3D anatomical model. The results section follows section 2, and it gives an account of the observations from our simulations. In section 3(discussion), we discussed our results and compared them to our findings in literature. The last section(conclusion) provides a summary of our work and the outcomes likely to result from it.

## II. METHODS

### A. *Single cell Biophysical Simulations*

Single cell AP simulations were performed using rabbit VM biophysical model by Mahajan et al. [17] and rabbit PC model by Aslanidi et al. [18]. Both models were paced at 500 ms basic cycle length (BCL) for 50 sec to attain steady state before they were used in simulations. $I_{Kr}$ was blocked from 0% (Control) to 100% (complete blockade) by applying corresponding scaling to the maximum conductance of $I_{Kr}$ and its effect on AP durations at 50% and 90% repolarization ($APD_{50}$ and $APD_{90}$, respectively) were studied in both tissue types.

### B. *3D Anatomical Simulations*

The 3D simulations were performed in a rabbit ventricular anatomical model. The model consists of a finite element tetrahedral mesh, based on the San Diego rabbit heart [19], consisting of 547,680 myocardial nodes (862,515 nodes including surrounding bath and cavities), with an average internodal spacing of 250 μm (see Figure 1). LV and RV stand for are left ventricle and right ventricle, respectively.

The PS comprised of a branching network of one-dimensional cubic Hermite elements. PS nodes were separated by discrete gap junctions that were modeled as fixed resistances. The purkinje-myocardial junctions (PMJs) were modeled as resistive junctions as described in [20]. The electrical activity in the tissue was modeled by bidomain

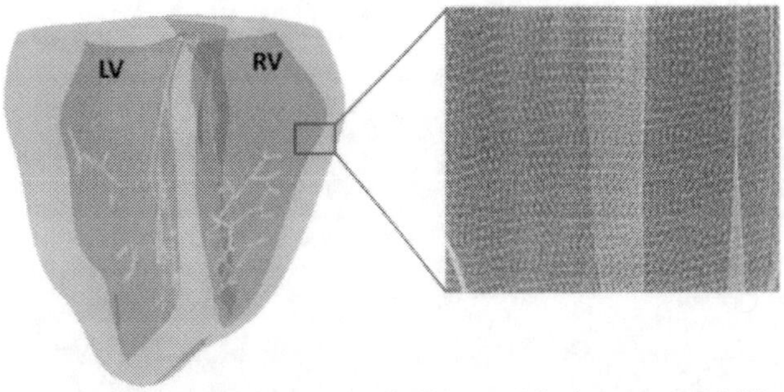


Figure 1. 3D computational mesh of rabbit ventricles integrated with PS (green color) used in our study. The inset shows the mesh discretization.

equations as described elsewhere [10][20]. The intracellular, $\Phi_i$ and extracellular, $\Phi_e$ potentials are related through the transmembrane current density, $I_m$ by the equations:

$$\nabla.(\bar{\sigma}_i + \bar{\sigma}_e)\nabla\Phi_e = -\nabla.\bar{\sigma}_i\nabla V_m - I_e \quad (1)$$

$$\nabla.\bar{\sigma}_i\nabla V_m = -\nabla.\bar{\sigma}_i\nabla\Phi_e + \beta I_m \quad (2)$$

$$I_m = C_m\frac{\partial V_m}{\partial t} + I_{ion}(V_m, v) - I_{trans} \quad (3)$$

, where $\bar{\sigma}_i$ and $\bar{\sigma}_e$ are the intracellular and extracellular conductivity tensors respectively, $\beta$ is the surface-to-volume ratio of the cardiac cells, $I_{trans}$ is the transmembrane current density stimulus as delivered by the intracellular electrode, $I_e$ is the extracellular stimulus current density, $C_m$ is the membrane capacitance per unit area, $V_m$ is the transmembrane voltage which is defined as $\Phi_i - \Phi_e$ and $I_{ion}$ is the current density flowing through the membrane ionic channels which depends on the transmembrane voltage and several other variables v [28].

The membrane biophysics of ventricular myocardium (V) was simulated by Mahajan et. al. model [17] whereas that of Purkinje network was simulated by Aslanidi et al. model [18].

To simulate sinus rhythm activity, stimulus was applied to the top nodes of His bundle with BCL of 500 ms for at least 5 sec before any simulation protocol was applied. To ascertain the cardiac activity in the presence of LQT2 phenotype, maximum conductance of $I_{Kr}$ in both V and PS was reduced by a percentage (25% block, 50% block and 100% block). Pseudo ECGs were generated by extrapolating the extracellular potentials to approximate limb locations for leads I, II and III.

### C. *Reentry Induction Protocol*

Reentry was simulated by S1-S2 protocol for Control and 100% $I_{Kr}$ block in V and PS. The myocardial conductivity in the model was reduced by 50% to slow the conduction and accommodate reentry wavelength in the tissue. Both models were paced at His with BCL of 500 ms for 5 sec to simulate sinus rhythm (S1). Then an ectopic stimulus (S2 stimulus) was delivered to a quarter region of myocytes on the right ventricle. The S1-S2 duration was varied between 200-300ms

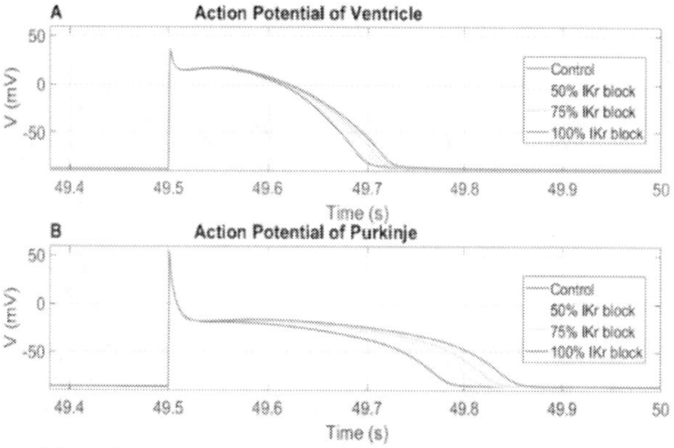


Figure 2. Action Potential Morphology. A: AP of ventricular myocyte for control, 50%, 75% and 100% $I_{Kr}$ block. B: AP of the purkinje cell for control, 50%, 75% and 100% $I_{Kr}$ block.

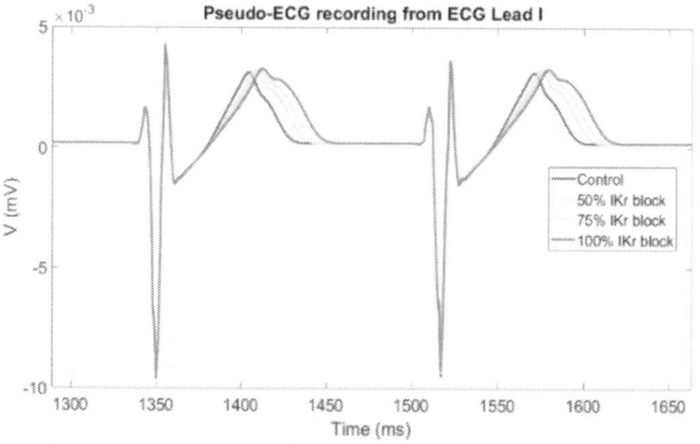


Figure 3. Lead I Pseudo ECG recording for Control,50%,75%, and 100% $I_{Kr}$ block during sinus rhythm.

in the steps of 10 ms to determine a window of vulnerability to reentry initiation. The S1-S2 duration was varied in steps of 1-5ms within the window of vulnerability to allow fine-grain control of the timing at which reentry occurs. The reentrant activations were classified as tachycardia if they were sustained beyond 500 ms duration.

The 3D simulations were performed using Cardiac Arrhythmia Research Package (CARP), an in-silico cardiac simulator [21]. Single cell simulations were performed using bench utility in OpenCARP simulator [21]. All simulations were performed on High Performance Computing (HPC) facilities of Old Dominion University (ODU) using 40 computing nodes and 2GB of physical memory per node.

## III. RESULTS

### A. *Ventricular myocyte and Purkinje cell action potential*

Figures 2A and B show the rabbit AP for both the VM and PC from the single cell simulations with varying $I_{Kr}$ block ranging from 0% (Control)to 100% (complete blockade). Both the VM and PC APs exhibited the characteristic spike and dome morphology. In VM, the $APD_{90}$ was prolonged by 13% as compared to the Control when $I_{Kr}$ was completely blocked (192 ms in Control vs. 216 ms in 100% block). The effect of $I_{Kr}$ block in PC was more severe in which the $APD_{90}$ was prolonged by 26% when $I_{Kr}$ was blocked completely

TABLE 1. $APD_{90}$ AND PERCENTAGE PROLONGATION FOR 0%, 50%, 75% AND 100% $I_{KR}$ BLOCK IN VENTRICULAR MYOCYTE (VM) AND PURKINJE CELL (PC) MODELS.

| $I_{Kr}$ block | VM | | PC | |
|---|---|---|---|---|
| | *$APD_{90}$ (ms)* | *% Prolongation* | *$APD_{90}$ (ms)* | *% Prolongation* |
| 0% (Control) | 192 | 0 | 267 | 0 |
| 50% | 203 | 6 | 299 | 12 |
| 75% | 209 | 9 | 317 | 19 |
| 100% | 216 | 13 | 336 | 26 |

(267 ms in Control vs. 336 ms in 100% block). Table 1 lists the percent prolongation in $APD_{90}$ for various extents of $I_{Kr}$ block in VM and PC models.

### B. *Pseudo-ECG Recordings During Sinus Rythm*

Pseudo-ECGs for the primary three leads (I, II and III) were derived during sinus rhythm for Control and $I_{Kr}$ block models. Figure 3 shows Lead I ECGs during sinus rhythm with aligned QRS for comparison. The QT prolongation was evident when $I_{Kr}$ was blocked, and the extent of QT prolongation increased with the extent of $I_{Kr}$ blockade.The QT duration measured was 94ms, 100 ms, 104 ms, and 114 ms for the control, 50% $I_{Kr}$, 75% $I_{Kr}$ and 100% $I_{Kr}$ block, respectively.

### C. *Window of Vulnerability to Reentry*

Figure 4 summarizes the outcome of S1-S2 stimulation in Control and 100% $I_{Kr}$ block models. If S2 stimulus occurred too soon, it was blocked by the refractory tissue (grey region). Whereas if S2 occurred too late, it was conducted by the entire ventricular tissue causing a premature excitation (blue region). When the S2 stimulus occurred when the tissue is partially excitable, more complex interactions were observed. In this case, the timing of the ectopic stimulus yielded the following consequences: 1) when myocytes in the vicinity of the stimulus were excitatory and right bundle branch (RBB) was excitatory, the ectopic stimulus induced activations in the right ventricle, which were picked up by the right distal purkinje fibers and conducted retrogradely through the PS.

The retrograde activations spread rapidly through the RBB exciting the left bundle branch (LBB) and the left ventricle, and 2) when myocytes in the vicinity of the stimulus were excitatory but the RBB was refractory, the right purkinje fibers blocked the activity from spreading through the RBB. The activations spread to the left ventricle via transseptal conduction instead. These two scenarios resulted in reentry and ventricular tachycardia (red region). It is also evident from the figure that the window of tachycardia occurrence is extended significantly when $I_{Kr}$ is

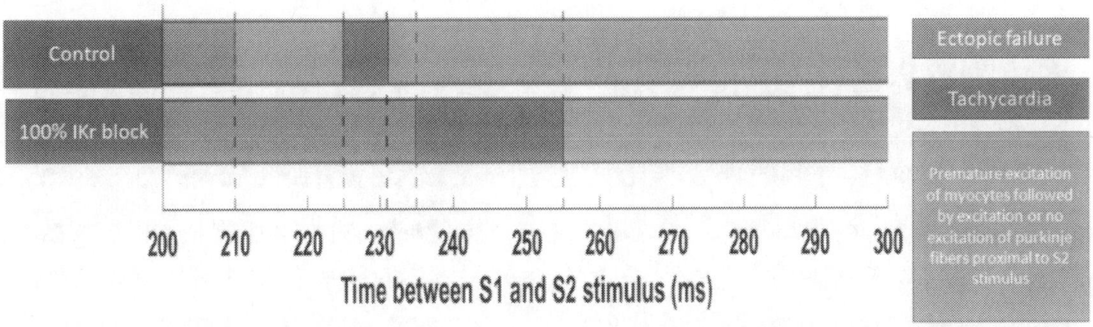


Figure 4. Conduction outcomes during reentry induction by S1-S2 window.

blocked. Thus, the ventricles are more susceptible to arrhythmia in presence of $I_{Kr}$ block induced LQT2 phenotype.

### *D. Simulated Reentry Mechanism*

Figure 5 shows a typical activation sequence in presence of 100% $I_{Kr}$ block for a reentry duration that lasted at least 500 ms hence was referred to as tachycardia. The ectopic stimulus was delivered when the S1-S2 interval was 240 ms. When the ectopic stimulus was applied, the RV myocytes in the vicinity of the stimulus were excitatory while the RBB was refractory (Figure 5A). The ectopic stimulus induced activations in ventricles which were picked up by right distal PS network (see Figure 5A black arrow, V- P).

However, the excitation within the PS was blocked by the refractory RBB, thus preventing retrograde propagation towards the LBB. Excitations spread to the left ventricle via transseptal conduction (Figure 5A, white arrow). Due to the slowed conduction in the septum, the LBB recovers completely before the activation is picked up by the left distal PS network (Figure 5B). The activation excites the LBB which conducts retrogradely to the RBB, thus exciting the right PS and RV (Figure 5B, white arrow).

At 5500 ms, stimulus from the His bundle is blocked by both the RBB and LBB because both branches are refractory. Retrograde propagation from the LBB to RBB between 5500 and 5700 ms (Figure 5C) experiences a conduction block (CB) (Figure 5C, blue arrow). Excitation spreads to the right via transseptal conduction. Both bundle branches were now excitable as excitation reached the right (Figure 5D). Excitation from the ventricle (Figure 5D, black arrow, V-P) excites the RBB. Retrograde propagation (Figure 5D, yellow arrow, P-P) through the RBB reached the LBB, exciting it and the LV. Similar excitation pattern continued throughout the duration of tachycardia.

## IV. DISCUSSION

In this study, we utilized single cell biophysical models of ventricular myocyte and Purkinje cell as well as 3D anatomical model of ventricles to investigate the susceptibility to arrhythmia in presence of HERG mutation leading to loss of $I_{Kr}$ function. The main findings of our numerical study include: 1) loss of $I_{Kr}$ function results in prominent QT prolongation in ECG, 2) the effects of $I_{Kr}$ blockade on AP morphology are more severe in cardiac purkinje cells than that in ventricular myocytes, 3) the loss of $I_{Kr}$ function increases the spatial dispersion of repolarization and refractoriness resulting into increased vulnerability to reentry and ventricular tachycardia, and 4) the His-Purkinje system plays an active role during maintenance of tachycardia.

### *A. AP Morphology in PC vs. VM*

The characteristic spike and dome morphology was more prominent in the rabbit PC than in VM. Higher peak density of transient outward current ($I_{to}$) has been reported in rabbit PCs than ventricles [22] which produces the characteristic early repolarization in PCs. The inward rectifying potassium current ($I_{K1}$), which is responsible for keeping the cell at rest, is smaller in PC [22] than in ventricles. This results in a larger diastolic membrane resistance in PC allowing small charge displacements to cause significant changes in the membrane voltage [23]. The higher resistance accounts for the more substantial change in $APD_{90}$ in PCs than VMs. $I_{Kr}$ is the prominent repolarizing current in PCs. PCs also exhibit lower repolarization reserve than in VMs [27], hence the effects of $I_{Kr}$ block on AP prolongation are more significant in PCs than VMs.

### *B. QT Prolongation in Pseudo-ECG*

The limited availability of more definitive tests for LQTS makes ECG very important in its diagnosis [6]. Single-cell studies can only determine how much an APD is altered and cannot quantify the percentage QT prolongation. The widespread distribution of electrical pulses throughout the ventricles is mediated by the PS, and there is a significant change in the behavior of PS when it is coupled to a large mass of ventricular muscle [14] due to electrotonic loading. Our 3D model comprised of an integrated His-PS network which is capable of reproducing myocardial loading effects. Our model was able to successfully reproduce the prolonged QT interval and prominent notching of the T in ECGs corresponding to the loss of $I_{Kr}$ as reported previously [6].

### *C. Arrhythmia in LQTS*

Repolarization in cardiomyocytes depends on a delicate balance between various ionic currents. Abnormal repolarization of the AP provides a substrate for life-threatening cardiac arrhythmias. Early afterdepolarizations

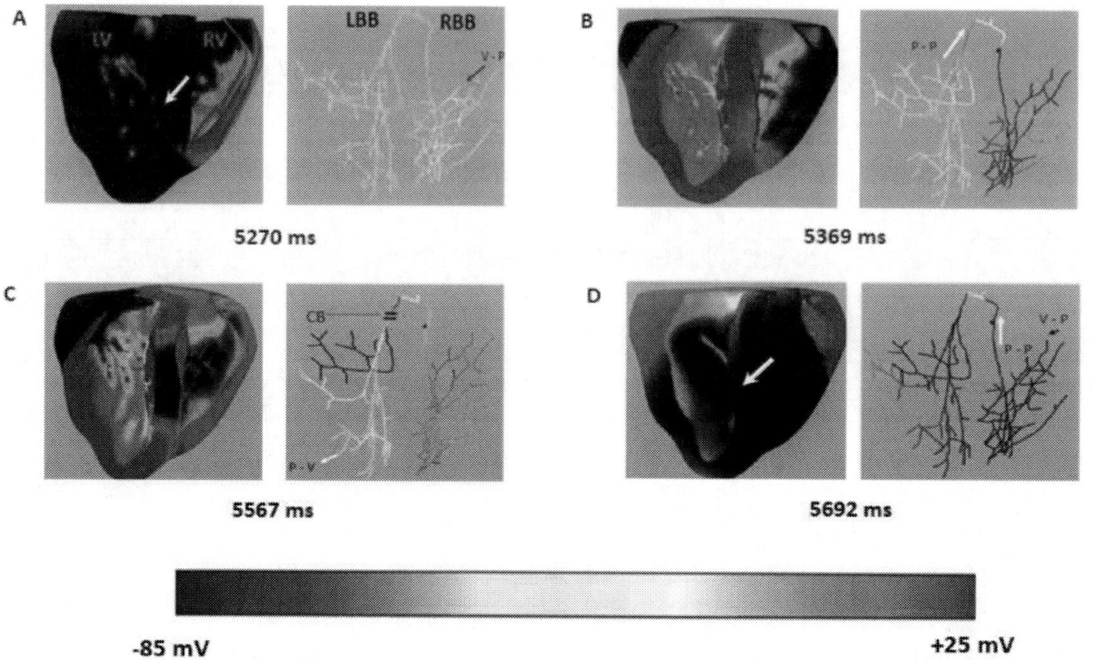


Figure 5. Reentry activations in the 3D ventricular model induced by an ectopic stimulus 270 ms post His-bundle activation. V-P: ventricular myocardium to Purkinje propagation; P-V: Purkinje to ventricular myocardium propagation; P-P: propagation within the Purkinje system; CB: conduction block.

(EADs), which are abnormal membrane depolarizations during the plateau or the repolarization phase of an AP, are thought to be responsible for arrhythmia initiation in LQTS. EADs increase substrate vulnerability (by increasing APD dispersion) and promote triggers for reentry formation [19]. In vivo monophasic AP recordings from the LV endocardium of rabbits induced with polymorphic ventricular tachycardia was preceded by deflections consistent with EADs in the monophasic APs [24]. The mutations in the HERG channel can prolong APD sufficient to generate EADs which may trigger life-threatening arrhythmias [25]. Electrophysiological studies of transgenic LQT1 and LQT2 rabbits reported prolonged APD and QT intervals; however atrioventricular (AV) blocks and polymorphic ventricular tachycardia were developed only in LQT2 rabbits [26].

In our study, we demonstrated tachycardia induction by applying a premature stimulus, which has a similar effect of EAD-induced tachycardia. More simulations are warranted to establish the mechanisms for increased susceptibility of the ventricular conduction system to trigger EAD-induced arrhythmia in LQT2 conditions.

## V. Conclusion

We presented a multiscale numerical simulation study to investigate the arrhythmogenic effects of HERG channel block producing an LQT2 phenotype. Our model was able to reproduce clinically observed QT prolongation in ECG as a result of $I_{Kr}$ block. Our study revealed that, a complete $I_{Kr}$ blockade results into more severe phenotype in Purkinje cells than in ventricular myocytes. The window of susceptibility to reentry that degrades into tachycardia was significantly prolonged in presence of $I_{Kr}$ block. Our simulation outcomes may provide vital insights into the mechanisms of arrhythmia susceptibility as observed in LQT2 patients.

## Acknowledgment

The study was supported by the National Institutes of Health (NIH) award no. 1R15HL145530-01A1.

## References

[1] S. G. Priori, R. Bloise, and L. Crotti, "The long QT syndrome," *Europace*, vol. 3, no. 1, pp. 16–27, 2001, doi: 10.1053/eupc.2000.0141.

[2] P. Kannankeril, D. M. Roden, and D. Darbar, "Drug-Induced Long QT Syndrome," vol. 62, no. 4, pp. 760–781, 2010, doi: 10.1124/pr.110.003723.electrophysiologic.

[3] M. D. Lemoine *et al.*, "Human Induced Pluripotent Stem Cell-Derived Engineered Heart Tissue as a Sensitive Test System for QT Prolongation and Arrhythmic Triggers," *Circ. Arrhythmia Electrophysiol.*, vol. 11, no. 7, pp. 1–15, 2018, doi: 10.1161/CIRCEP.117.006035.

[4] Y. Rudy and J. R. Silva, "Computational biology in the study of cardiac ion channels and cell electrophysiology," *Q. Rev. Biophys.*, vol. 39, no. 1, pp. 57–116, 2006, doi: 10.1017/S0033583506004227.

[5] C. Carter and M. Shah, "Long QT syndrome: A therapeutic challenge," *Ann. Pediatr. Cardiol.*, vol. 1, no. 1, p. 18, 2008, doi: 10.4103/0974-2069.41051.

[6] M. Deo *et al.*, "Relative contribution of changes in sodium current versus intercellular coupling on reentry initiation in 2-dimensional preparations of plakophilin-2deficient cardiac cells," *Hear. Rhythm*, vol. 8, no. 11, pp. 1740–1748, 2011, doi: 10.1016/j.hrthm.2011.06.029.

[7] M. Deo *et al.*, "KCNJ2 mutation in short QT syndrome 3 results in atrial fibrillation and ventricular proarrhythmia," *Proc. Natl. Acad. Sci. U. S. A.*, vol. 110, no. 11, pp. 4291–4296, 2013, doi: 10.1073/pnas.1218154110.

[8] L. Hou *et al.*, "A major role for hERG in determining frequency of reentry in neonatal rat ventricular myocyte monolayer," *Circ. Res.*, vol. 107, no. 12, pp. 1503–1511, 2010, doi: 10.1161/CIRCRESAHA.110.232470.

[9] M. Deo, P. Boyle, G. Plank, and E. Vigmond, "Arrhythmogenic mechanisms of the Purkinje system during electric shocks: A modeling study," *Hear. Rhythm*, vol. 6, no. 12, pp. 1782–1789, 2009, doi: 10.1016/j.hrthm.2009.08.023.

[10] M. Deo, P. M. Boyle, A. M. Kim, and E. J. Vigmond, "Arrhythmogenesis by single ectopic beats originating in the Purkinje system," *Am. J. Physiol. - Hear. Circ. Physiol.*, vol. 299, no. 4, pp. H1002–H1011, 2010, doi: 10.1152/ajpheart.01237.2009.

[11] V. Iyer, K. J. Sampson, and R. S. Kass, "Modeling tissue- and mutation- specific electrophysiological effects in the long QT syndrome: Role of the Purkinje fiber," *PLoS One*, vol. 9, no. 6, p. e97720, 2014, doi: 10.1371/journal.pone.0097720.

[12] G. Seemann, D. L. Weiß, F. B. Sachse, and O. Dössel, "Simulation of the long-QT syndrome in a model of human myocardium," *Comput. Cardiol.*, vol. 30, pp. 287–290, 2003, doi: 10.1109/cic.2003.1291147.

[13] I. Itzhaki *et al.*, "Modelling the long QT syndrome with induced pluripotent stem cells," *Nature*, vol. 471, no. 7337, pp. 225–230, 2011, doi: 10.1038/nature09747.

[14] A. D. Akwaboah *et al.*, "An in silico hiPSC-Derived Cardiomyocyte Model Built With Genetic Algorithm," *Front. Physiol.*, vol. 12, pp. 1–24, 2021, doi: 10.3389/fphys.2021.675867.

[15] G. Salama and B. London, "Mouse models of long QT syndrome," *J. Physiol.*, vol. 578, no. 1, pp. 43–53, 2007, doi: 10.1113/jphysiol.2006.118745.

[16] D. Fedida and L. Macdonald, "hERG long QT syndrome type 2 mutants need more than a chaperone to dance," *J. Physiol.*, vol. 594, no. 15, pp. 4095–4096, 2016, doi: 10.1113/JP272417.

[17] A. Mahajan *et al.*, "A rabbit ventricular action potential model replicating cardiac dynamics at rapid heart rates," *Biophys. J.*, vol. 94, no. 2, pp. 392–410, 2008, doi: 10.1529/biophysj.106.98160.

[18] O. V. Aslanidi, R. N. Sleiman, M. R. Boyett, J. C. Hancox, and H. Zhang, "Ionic mechanisms for electrical heterogeneity between rabbit purkinje fiber and ventricular cells," *Biophys. J.*, vol. 98, no. 11, pp. 2420–2431, 2010, doi: 10.1016/j.bpj.2010.02.033.

[19] F. J. Vetter and A. D. McCulloch, "Three-dimensional analysis of regional cardiac function: A model of rabbit ventricular anatomy," *Prog. Biophys. Mol. Biol.*, vol. 69, no. 2–3, pp. 157–183, 1998, doi: 10.1016/S0079-6107(98)00006-6.

[20] P. M. Boyle, M. Deo, G. Plank, and E. J. Vigmond, "Purkinje-mediated effects in the response of quiescent ventricles to defibrillation shocks," *Ann. Biomed. Eng.*, vol. 38, no. 2, pp. 456–468, 2010, doi: 10.1007/s10439-009-9829-4.

[21] A. Prassl *et al.*, "- User's Manual - Anton Prassl," 2020.

[22] D. J. Huelsing, K. W. Spitzer, J. M. Cordeiro, and A. E. Pollard, "Conduction between isolated rabbit Purkinje and ventricular myocytes coupled by a variable resistance," *Am. J. Physiol. - Hear. Circ. Physiol.*, vol. 274, no. 4 43-4, pp. 1163–1173, 1998, doi: 10.1152/ajpheart.1998.274.4.h1163.

[23] I. Schafferhofer-Steltzer, E. Hofer, D. J. Huelsing, S. P. Bishop, and A. E. Pollard, "Contributions of Purkinje-myocardial coupling to suppression and facilitation of early afterdepolarization-induced triggered activity," *IEEE Trans. Biomed. Eng.*, vol. 52, no. 9, pp. 1522–1531, 2005, doi: 10.1109/TBME.2005.851528.

[24] L. Carlsson, C. Abrahamsson, L. Drews, and G. Duker, "Antiarrhythmic effects of potassium channel openers in rhythm abnormalities related to delayed repolarization," *Circulation*, vol. 85, no. 4, pp. 1491–1500, 1992, doi: 10.1161/01.CIR.85.4.1491.

[25] C. E. Clancy and Y. Rudy, "Cellular consequences of HERG mutations in the long QT syndrome: Precursors to sudden cardiac death," *Cardiovasc. Res.*, vol. 50, no. 2, pp. 301–313, 2001, doi: 10.1016/S0008-6363(00)00293-5.

[26] K. E. Odening *et al.*, "Electrophysiological studies of transgenic long QT type 1 and type 2 rabbits reveal genotype-specific differences in ventricular refractoriness and His conduction," *Am. J. Physiol. - Hear. Circ. Physiol.*, vol. 299, no. 3, pp. H643–H655, 2010, doi: 10.1152/ajpheart.00074.2010.

[27] R. Dumaine and J. M. Cordeiro, "Comparison of K+ currents in cardiac Purkinje cells isolated from rabbit and dog," *J. Mol. Cell. Cardiol.*, vol. 42, no. 2, pp. 378–389, 2007, doi: 10.1016/j.yjmcc.2006.10.019.

[28] E. J. Vigmond, R. Weber dos Santos, A. J. Prassl, M. Deo, and G. Plank, "Solvers for the cardiac bidomain equations," Prog. Biophys. Mol. Biol., vol. 96, no. 1–3, pp. 3–18, 2008, doi: 10.1016/j.pbiomolbio.2007.07.012.

# Evaluation of Spinal Anatomy Segmentation Methods using Synthetic Computed Tomography Volumes

Austin Tapp and Michel Audette
Biomedical Engineering Institute,
Computational Modeling and Simulation Engineering
Old Dominion University
Norfolk, VA, USA
e-mail: atapp001@odu.edu

*Abstract*— **Severe adolescent idiopathic scoliosis (AIS) is corrected by surgical procedures that necessitate ligament releases. To determine appropriate release allotments, soft tissues must be localized on a patient-specific basis. However, routine computed tomography (CT) imaging precludes traditional, voxel-based soft tissue localization. Fortunately, recent studies have proposed top-down segmentation methods, which elucidate soft tissues using pre-operative CT volumes. While the accuracy of vertebral segmentations obtained from these methods has been determined, the accuracy of soft tissue segmentations has not. To ensure the soft tissue segmentation methods are clinically applicable, soft tissue validation must occur. This study presents an evaluation measure for surmised soft tissues, accomplished through the use of synthetic CT (sCT) volumes. The sCTs have geometrically scoliotic shapes and provide ground truth information, which was used to evaluate soft tissue segmentations and establish their clinical utility. This proposed validation method is achieved fully *in silico* and is generically applicable, allowing future soft tissue elucidation methods to be assessed.**

***Keywords-patient-specific modeling; osseoligamentous mesh; synthetic CT; in silico validation; adolescent idiopathic scoliosis.***

## I. INTRODUCTION

### A. Background

Adolescent idiopathic scoliosis (AIS) affects about 30 million individuals worldwide [1]. If not resolved, AIS can lead to serious back problems, decreased lung capacity, and heart damage. AIS treatments depend on the patient's primary, lateral spine curvature. Severe curvatures, defined by angles greater than 45 degrees, are resolved with invasive surgical interventions like posterior spinal fusion (PSF) [1][2]. PSF surgical outcomes seek to prevent progression, maintain coronal and sagittal alignment, level the shoulders, correct the spinal deformity, and preserve motion segments [1]. Prior to PSF operations, computed tomography (CT) or biplanar X-ray imaging is used to evaluate curvature angles and determine correction strategies [3]. Unfortunately, such images provide little understanding as to how patients will respond intraoperatively during corrective procedures [4]. Thus, extra steps to mobilize the spine are performed, resulting in increased morbidity, operating room time, and patient blood loss [5]. To make operations safer and more efficient, patient-specific, biomechanical, finite element (FE) simulations may be used to explore various corrective strategies and approaches [6]. FE biomechanical simulation offers risk-free ways to determine necessary corrective forces when multi-material, volumetric meshes encompass all patient anatomy, including soft tissues [7]. Unfortunately, the nature of pre-operative CT and X-ray imaging modalities makes it nearly impossible to localize soft tissues and determine required ligament releases needed to mobilize the spine during PSF correction.

### B. Related Work

A recent method for ligament segmentation using a top-down segmentation approach, based on anatomy that is conspicuous in CT imaging, has been proposed [8]. By exploiting an osseoligamentous computer-aided designed (CAD) mesh, context-aware deformable registration of the osseoligamentous mesh onto vertebral anatomy of CT imaging allows for the position of volumetric soft tissues, including ligaments, to be surmised on a patient-specific basis. Fig. 1 shows the method. While registration accuracy of this method has been evaluated for anatomy conspicuous in CT and magnetic resonance imaging (i.e., vertebrae and intervertebral discs, respectively), validation of the ligament positioning has not been performed. Such validation requires that ground truth segmentations of ligaments within CT images be known. However, if ground truth ligament segmentations could be obtained manually, the need for top-down segmentation would be obviated: bottom-up, voxel-based methods would be sufficient to determine ligament positions. The inability to obtain expertly segmented ground truth ligaments presents a serious roadblock. One option for the elucidation of ligament ground truths is through synthetic CT (sCT) imaging. Literature describing synthetic image creation is often focused on the conversion of sCTs from other imaging modalities, namely magnetic resonance imaging (MRI). Methods creating sCTs are wide-ranging and use simple algorithms or computationally expensive, conditional generative adversarial networks [9][10][11]. However, these methods disregard the soft tissues that are conspicuous within MRIs but are non-conspicuous in CTs and do not transfer soft tissues information during MRI to sCT conversion.

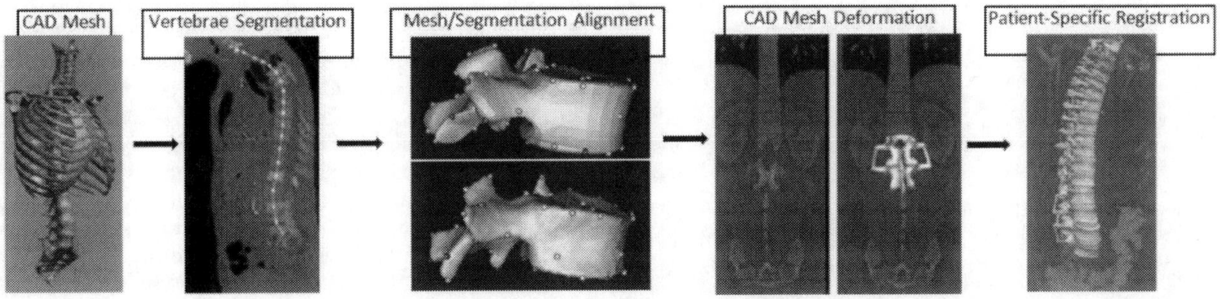


Figure 1. Tapp et al. overview [8]. (Left to right) The method begins with an osseoligamentous CAD torso, with red and green coloring for bones and soft tissues, respectively. Then a patient CT is fed to a neural network, which automatically outputs vertebrae segmentations. CAD vertebrae and vertebrae segments are affinely aligned using a corresponding particles system. This is followed by elastic deformations of the CAD to a patient-specific mesh.

Therefore, an alternative scoliotic sCT volume creation method that maintains soft tissue positioning information is necessary [12]. The method benefits from having its foundation rooted in FE analyses. While many FE studies have explored AIS etiology, they end after scoliotic induction is completed [4][13][14]. If post-study FE meshes containing volumetric or 3-dimensional (3-D) ligaments are converted to sCT volumes, the ligament ground truth segmentation roadblock may be circumvented. AIS-shaped sCT volumes would have corresponding ligament ground truths, provided by the FE meshes. The ligament positions surmised by the top-down segmentation approach could then be validated with the FE mesh-based ground truths. This validation would assist in substantiating methods that localize ligaments in routine CT and X-ray imaging; again, these methods provide a critical step toward determining the minimum number of ligament releases required to mobilize the spine when AIS patients undergo PSF operations.

This study examined the accuracy of all anatomy generated by the top-down segmentation approach using an sCT-based validation measure, which provided 3-D ground truth segmentations for vertebrae, intervertebral discs (IVDs) and other soft tissues. sCT volumes were generated for the lumbar and thoracolumbar sections of the spine with a conversion method that harnesses FE meshes, which contain 3-D bone and soft tissue structures and have been deformed by FE analysis methods to appear geometrically scoliotic. After applying the top-down segmentation method of Tapp et al. to the sCT volumes, the surmised, patient-specific anatomy is compared to its respective ground truths. This contribution provides the medical image analysis community with the means to verify the accuracy of methods surmising soft tissues, which are practically impossible to manually segment.

## II. METHODS

### A. *Creating Synthetic CT Volumes*

The FE spine mesh with 3-D ligaments was developed into a synthetic CT volume that is geometrically scoliotic with the process seen in Fig. 2. The process begins by running FE analyses on FE spine meshes. All FE spine meshes contain tetrahedral, 4-node elements that represent: cortical bone, trabecular bone, posterior bone, vertebral endplates, cartilaginous endplates, nucleus pulposus, annulus matrices, annulus fibers and any spinal ligaments. Material properties for elements of all the FE spine mesh are derived from published studies and are shown in Table 1 [15][16][17][18]. A neo-Hookean model represents only trabecular and posterior bone, the nucleus pulposus and both endplates. Cortical bone uses an orthotropic elastic material. The annulus fibrosus is represented with a compressible Holmes-Mow matrix model and fiber components that apply an exponential power law to describe strain energy density. All 3-D ligaments use the same viscoelastic, coupled, transversely-isotropic Mooney-Rivlin material, which was experimentally determined [17][18]. This study utilized FEBio for FE analysis because of its credibility and open-source availability [19]. Scoliotic shapes were induced phenomenologically, by applying simplistic boundary conditions to FE spine meshes. Linear, prescribed, transverse displacement was applied to all nodes comprising the bony structure of the most central vertebra. To imitate that FE spine was part of a larger column, upper vertebral endplates of the most superior vertebrae and lower vertebral endplates of the most inferior vertebra were fixed. Linear boundary conditions were continuously applied in a transient manner until a subsequent time step caused deformations that prematurely terminated the run of the FE analysis.

Once the FE spine meshes undergo FE analyses to appear scoliotic, meshes are converted to sCT volumes. First, FE spine meshes are exported as triangular surface meshes, and the surface mesh is resampled into a volume using a true CT. The resampling maintains the mesh's structure but adjust its size and spacing to match that of the true CT. Then, using Elastix, the true CT is deformably registered onto the newly created mesh volume, which is structurally identical to the surface mesh it was created from [20]. This volume-to-volume registration method consistently transfers Hounsfield unit values from the true CT to the sCT. A mask that obscures bone bereft portions of the true CT will explicitly preserve the original image intensity values that surround bony structures of the true CT and rapidly produce sCT volumes with Hounsfield unit (HU) intensity values for all portions of the image. The triangular surface mesh that was exported after the FE analysis is the ground truth for the sCT. The ground truth can be stripped of bone or soft tissues to allow for the use of each type of anatomy, as needed.

TABLE I. MATERIAL PROPERTY CONSTANTS OF THE FE MESHES

| Structure | Materials | Property Constants | Ref |
|---|---|---|---|
| Cortical bone | Orthotropic elastic | $E_1$ = 8k MPa, $E_2$ = 8k MPa, $E_3$ = 12k MPa, $v_{12}$ = 0.4, $v_{23}$ = 0.3, $v_{31}$ = 0.35 | 15,16 |
| Trabecular bone | Neo-Hookean | E = 100 MPa, v = 0.2 | 15,16 |
| Posterior bone | Neo-Hookean | E = 3500 MPa, v = 0.3 | 15,16 |
| Vertebral endplate | Neo-Hookean | E = 1000 MPa, v = 0.3 | 15,16 |
| Cartilaginous endplate | Neo-Hookean | E = 23.8 MPa, v = 0.42 | 15,16 |
| Nucleus pulposus | Neo-Hookean | E = 1 MPa, v = 0.49 | 15,16 |
| Facet cartilage | Neo-Hookean | E = 30 MPa, v = 0.4 | 15,16 |
| Annulus matrix | Holmes-Mow | E = 1 MPa, $ß^1$ = 3.4 | 15,16 |
| Annulus fibers | Fiber-exp-power | $\alpha^2$ = 65, $ß^3$ = 2, $\xi^4$ = 0.296 MPa | 15,16 |
| **3-D Ligaments** | Coupled transversly-isotropic Mooney-Rivlin | $c_1$ = 2.1660 MPa, $c_3$ = 0.2677 MPa, $c_4$ = 83.0594, $c_5$ = 535.5720, $k^5$ = 436.845 MPa, $\lambda^6$= 1.0498 | 17,18 |

a. For 3-D ligaments: 1: exponential stiffening coefficient, 2: coefficient of exponential argument, 3: power of exponential argument, 4: fiber modulus, 5: bulk modulus, 6: max fiber straightening stretch

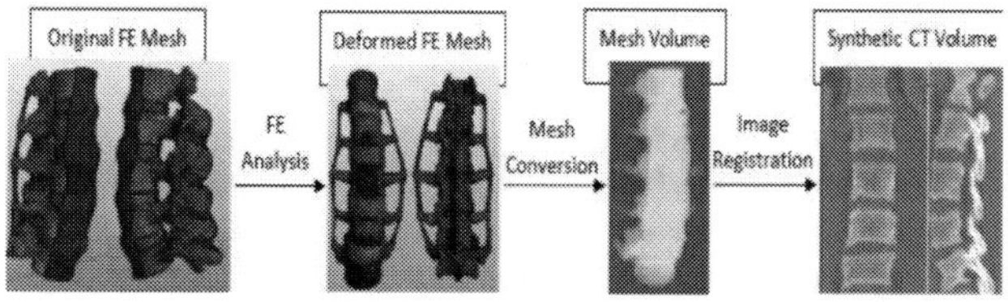


Figure 2. Overview of the FE mesh to sCT volume method [12]. The FE mesh is deformed, converted to an image registered with a true CT volume.

## B. *Generating Volume-Specific, Osseoligamentous Meshes*

While more details can be found in the manuscript by Tapp et al., a brief outline of how to develop a volume-specific osseligamentous spine mesh is described below. As mentioned, because of the inconspicuous presentation of soft tissues in CT imaging, segmenting ligaments by intrinsic voxel-based or neural network (NN) techniques is precluded. Therefore, the top-down, segmentation approach must begin with an anatomist-developed CAD mesh of a torso. The torso's structure is characteristic of a healthy, average, adult human and contains bone, ligament, and some other soft tissues, but no muscle. The deformable registration process of the CAD mesh first requires it to be approximately positioned within the CT image space. To accomplish this, vertebral segmentations, attained from the sCT using a deep learning NN, are utilized as a basis for the positioning of the CAD mesh vertebrae. The deep learning NN obtains vertebral segmentations in a fully automatic, 3-step, coarse-to-fine process [21]. The first step predicts approximate x and y coordinates of the spine as $\hat{x}_{spine} \in \mathbb{R}^2$ using a U-Net variant. The second step localizes the center of the vertebral bodies through a Spatial-Configuration-Net (SC-Net), which is comprised of 2 components that work together to determine local landmark appearance while considering the landmark's spatial configuration. The predicted spine coordinate $\hat{x}_{spine}$ of the first step is used to narrow the portions of the sCT processed. Finally, individual vertebrae are segmented with the same U-Net variant as in Step 1. The centroids output by SC-Net provide a semantic label that crops the region around the landmark, allowing vertebrae to be segmented at full resolution and independently of one another. The resulting output segmentations are resampled to their original input position in the overall sCT volume. The CAD meshes are then aligned to relevant sCT image space by an affine transformation that exploits these NN-derived vertebrae segmentations. The CAD vertebrae meshes and the NN vertebrae segmentations are populated with surface particles that spatially correspond between both vertebrae's surfaces [22]. The particles guide an initial affine transform.

After the affine transform of the CAD mesh onto relevant sCT space, the CAD mesh is deformably registered [23]. This occurs by lumping all CAD mesh vertices as a single mass component, which is driven toward pertinent CT voxels. The meshes' vertex motions are solved using an implicit Euler scheme that determines Newtonian dynamics-based forces described by $f_i = \alpha_i(R_i - P_i)$, where $P_i$ is a vertex position and $f_i$ is the force that attracts $P_i$ towards its target vertex, $R_i$. Weighting factors consider image gradients and upper-quartile voxel intensities to encourage CAD vertebrae deformation toward highly conspicuous aspects of the sCT, i.e., the sCT's vertebrae. Simultaneously, anatomy around the vertebral portions of the CAD mesh is locally deformed due to the vertices mass grouping, surmising positions of soft tissues, such as ligaments, that are inconspicuous in the sCT.

## C. *Validation Metrics*

Several validation metrics were employed to evaluate the volume-specific meshes generated through the deformable registration of the osseoligamentous CAD mesh onto sCT volumes. The metrics compare the post-registered meshes with their respective ground truth segmentations, which are given during the FE spine mesh to sCT conversion pipeline. The volume-specific meshes are converted to segmentations prior to comparison to their ground truths. For more detailed descriptions of the comparisons utilized, we refer the reader to Yeghiazaryan & Voiculescu [24]. Briefly, three accuracy metrics for segmentation that are commonly considered to be gold standards are described. The first metric, Dice similarity coefficient (DSC), volumetrically compares the number of segment elements that overlap with the total elements found in the ground truth segmentations; the DSC of a segment compared to itself would be 1. A second metric, average Hausdorff distance (aHD), compares the overall surfaces of segmentations, measuring disparity, in millimeters (mm), between the surface a segmentation and the corresponding surface of its ground truth. The third metric is Intersection over Union (IoU), also known as Jaccard similarity. This metric is quite similar to DSC, but penalizes false positives to a greater degree. Again, a segment compared to itself is equal to 1. Additional metrics that are not described in detail are: $95^{th}$ percentile HD (95%) in mm, sensitivity (SE), specificity (SP), false positive rate (FP) and false negative rate (FN).

## III. RESULTS

### A. *Synthetic CT Volumes*

The CAD-based FE meshes with 3-D ligaments were deformed using prescribed displacement to create a scoliotic curve profile. For the CAD-based lumbar mesh, the L3 vertebra was displaced by 5.1 mm and for the CAD-based thoracolumbar mesh, the T10 vertebra was displaced 6.5 mm. The two CAD-based meshes were then successfully converted into two sCT images using true CT volumes from their respective anatomical regions. The lumbar sCT volume is seen in Fig. 2 and the thoracolumbar sCT volume is shown next to its true CT in Fig. 3. Both sCT volumes had voxel intensity values that remained consistent with their true CT counterparts. sCT voxel values ranged from -1272 to 1716 HUs. Fig. 4 shows histograms that reflect HUs of the lumbar and thoracolumbar sCT volumes and their true CTs.

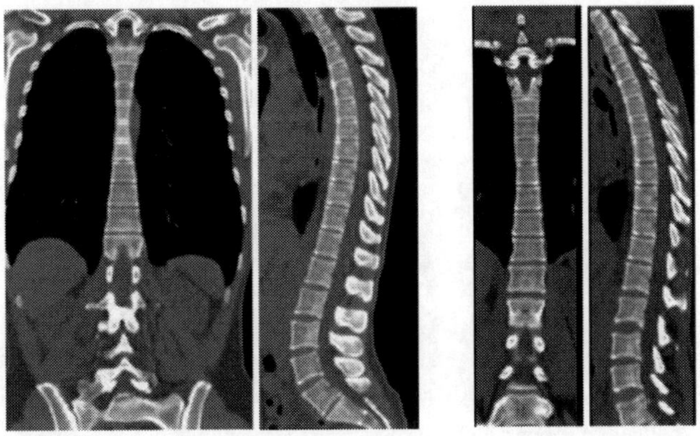

Figure 3. The thoracolumbar sCT (right side) and its true CT (left side).

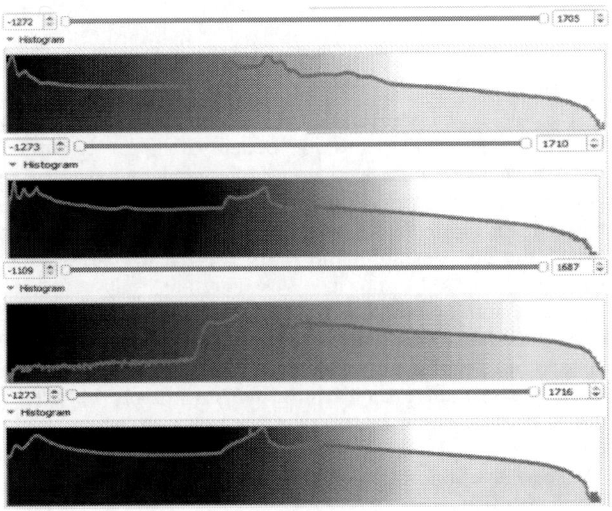


Figure 4. From top to bottom: histograms of the true lumbar CT, lumbar synthetic CT, true thoracolumbar CT and thoracolumbar synthetic CT.

### B. *Validating Volume-Specific, Osseoliagmentous Meshes*

NN training was done with CT data of MICCAI's VerSe grand challenge (verse2020.grand-challenge.org/). Training and testing was performed with Tensor-flow using a mini-batch size of 1 for all networks, 10,000 iterations for the spine localization network, 50,000 iterations for the vertebrae localization network and 50,000 iterations for the segmentation network. The Adam optimizer with a $10^{-4}$ learning rate was used for Modified U-Nets; the Nesterov optimizer at a $10^{-8}$ learning rate was used for SC-Net [21].

Both volume-specific, osseoligamentous meshes were evaluated with the metrics described in section 2C. The osseoligamentous meshes were assessed as a whole, with the soft tissues removed (i.e., only comparing vertebrae), and with the bone removed (i.e., only comparing soft tissues). Further, to provide a frame of reference and determine the necessity of the affine and deformable registration methods, the NN-derived vertebrae segmentations were also evaluated with bone-only ground truths. Table 2 contains a summary of detailed results for each of these four evaluations. Fig. 5 shows a qualitative view of the 3 ground truth segmentations compared to their meshes during lumbar spine evaluation. Briefly, DSC, aHD and IoU of all anatomy evaluation was determined to be 0.72, 2.4mm and 0.55, respectively for the lumbar meshes and 0.68, 2.1mm and 0.52, respectively for the thoracolumbar meshes. For the vertebrae only evaluation, it is important to note the whole vertebrae, not just vertebral bodies of vertebrae, were evaluated. DSC, aHD and IoU of the vertebrae was determined to be 0.66, 2.27mm and 0.50, respectively for the lumbar meshes and 0.64, 1.97mm and 0.48, respectively for the thoracolumbar meshes. For the soft tissue only comparison, all 3-D ligaments and the IVDs were examined. For the soft tissues of the lumbar patient-specific mesh DSC was 0.46, aHD was 4.5mm and IoU was 0.30. For the soft tissues of the thoracolumbar patient-specific mesh, DSC was 0.50, aHD was 2.9mm and IoU was 0.34. Finally, for unassisted, NN-derived vertebrae segmentations in the lumbar mesh DSC was 0.58, aHD was 2.61mm and IoU was 0.41 while in the thoracolumbar mesh DSC was 0.54, aHD was 3.47mm and IoU was 0.37.

TABLE II. QUANTITATIVE RESULTS SUMMARY. L AND T ARE LUMBAR AND THORACOLUMBAR EVALUATIONS, RESPECTIVELY. ST IS SOFT TISSUE, 8 IS VERETBRAE MESHES OBTAINED WITH [8]'S METHOD, 21 IS VERTBRAE MESHES OBTAINED WITH THE NN. 2C DEFINES ABBREVATIONS AND UNITS.

| Mesh | DSC | aHD | IoU | 95% | SP | SE | FP | FN |
|---|---|---|---|---|---|---|---|---|
| L-all | 0.72 | 2.40 | 0.55 | 6.38 | 0.98 | 0.63 | 0.02 | 0.37 |
| L-ST | 0.46 | 4.46 | 0.30 | 12.4 | 0.99 | 0.33 | 0.01 | 0.67 |
| L-8 | 0.66 | 2.27 | 0.50 | 5.74 | 0.97 | 0.60 | 0.03 | 0.40 |
| L-21 | 0.58 | 2.61 | 0.41 | 5.84 | 1 | 0.41 | 0.00 | 0.59 |
| T-all | 0.68 | 2.08 | 0.52 | 5.67 | 0.97 | 0.63 | 0.02 | 0.37 |
| T-ST | 0.50 | 2.90 | 0.34 | 8.02 | 1 | 0.39 | 0.00 | 0.61 |
| T-8 | 0.64 | 1.97 | 0.48 | 5.31 | 0.98 | 0.60 | 0.02 | 0.40 |
| T-21 | 0.54 | 3.47 | 0.37 | 13.2 | 1 | 0.37 | 0.00 | 0.63 |

## IV. Discussion

The presented evaluation demonstrated that the published method achieves a somewhat decent agreement when comparing all anatomical structures – the soft tissues and the vertebrae. The method also reported better overall scores compared to the current MICCAI vertebrae segmentation challenge winning network for vertebrae in the sCT [21]. The network seems to have struggled significantly when segmenting the sCT volumes, possibly due to their synthetic nature, their zoomed cropping around the region of the spine, or their structurally adjusted shape. Regardless, the poor segmentations caused the downstream methods to perform significantly worse than in previously published studies. In particular, Fig. 5 shows the NN's segmentation results for the transverse processes of the vertebrae guided a completely incorrect placement of the transverse ligaments. Typically, the NN performs quite well on patient CT volumes and allows the downstream affine and deformable registration processes to outperform state of the art methods in related studies. Unfortunately, there are no studies that evaluate all spinal soft tissues, so comparison or discussion of these results is extremely limited. However, given DSC and aHD are weakest in soft tissue evaluations, additional work will need to be considered for better soft tissue fitting. Further, as seen in Fig. 5. the subtraction technique performed to obtain soft tissue ground truths may not be ideal. Alternatively, soft tissues should be exported as their own mesh; the present study subtracted the fully included anatomy ground truth by the bone only ground truth to provide soft-tissue ground truth data and may have resulted in the noted underperformance due to additional, inaccurate "ground truth" information. Finally, scoliotic geometry of sCT volumes were minor. sCT with geometry of moderate to severe scoliotic spines should be tested with Tapp et al. and Payer et al.'s methods [8][21].

### A. *Conclusion*

This study implemented previously published methods to evaluate the spinal anatomy segmentations derived from the MICCAI vertebral segmentation challenge winning NN and from an emerging top-down segmentation approach. The top-down approach surmises the position of ligaments and soft tissues by exploiting bone structures, like vertebrae, that are conspicuous in CT imaging. By using a sCT that provides 3-D soft tissue ground truths, all portions of patient-specific osseoligamentous meshes developed with the top-down approach can be evaluated. The presented technique quantitatively evaluates the soft tissue positions obtained by the top-down segmentation approach completely *in silico.* This validation technique is required for advancing scoliosis interventions, like PSF, which currently necessitate unknown numbers of ligament releases. Ligaments must first be accurately localized on a patient-specific basis to develop a full patient-specific model that will help to determine ideal ligament release strategies. Corrective procedures like PSF, can be made safer and more efficient by yielding models that contain 3-D ligaments and calculate the number of ligament releases required to mobilize the spine during surgical interventions. Aside from its capability to verify soft tissues in the spinal column, the presented method is broadly applicable for validating the presence of other soft tissues and may be especially beneficial for future studies performed on areas of the knee, shoulder, hand, and foot.

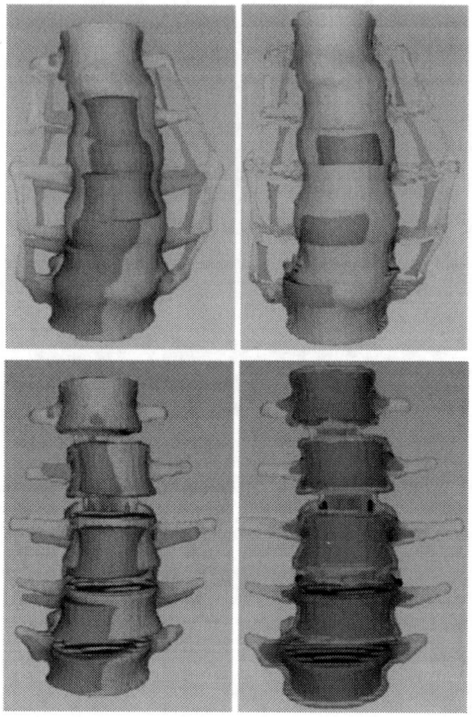

Figure 5. Lumbar Qualitative results. Ground truth is green, meshes evaluated are gray. (top left) All anatomy evaluated, including bone and soft tissue. Then, (top right) soft tissues evaulated; vertebrae are removed. Finally, (bottom left) vertebrae only evaluation using the method of [8] compared to [21]'s segmentations (bottom right).

### B. *Future Work*

Parameters of the top-down segmentation methodology need to be updated to provide better soft-tissue alignment. The FE meshes must also undergo varied analyses to see what kinds of severe scoliotic curve geometries can be induced. FE meshes with more than one curve are also being considered for development. This breadth of FE meshes, which will be used to produce sCT volumes, may be utilized for additional methodological validation. sCT volumes should encompass an entire spinal column, from the skull to the sacrum for future validation work. Further, the sCT volumes and their ground truths will ultimately be used to train a deep learning neural network that performs one-shot segmentations given the sCT image and the ground truth. The segmentations may include all anatomy or exclusively output soft tissues.

## REFERENCES


[1] M. Mohamed, J. Trivedi, N. Davidson, and S. Munigangaiah, "Adolescent idiopathic scoliosis: a review of current concepts," Orthopaedic and Trauma, vol. 34, pp. 338-345, Dec. 2020, doi:10.1016/j.mporth.2020.09.003.

[2] Z. B. Cheung, S. Selverian, B.H. Cho, C. J. Ball, S. Kang-Wook and Cho, S. "Idiopathic Scoliosis in Children and Adolescents: Emerging Techniques in Surgical Treatment," World Neurosurgery, vol. 130, pp. e737-742, Oct. 2019, doi:10.1016/j.wneu.2019.06.207.

[3] T. Illés and S. Somoskeöy, "The EOS$^{TM}$ imaging system and its uses in daily orthopaedic practice," International Orthopaedics, vol. 36, pp. 1325-1331, Feb. 2012, doi:10.1007%2Fs00264-012-1512-y.

[4] J. P. Little and C. Adam, "Patient-specific computational biomechanics for simulating adolescent scoliosis surgery: Predicted vs clinical correction for a preliminary series of six patients," International Journal for numerical Methods in Biomedical Engineering, vol. 27, pp. 347-356. Mar. 2011, doi:10.1002/cnm.1422.

[5] L. G. Lenke, et al., "Adolescent idiopathic scoliosis. A new classification to determine extent of spinal arthrodesis," The Journal of Bone & Joint Surgery, vol. 83, pp. 1169-1181, Aug. 2001, doi:10.2106/00004623-200108000-00006.

[6] L. La Barbera, A.N. Larson, J. Rawlinson, and C. E. Aubin, "*In silico* patient-specific optimization of correction strategies for thoracic adolescent idiopathic scoliosis," Clinical Biomechanics, vol. 81, pp. unlisted Jan. 2021, doi:10.1016/j.clinbiomech.2020.105200.

[7] M. Audette, J. Schmid, C. Goodmurphy, M. Polanco, S. Bawab, et al., "Towards a deformable multi-surface approach to ligamentous spine models for predictive simulation-based scoliosis surgery planning," Computational Methods and Clinical Applications for Spine Imaging, vol. 11397, pp. 90-102, Mar. 2019, doi:10.1007/978-3-030-13736-6_8.

[8] A. Tapp, C. Payer, J. Schmid, M. Polanco, et al., "Generation of patient-specific, ligamentoskeletal, finite element meshes for scoliosis correction planning," LNCS., in press.

[9] N. Chegeni, M. Birgani, F. Birgani, D. Fatehi, G. Akbarizadeh, and M. Tahmasbi, "Introduction of a simple algorithm to create synthetic-Computed tomography of the head from magnetic resonance imaging," Journal of Medical Signals and Sensors, vol. 9, pp. 123-129, Apr. 2019, doi:10.4103/jmss.JMSS_26_18.

[10] A. Baydoun, et al., "Dixon-based thorax synthetic CT generation using Generative Adversarial Network," vol. 3-4, pp. unlisted, Dec 2020, doi: 10.1016/j.ibmed.2020.100010.

[11] J. Mangalagiri, "Toward Generating Synthetic CT Volumes using a 3D-Conditional Generative Adversarial Network," ArXivorg, Jan 2021 , https://par.nsf.gov/biblio/10232074.

[12] A. Tapp, M. Polanco, I. Kumi, S. Bawab, et al., "Generating scoliotic computed tomography volumes from finite element spine models," LNCS., in press.

[13] L. Shi, et al., "Biomechanical analysis and modeling of different vertebral growth patterns in adolescent idiopathic scoliosis and healthy subjects," Scoliosis, vol. 6, pp. unlisted, May 2011, doi:10.1186/1748-7161-6-11.

[14] J.F. Sarwark, R. M. Castelein, A. Maqsood, C. E. Aubin, "The Biomechanics of Induction in Adolescent Idiopathic Scoliosis: Theoretical Factors," Journal of Bone and Joint Surgery, vol. 101, pp. e22, Mar 2019, doi:10.2106/JBJS.18.00846.

[15] S.M. Finley, D.S. Brodke, N.T. Spina, C.A. DeDen, and B.J. Ellis, "FEBio finite element models of the human lumbar spine," Computer Methods in Biomechanics and Biomedical Engineering, vol. 21, pp. 444-452, Jan 2018, doi:10.1080/10255842.2018.1478967.

[16] H. Kim, H. Chun, et al., "A validated finite element analysis of nerve root stress in degenerative lumbar scoliosis," Medical & Biological Engineering & Computing, vol. 47, pp. 599-605, Mar. 2009, doi: 10.1007/s11517-009-0463-y.

[17] M. Hortin, Ligament model fidelity in finite element analysis of the human lumbar spine. [Online]. Available from: scholarsarchive.byu.edu/etd/5254. Accessed 09/09/2021.

[18] E. Peña, B. Calvo, M. A. Martínez, M. Doblaré, "A three-dimensional finite element analysis of the combined behavior of ligaments and menisci in the healthy human knee joint," Journal of Biomechanics, vol. 39, pp.1686-1701, doi:10.1016/j.jbiomech.2005.04.030.

[19] S. A. Maas, B. J. Ellis, G.A. Ateshian, J.A. Weiss, "FEBio: Finite elements for biomechanics," Journal of Biomechanical Engineering, vol. 134, Feb. 2012, doi:10.1115/1.4005694.

[20] S. Klein, M. Staring, K. Murphy, M. A. Viergever, and J. P. W. Pluim, "elastix: A Toolbox for Intensity-Based Medical Image Registration," in IEEE Transactions on Medical Imaging, vol. 29, pp. 196-205, Jan. 2010, doi: 10.1109/TMI.2009.2035616.

[21] C. Payer, D. Štern, H. Bischof, M. Urschler, "Coarse to fine vertebrae localization and segmentation with SpatialConfiguration-Net and U-Net," VISIGRAPP, vol. 5, pp. 124-133, Feb. 2020, doi:10.5220/0008975201240133.

[22] J. Cates, S. Elhabian, R. Whitaker, "ShapeWorks: Particle-Based Shape Correspondence and Visualization Software," Statistical Shape and Deformation Analysis, vol. 1, pp. 257-298, Jan. 2017, doi:10.1016/B978-0-12-810493-4.00012-2.

[23] D. Damopoulos, et al., "Segmentation of the proximal femur in radial MR scans using a random forest classifier and deformable model registration," International Journal of Computer Assisted Radiology and Surgery, vol. 14, pp. 545-561, Jan. 2019, doi:10.1007/s11548-018-1899-z.

[24] V. Yeghiazaryan, I. Voiculescu, "Family of boundary overlap metrics for the evaluation of medical image segmentation," Journal of Medical Imaging, vol. 5, pp. 015006, Feb. 2018, doi:10.1117/1.jmi.5.1.015006.

# Simulative Comparison of Scheduling at Krones AG with Shortest Slack

Frank Herrmann
Ostbayerische Technische Hochschule Regensburg - University of Applied Sciences Regensburg
Innovation and Competence Centre for Production Logistics and Factory Planning (IPF)
PO Box 120327, 93025 Regensburg, Germany
E-Mail: Frank.Herrmann@OTH-Regensburg.de

*Abstract*— **Final assembly at Krones AG must make the best possible use of its production space, and meeting the specified customer due dates is critical. Via a self developed simulation tool, the present scheduling procedure is compared with the one by priority rule shortest slack. As a consequence slack should have a higher importance in the planning.**

***Keywords- Simulation of scheduling; unused area; tardiness.***

## I. Introduction

At Krones AG, the world market leader in the beverage industry, orders with very large area requirements have to be produced. Despite very high investments in suitable halls, the available area is a major bottleneck. This is also the case for other companies.

Despite the use of planners, at least 21% of orders at Krones have consistently been late in recent years. Delays result in significant penalties and undermine the goal of getting every plant up and running on time. For many orders, delays were only avoided because process accelerations were made in the mostly long production processes through measures such as overtime.

Krones now wanted to know more precisely:
- How good is the actual quality of planning?
- How good is planning that (primarily) follows due dates?

Due to the improvement of planning within the production execution, the production result are not representative of the planning quality in terms of meeting due dates. Therefore, these questions should be answered by a simulation study.

This article is structured as follows. In section 2, the previous planning procedure at Krones is explained and section 3 contains the relevant literature. In section 4 the self-developed simulation tool is explained. Section 5 contains an analysis of the simulation results. Finally, in section 6, a summary is given and planned further work is described.

## II. Production and Planning at Krones AG

Krones AG, headquartered in Neutraubling, Germany, employs around 15,000 people worldwide. It has been producing components, lines and systems for beverages and liquid food since 1951. It is assigned to the machinery and plant engineering sector, and it is a leading manufacturer in packaging and filling technology. The company covers every step of the production process, from product and container manufacturing, through filling and packaging, to material flow and container recycling. One of the last steps is the final assembly of filling machines in plant hall 5.

The following description of the assembly serves to illustrate the area requirements, which can increase and decrease over time. At the same time, it mentions technical restrictions due to which processing times are not known in advance and are constant.

Only one machine at a time can enter or leave the plant hall through the plant gates. Before starting the final assembly of a machine, a final assembly station with sufficient area is determined depending on the machine size. For example, in Figure 1, three fillers are to be assembled. Such a hall allocation is representative for the entire plant. All subassembly parts and materials of all machines are delivered to the delivery spots (i.e., "delivery spot" in Figure 1). Materials from different machines and assemblies can be mixed here; indicated by "Assembly" in Figure 1. These outdoor delivery areas are limited, but can be used by any type of machine and material.

The sub-assemblies and materials are divided into two groups of master material types. The first group of assemblies, due to design and/or weight, can only be lifted into the factory facility with the main crane (in Figure 1, materials with solid border lines). Mostly these parts are main machine parts. The second group of materials can be brought to their target material location by operators (in Figure 1 materials with dashed border lines). These are assembly parts sorted in trolleys or bins. These parts can be lifted by auxiliary cranes to their final place in the machine and are assigned to a single machine in the inside material place. These indoor material spots are physically fixed according to the final assembly station and are individual for each machine with materials.

Final assembly stations are physically fixed and are individual for each machine with materials. After completion of the final assembly process, the finished machine can only be transported out of the hall by the main crane. The main crane and the outrigger cranes operate at different levels so that blocking is not possible. Support cranes are divided between the right and left sides of the plant and cannot pass each other on either side.

Due to this area demand and the large dimensions of the assembled machines with diameters from 1.0 m to 7.2 m, plant hall 5 has an overall length of 105 m and a width of 30 m and the area usable for assembly consists of 2208 m².

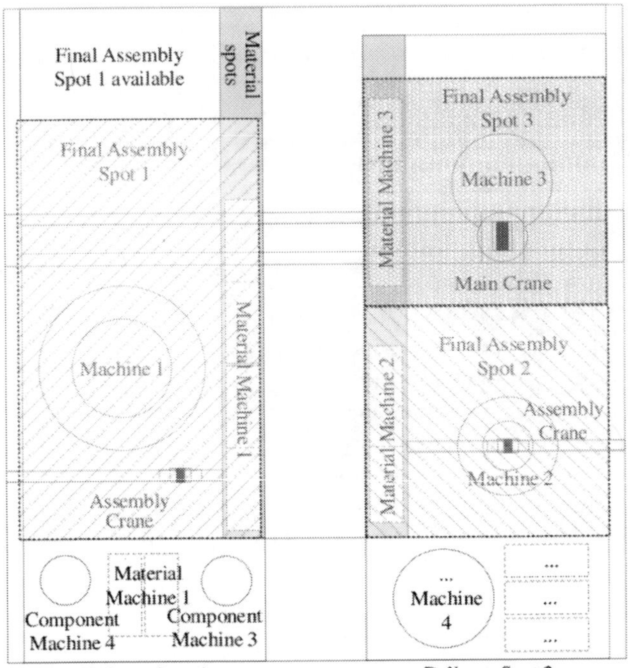


Figure 1: Detail of the factory layout of the final assembly of the filling technology.

In 2020, 145 machines were assembled and a higher number is expected in the next few years. The processing time of the assembly orders varies between 6 weeks and 19 weeks with a mean value of 10.24 weeks and a deviation of 2.5 weeks. At the end of a week, the plants leave the hall.

Planning is done, as is standard for companies, by configuring the SAP system specifically for Krones AG. Its main components are listed in Figure 2. Its main service is ensuring the availability of materials. As analysed in the literature, e.g., [9], this planning provides insufficient results when taking into account the limited capacity. Just very simple procedures are used; which are listed in Figure 2. As discussed in the literature, e.g., [1], [3], [8], [9] and [11], scheduling is needed as an additional planning procedure between capacity planning and manufacturing execution.

In principle, scheduling of the assembly orders of the hall at Krones is currently carried out by means of the following procedure:

Planning is performed always at the beginning of a week. The worklist covers 12 weeks. This worklist is the result of the capacity planning by the SAP system, which is executed every day. At the beginning of each week, a machine can be allocated into the hall, provided that the necessary area is available, without having to reposition the machines already in the hall. A planner uses a printed layout of the plant hall in which the previously scheduled lines are drawn. The plant data, such as length, width, (customer) due date, are located in Krones' SAP system.

Due to planning by the SAP system, the worklist is already ordered. A planner schedules the machines into the hall according to this list, provided availability is assured. The SAP system provides an order list (or machine list) for each day. The SAP system does not determine a sequence between the orders of a single day. A planner orders the machines of such a day. For this, she/he prefers larger required area or processing time over smaller ones. This follows the assumption that smaller machines, in terms of space requirements and/or processing times, can be more easily planned into a partially occupied hall than larger ones.

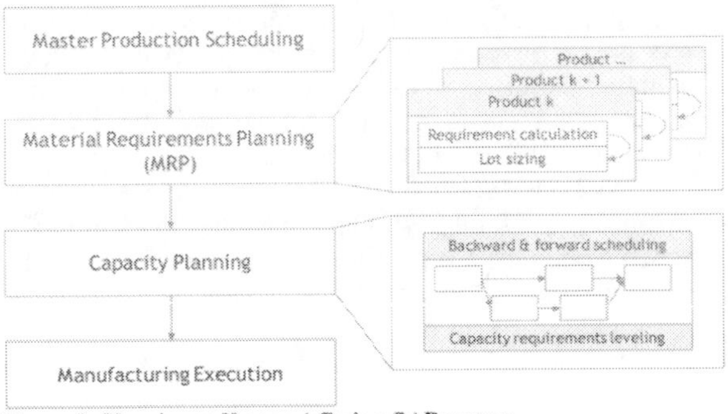


Figure 2: Planning at Krones AG via a SAP system.

## III. Literature Review

According to the literature and the experience of planner in companies, there is a conflict of objectives between minimizing the unused area, minimizing the number of workers, and minimizing the tardiness; as seen in the scheduling trilemma; see also [8].

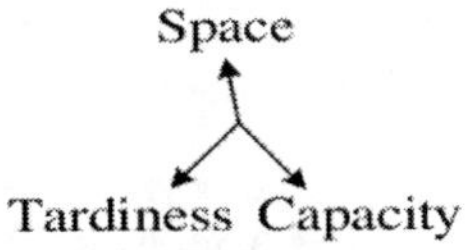


Figure 3: Trilemma

In the literature there are numerous works on scheduling as in [8] or [11] and on layout planning as in [2] or [4]. In combinations of both problems, either scheduling or layout planning dominates. An example is project planning for ships in [5] and [6] where well-used spatial layout is most important. The class of problem considered here consists not of projects, but of independent individual assembly orders.

The proceedings of the annual winter simulation conferences contain many articles on simulation that are relevant to this work. Particularly relevant for this research work were [13] and the description of a process simulation as part of modelling in [12].

The real application operates in dynamic environments where real time events like station failure, tool breakage, arrival of new orders with high priority, changes of due dates etc., may turn a feasible schedule into an infeasible one; examples can be found in [8] and [11]. A feasible schedule of jobs is achieved by a priority rule like Earliest Due Date (EDD), because a priority rule orders a queue of jobs in front of a station quasi immediately; for its description and the one of other widely used priority rules see [3]. Thus, priority rules are still analysed in many studies on scheduling; one example of a recent one is [10] and [1].

In addition to this facts, priority rules are also a first choice in the case of complex scheduling problems; especially in industrial practice. Thus, in [14] for a complex scheduling problem the performance of priority rules is analysed. Another example is the application of priority rules for the dispatching of AGVs in flexible job shops in [7]. It might be that in the near future several such problems will be solved by more sophisticated heuristics as genetic algorithms for example.

## IV. Simulation Tool

For the simulation study, common commercially available simulation tools such as Plant Simulation from Siemens were first evaluated against a proprietary development. The tools allow extensive visualisations of the processes. However, they cannot significantly reduce the development effort required to control the scheduling of randomly arriving customer orders in the factory hall compared to an in-house development.

A tool is developed to simulate and analyse various sequences of assembling filling machines in plant hall 5. It is implemented in Excel (in VBA) and one Excel sheet represents an allocation of plant hall 5. The hall is represented in Excel by a rectangle of cells, where each cell represents an area over 1m² in the plant hall. An assignment of 0 means an unused area (over 1m²) and a 1 means an allocation by a machine; other areas, such as those of passageways, office area, etc., are coded in Excel by 80. The total area required by a filling machine is then a rectangle of 1-s in an Excel sheet. A sequence simulation creates such a sheet for each week (period) of the simulation horizon. It ends if the last machine of a set of orders, called workload, which is known at the beginning of the simulation run, has been assembled.

For a sequence of orders elaborated by a planner or by the slack rule, the machines (orders) are iteratively assigned to plant hall 5 as follows. For an order (i.e., machine), the production area is searched from left to right and then from top to bottom until a sufficiently large free area is found. This area must also be free in the coming periods, as scheduling sequences are usually not sorted by release date. In the positive case, the allocation takes place, as far left-up as possible. In the negative case, this allocation attempt is repeated as soon as a machine is assembled and has left the hall; this could just happen at the of a week (period).

After a successful simulation run, for each order its tardiness (actual completion date minus due date) and for each period the occupied area (or free area) are calculated.

## V. Results

The basis for the simulation experiments is the order data in 2020. The direct use of these data resulted in a very high standard deviation of mean tardiness and other key figures named below and used in the analysis. As a result, it was not possible to identify statistically significant results.

In order to obtain meaningful results, the sequence of incoming orders over all weeks was examined more closely. It shows that there are periods in which the due dates can easily be met because the time available for processing (i.e., due date minus release date) is high compared to the net processing time. In contrast, in other periods this ratio (quotient) of available time and net processing time is closer to one or even less than one (and thus critical); note: in the first case this quotient is significantly higher than 1.

TABLE I. KEY FIGURES FOR THE TWO CLASSES OF WORKLOADS

| Workload | WL1 | WL2 |
|---|---|---|
| Number of orders | 50 | 50 |
| Processing time: minimum / maximum [weeks] | 6 / 17 | 8 / 19 |
| Processing time: mean / standard deviation [weeks] | 9.1 / 2.0 | 11.4 / 2.5 |
| Product width: minimum / maximum [meter] | 3 / 15 | 3 / 18 |
| Product width: mean / standard deviation [meter] | 7.2 / 2.7 | 8.5 / 2.9 |
| Product length: minimum / maximum [meter] | 3 / 12 | 3 / 12 |
| Product length: mean / standard deviation [meter] | 8.9 / 2.1 | 10.2 / 2 |
| Due date: minimum / maximum [weeks] | 11 / 23 | 11 / 23 |
| Due date: mean / standard deviation [weeks] | 14.3 / 2.8 | 14.3 / 2.8 |

TABLE II. KEY FIGURES FOR THE SIMULATION RUNS FOR WORKLOAD WL 1

| | Planner | slack |
|---|---|---|
| Cumulative tardiness | | |
| minimum [weeks] | 71 | 76 |
| mean value [weeks] | 74.3 | 77.6 |
| maximum [weeks] | 78 | 75 |
| standard deviation [weeks] | 2.37 | 2.76 |
| Cumulative free area | | |
| minimum [meter²] | 18920 | 21128 |
| mean value [meter²] | 20392 | 24808 |
| maximum [meter²] | 21128 | 27752 |
| standard deviation [meter²] | 1040.86 | 2753.86 |
| Makespan | | |
| minimum [weeks] | 23 | 24 |
| mean value [weeks] | 23.6 | 25.6 |
| maximum [weeks] | 24 | 27 |
| standard deviation [weeks] | 0.47 | 1.25 |
| Mean free area per week | | |
| minimum [meter²] | 822.61 | 880.33 |
| mean value [meter²] | 861.09 | 963.55 |
| maximum [meter²] | 880.33 | 1027.85 |
| standard deviation [meter²] | 27.21 | 61.69 |

On the basis of this analysis, two classes of workloads were created. Each consists of a high number of sets of orders. Each of them is planned by a planner and by the slack rule. The key figures shown in Table 1 are calculated for all sets of orders. Both workloads have the same key figures for the due dates. Therefore, higher processing times for workload 2 result in a more critical due date situation. The results achieved by the planners and the slack rule result in the key figures given in Table 2.

TABLE III. KEY FIGURES FOR THE SIMULATION RUNS FOR WORKLOAD WL 2

| | Planner | Slack |
|---|---|---|
| Cumulative tardiness | | |
| minimum [weeks] | 287 | 266 |
| mean value [weeks] | 290.5 | 270 |
| maximum [weeks] | 294 | 304 |
| standard deviation [weeks] | 3.50 | 2.70 |
| Cumulative free area | | |
| minimum [meter²] | 26989 | 24781 |
| mean value [meter²] | 29197 | 25885 |
| maximum [meter²] | 31405 | 26989 |
| standard deviation [meter²] | 2208 | 1104 |
| Makespan | | |
| minimum [weeks] | 35 | 34 |
| mean value [weeks] | 36 | 34.5 |
| maximum [weeks] | 37 | 35 |
| standard deviation [weeks] | 1.00 | 0.50 |
| Mean free area per week | | |
| minimum [meter²] | 771.11 | 728.85 |
| mean value [meter²] | 809.95 | 749.98 |
| maximum [meter²] | 848.78 | 771.11 |
| standard deviation [meter²] | 38.83 | 21.13 |

As said earlier, a planner prefers larger required area or processing time over smaller ones. Meeting due dates is thus only implicitly relevant in the best case. A detailed analysis of the individual plans shows: Responsible for the differences is that a planner prefers area requirements over tardiness avoidance. This is more likely to be the case with sets of orders causing high time pressure. Conversely, there are situations in which the planner achieves better results because she/he achieves faster processing of orders through better utilisation of plant hall 5. Note: the figures for the mean free area are based on makespan.

## VI. CONCLUSION

Scheduling in the literature mainly considers a bottleneck, such as the limited capacity of the machines. Requirements for the use of limited area for the assembly of machines is dealt with in other publications. Responsible for this are different approaches to these two problem classes.

For the final assembly at Krones AG, both planning problems have to be considered simultaneously. Two experienced planners are used for this purpose. A simulation tool was developed to analyse the possibilities for improvements. The simulation experiments so far show that planners often find a good balance between using the limited area and avoiding tardiness. In situations with high time pressure, a preference for meeting due dates will already provide better results through the slack rule. The two planners are therefore encouraged to consider an allocation decision through slack. The two planners are therefore encouraged to consider an allocation decision through slack.

The results so far show a significant difference in the use of free areas. Therefore, combinations of priority rules to meet due dates with rules to avoid unused areas are to be designed and simulatively investigated.

## REFERENCES

[1] A. El-Bouri, “A cooperative dispatching approach for minimizing mean tardiness in a dynamic flowshop”, in Computers & Operations Research, Volume 39, Issue 7 (July), p. 1305–1314, 2012.

[2] A. Drira, H. Pierreval, and S. Hajri-Gabouj, “Facility layout problems: A survey”, in Annual Reviews in Control Volulme 31 Issue 2, p. 255-267, 2007.

[3] S. Engell, F. Herrmann, and M. Moser, “Priority rules and predictive control algorithms for on-line scheduling of FMS”, in Computer Control of Flexible Manufacturing Systems, S.B. Joshi and J.S. Smith (Eds.). Chapman & Hall, London, p. 75–107, 1994.

[4] C. Garcia and G. Rabadi, “Approximation Algorithms for Spatial Scheduling”, in International Series in Operations Research and Management Science Volume 236, p. 1-16, 2016.

[5] Y. Ge and A. Wang, “Spatial scheduling for irregularly shaped blocks in shipbuilding”, in Computers & Industrial Engineering Volume 152 Issue November 2020, p. 1–14, 2020.

[6] Y. Ge and A. Wang, “Spatial scheduling strategy for irregular curved blocks based on the modified genetic ant colony algorithm (MGACA) in shipbuilding”, in International Journal of Production Research, 56:9, p. 3099-3115, 2018.

[7] J. Heger and T. Voß, “Dynamic priority based dispatching of AGVs in flexible job shops”, in Procedia CIRP, Volume 79, p. 445–449, 2019.

[8] F. Herrmann, “Operative Planung in IT-Systemen für die Produktionsplanung und -steuerung. Regensburg“, Germany: Vieweg+Teubner, 2011.

[9] F. R. Jacobs, W. Berry, D. Whybark, and T. Vollmann, “Manufacturing Planning and Control for Supply Chain Management”, in McGraw-Hill/Irwin (New York), 6 edition, 2010.

[10] C. Koulamas and S. S.Panwalkarb, “New index priority rules for no-wait flow shops”, in Computers & Operations Research, Volume 115, pp. 647–652, 2018.

[11] M. Pinedo, “Scheduling: Theory, Algorithms and Systems”, Fifth Edition. New York, USA: Springer Science+Business Media, 2016

[12] C. Pruncu and J. Jiang, “Modeling and Optimization in Manufacturing – Toward Greener Production by Integrating Computer Simulation”. Wiley-VCH, Weinheim, Germany, 2021.

[13] T. Sobottka, F. Kamhuber, J. Henjes, and W. Sihn, “A case study for simulation and optimization based planning of production and logistics systems”, in Proceedings of the 2017 Winter Simulation Conference W. K. V. Chan, A. D'Ambrogio, G. Zacharewicz, N. Mustafee, G. Wainer, and E. Page, eds., pp. 3495–3506, 2017.

[14] K. D. Sweeney, D. C. Sweeney, and J. F. Campbell, “The performance of priority dispatching rules in a complex job shop: A study on the Upper Mississippi River”, in International Journal of Production Economics, Volume 216, pp. 154–172, 2019.

# Optimisation Modelling with Excel and CMPL2

Mike Steglich
Technical University of Applied Sciences Wildau
15745 Wildau, Germany
e-mail: mike.steglich@th-wildau.de

*Abstract* – **In companies and other organisations, spreadsheet programs are essential tools for preparing and supporting decisions, as they are easy to use and available in most workplaces. For complex problems, optimisation software is used. This offers a wide range of modelling capabilities but relies on external data, such as that maintained in spreadsheets. It therefore makes sense to combine spreadsheets and optimisation software. Add-ins in spreadsheet programs such as Excel solver are relatively widespread. They allow interactive work, although the method of modelling using cell ranges does not seem to be suitable for complex models. Another possibility is to use the spreadsheet interfaces of algebraic modelling languages, which are excellent for modelling complex problems. Unfortunately, as pure data interfaces, they do not allow interactive work. There are some approaches that combine modelling languages with Excel in the form of an Excel add-in, thus combining interactive work with the modelling possibilities of the modelling languages. Unfortunately, these solutions are only available for Windows and some of them seem to have been discontinued. The consideration of all the advantages and disadvantages of the available tools led to the motivation to create an easy-to-use interface between the open-source modelling language CMPL and Excel, which allows interactive work and is available for Windows and macOS. This paper describes this interface.**

***Keywords – spreadsheet optimisation; algebraic modelling language; interactive decision-making process; optimisation.***

## I. Introduction

To solve optimisation problems, the optimisation routines must be addressed, as well as the provision and organisation of the required data. This is often done in companies or other organisations with spreadsheet programs. This is the reason why a variety of software solutions have emerged that combine spreadsheet programs and optimisation environments. These solutions can be divided into spreadsheet add-ins and data interfaces.

The best-known spreadsheet add-in is the freely available Excel solver [1] and its commercial version by Frontline [2]. Similar solutions include the solver in LibreOffice/Calc [3], the open-source solution OpenSolver [4] [5], Frontline's add-in for Google Sheets [6], the Excel add-in Evolver by Palisade [7], Lindo's Whats'sBest! [8] and XLOPTIM by Addinsoft and LocalSolver [9].

In all these approaches, after organising the data, the user has to define the objective function, the variables and the constraints in a user dialogue, as shown in Figure 1. These definitions are made in the form of cell references. After optimisation, the solution is written in the spreadsheet cells defined for the variables. Further outputs, such as reduced costs and shadow prices can be written in separate tables.

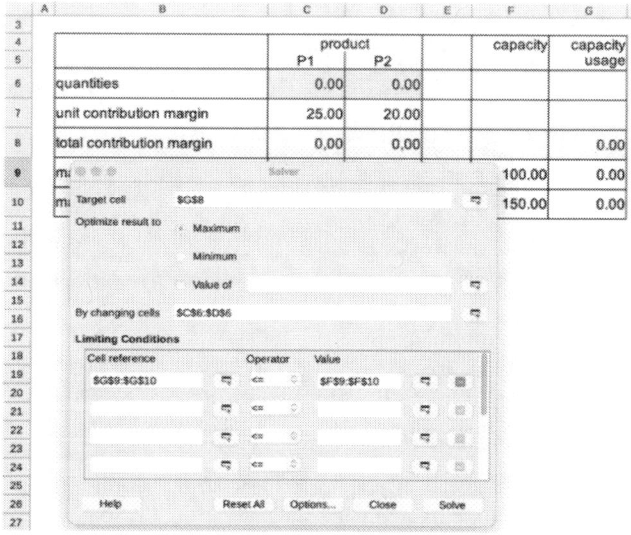

Figure 1. Solver add-in in LibreOffice.

With such solver add-ins, data and models can be easily combined and shared as needed. Since changes to the data lead to new solutions after new optimisation, interactive work is possible. On the other hand, the formulation of model relationships in the form of cell references is not suitable for complex models. Debugging models is also rather complicated [10]. Another disadvantage is that some of these add-ins are only available for Windows (e.g., What'sBest! and Evolver) and not for macOS.

Another widely used approach is algebraic modelling languages, which are more suitable for modelling and solving optimisation problems in terms of their functionality and flexibility than the solver add-ins. Most of these optimisation environments, such as AMPL [11], MPL [12], AIMMS [13], GAMS [14], OPL [15], MOSEL [16] and SAS [17] , offer an interface with which data can be read from spreadsheet files and results can be written to it. These interfaces allow the user to combine the capabilities of the languages with a widely available data source and to use the possibilities of a spreadsheet program to further process a solution that has been found. Unfortunately, these interfaces do not usually allow interactive work, as the spreadsheet files cannot be used by other processes while they are being written and thus cannot be opened. Some of these software solutions (e.g., MPL, MOSEL) offer a VBA library for Microsoft Excel that allows these languages to be used within Excel [18] [19]. But such approaches are more suitable for programmers than for typical corporate decision-makers.

The combination of both an algebraic modelling language and Excel in an interactive mode seems to be a good approach to many real decision-making problems in companies and other organisations. In this context, it is worth mentioning the commercially available AIMMS Excel add-in [20] and SolverStudio [10] [21], which is available free of charge. Microsoft's Solver Foundation was an interesting offer which is evidently not being continued [22].

After choosing certain settings like the project file and licence server, a user of the AIMMS Excel add-in has to define so-called execution sequences to determine the sets and parameters to be read into the AIMMS project, the execution of the problem and the reading back of the results into the Excel spreadsheet. This facilitates interactivity in the process of formulating, solving and interpreting an optimisation problem, albeit in a rather complex way. SolverStudio offers a simpler approach. This Excel add-in allows several algebraic modelling languages (PuLP, Pyomo, AMPL, GMPL, GAMS, CMPL and Gurobi via its Python modelling interface) to be used within Excel [21]. The first step is to select one of the modelling languages and formulate the optimisation model. Then, as shown in Figure 2, the Data Item Editor is used to define the sets and parameters that are to be read into the optimisation model and the solution elements to be written into the Excel spreadsheet after the optimisation is completed. The optimisation is started either by clicking the smiley in the toolbar or via the language menu [10].

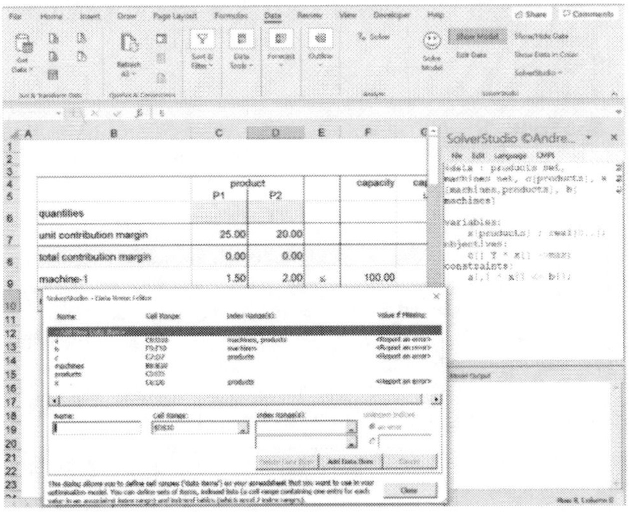

Figure 2. SolverStudio.

SolverStudio is an excellent and very convenient tool, but unfortunately the project does not seem to have been continued seriously, as the last update was in 2016. The interfaces to the languages depend on IronPython 2.7 which is no longer up to date. They would have to be redeveloped for IronPython 3.4, which is currently only available as an alpha version [23]. Another disadvantage is that both SolverStudio and the AIMMS Excel add-in are only available for Windows and not for macOS.

One of the languages supported by SolverStudio is CMPL [24], whose interface to SolverStudio was developed by the author of this paper. The problem with the non-updated SolverStudio and the consideration of all the advantages and disadvantages of all available tools led to the motivation to create an easy-to-use interface between this modelling language and Excel, which allows interactive work and is available for Windows and macOS.

This paper describes this interface. After a short introduction to CMPL, the interface CmplXlsData is explained, followed by an example.

## II. CMPL

<Coliop|Coin> Mathematical Programming Language (CMPL) is a mathematical programming language and a system for the mathematical programming and optimisation of linear and quadratic optimisation problems. The CMPL syntax is similar in formulation to the original mathematical model but also includes syntactic elements from modern programming languages. CMPL is intended to combine the clarity of mathematical models with the flexibility of programming languages [25].

A typical LP problem is the product-mix problem. The aim is to find an optimal quantity for the products, depending on given capacities. The objective function is defined by the profit contributions per unit $c$ and the variable quantity of the products $x$. The constraints consist of the use of the capacities and the ranges for the decision variables. The use of the capacities is given by the product of the coefficient matrix $a$ and the vector of the decision variables $x$ and restricted by the vector of the available capacities $b$. The simple example

$$
\begin{aligned}
&25x_1 + 20x_2 \to \max! \\
&s.t. \\
&1.5x_1 + 2x_2 \leq 100 \\
&12x_1 + 5x_2 \leq 150 \\
&x_1, x_2 \geq 0
\end{aligned}
$$

can be formulated in CMPL as follows:

```
par:
  c := (25, 20);
  a := ((1.5,  2), (12, 5));
  b := (100, 150);
var:
  x[defset(c)] : real[0..];
obj:
  c^T * x ->max;
con:
  a * x <=b;
```

Listing 1. The product-mix problem in CMPL

A CMPL model usually consists of four sections. In the `par` section (lines 01–04), sets and parameters (here the vectors $c$ and $b$ and the matrix $a$) must be specified. The `var` section (lines 05–06) is used to define the variables of the problem. In line 06, a vector `x` of non-negative continuous variables is defined using the definition set of the parameter vector `c`. The objective function in the `obj` section (lines 07–08) and the constraints in the `con` section (lines 09–10) are specified by vector and matrix multiplications.

CMPL executes CBC, GLPK, Gurobi, SCIP or CPLEX directly to solve the generated model instance. Because it is also possible to transform the mathematical problem into MPS or Free-MPS, alternative solvers can be used.

CMPL is a COIN-OR [26] open-source project initiated by the Technical University of Applied Sciences Wildau. Binaries for Windows, macOS and Linux can be downloaded free of charge from http://coliop.org/.

The CMPL distribution contains Coliop, which is CMPL's Integrated Development Environment (IDE), application programming interfaces (APIs) for Python3 and Java (pyCmpl and jCmpl) and, in CMPLServer, [27] an XML-RPC-based web service for distributed and grid optimisation.

## III. CmplXlsData

CmplXlsData was introduced with CMPL version 2.0 and is CMPL's interface for reading sets and parameters from an Excel file and for writing optimisation results to an open Excel file. If the Excel file is not open, CMPL will open it automatically and the results of the optimisation can be seen immediately. Please note, this feature is only available on Windows and macOS if Microsoft Excel is installed. CmplXlsData is mainly implemented with Python3 using the (open-source) Python for Excel library by xlwings [28].

As in SolverStudio or the AIMMS Excel add-in, a user must specify which data from an Excel file should be read into a CMPL model and which results should be written back. These specifications are made in a CmplXlsData file. A CmplXlsData file is a plain text file that contains the definition of parameters and sets with the cell addresses of their values in the specified Excel file in a particular syntax. Additionally, the optimisation results to be written to Excel with their cell addresses can be specified in this file.

A CmplXlsData file contains usually the three sections `@source`, `@input` and `@output`.

The `@source` section is intended to specify the Excel file and optionally the sheet to be used to read sets and parameters and to write the optimisation results.

| | |
|---|---|
| **@source** | Section for specifying the Excel file and the default sheet |
| **%file** <*fileName*> | Name of the Excel file |
| *[***%sheet** <*sheetName*>*]* | Optional argument to specify the name of the active sheet<br>In each entry for the inputs and the outputs, the sheet can be specified directly. |

Listing 2. Source section

In the `@input` section, the sets and parameters to be read into the CMPL model have to be specified with their cell ranges.

| | |
|---|---|
| **@input** | Section for specifying sets and parameters to be read into CMPL |
| %*name* <*cell*> | A scalar parameter `name` is assigned a single string or number available in Excel at the specified cell. |
| %*name* **set***[***[***rank***]***]* ↲<br><*cellRange*> | Definition of an $n$-tuple set<br>A set definition starts with the name followed by the keyword set. For $n$-tuple sets with $n > 1$ the rank of the set is to be specified enclosed by square brackets.<br>The set is assigned the entries available in Excel in the cells specified in the cell range reference. |
| %*name[set[,set1,* ↲<br>*...]]* <*cellRange*> | Definition of a parameter array<br>The specification of a parameter array starts with the name followed by one or more sets, over which the array is defined. The data entries can be strings or numbers and have to be found at the specified cell range reference in Excel. |

Listing 3. Input section

The `@output` section specifies the optimisation result elements to be written to the Excel file. These results are displayed directly in the Excel file.

| | |
|---|---|
| **@output** | Section for specifying the optimisation results to be written to Excel |
| %*name*.**activity** ↲<br><*cell*><br>%*name*.**type** <*cell*><br>%*name*.**lowerBound** ↲<br><*cell*><br>%*name*.**upperBound** ↲<br><*cell*><br>%*name*.**marginal** ↲<br><*cell*> | Singleton variable or constraint<br>For a singleton variable or constraint named `name`, the activity, type, limits and dual values can be written to Excel in the `cell`.<br>The name is followed by a dot and one of the keywords (`activity`, `type`, `lowerbound`, `upperbound`, `marginal`) for the information to be written to Excel. |
| %*name***[***set[,set1,* ↲<br>*...]***]***.***activity** ↲<br><*cellRange*> | Arrays of variables or constraints<br>A complete array of variables or constraints named `name`, the activity, type, limits and dual |

| | |
|---|---|
| %name[set[,set1, ↵ ...]].type ↵ <cellRange><br>%name[set[,set1, ↵ ...]].lowerBound ↵ <cellRange><br>%name[set[,set1, ↵ ...]].upperBound ↵ <cellRange><br>%name[set[,set1, ↵ ...]].marginal ↵ <cellRange> | values can be written to Excel in the specified cell range.<br>The specification of an array of variables or constraints starts with the name followed by one or more sets, over which the array is defined. This is followed by a dot and one of the keywords for the attributes activity, type, lowerbound, upperbound, marginal of the result information to be written to Excel. |
| %objName <cell> | Writes the name of the objective function to Excel in the specified cell |
| %objSense <cell> | Writes the objective sense |
| %objValue <cell> | Writes the objective function value |
| %objStatus <cell> | Writes the status of the objective function |
| %nrOfVars <cell> | Writes the number of the variables |
| %nrOfCons <cell> | Writes the number of the constraints |
| %solverName <cell> | Writes the name of the solver |
| %solverMsg <cell> | Writes a message of the solver |

Listing 4. Output section

To connect a CmplDataFile with the CMPL model, the command line option `xlsdata` is used. The arguments of this command line option define parameters and sets for CMPL, whose source Excel file and the corresponding cell ranges are specified in a CmplXlsData file. It is recommended that this command line option be used in the CMPL header.

```
%xlsdata [filename] : [set1 set[[rank]]] ↵
        [, set2 set[[rank]] , ... ]

%xlsdata [filename] : [param1] ↵
        [, param2 , ... ]

%xlsdata [filename] : [paramArray1[set]] ↵
        [, paramArray2[set] , ... ]
```

Listing 5. CmplXlsData in CMPL header

The first argument is the file name. If the file name contains white spaces, the name must be enclosed in double quotes. If *filename* is not specified, the generic name *model*.xdat is used, where *model*.cmpl is the name of the CMPL file. After the colon, the sets, scalar parameters and parameter arrays to be read can be specified and separated by commas.

## IV. CMPLXLSDATA EXAMPLE

In this section, a transhipment problem is used to illustrate the functionalities of CmplXlsData. A transhipment model is intended to organise an optimal supply of a homogeneous good between a set of sources (origins, suppliers), a set of transhipment nodes and a set of sinks (destinations, customers) in order to minimise the total transportation cost (or distances, times, etc.) [29].

In this example, a transport plan between three plants, two warehouses and four distribution centres is to be determined to minimise the total transport costs. The unit transport costs are shown in the picture below as weights at the edges. The capacity of each possible road (edge) is restricted to 500 units due to the vehicle pool.

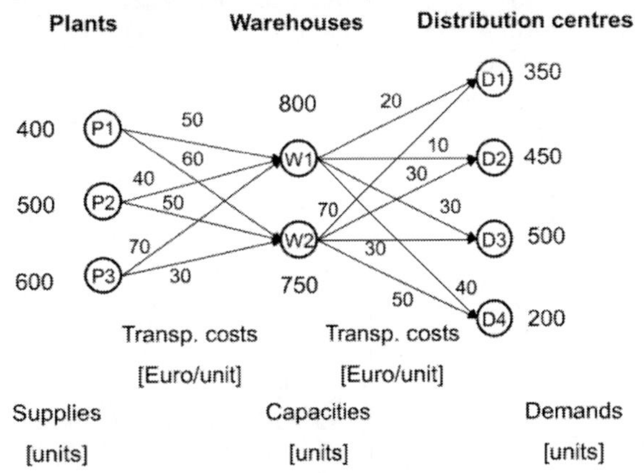


Figure 3. Transhipment problem example.

In the first step, an Excel file `transhipment.xlsx` containing the sheet `transhipment` is created. As shown in Figure 4, the IDs, supplies and demands of the nodes are given in the columns A to C. Please note that the transhipment nodes W1 and W2 have to be split (W1a, W1b, W2a, W2b) owing to their capacities and the fact that the min-cost flow model does not allow capacities for nodes [30]. Therefore, each transhipment node must be split into two nodes, with a cost-free edge connecting the two nodes. The maximum flow on such an edge equals the capacity of the transhipment node. Consequently, the definition of the 2-tuple set of the edges in the columns F and G also contains these two auxiliary edges W1a to W1b and W2a to W2b in addition to the normal edges.

The corresponding cost rates, minimum and maximum capacities of these edges are given in columns H to J. The columns K and M are for the activities and marginal values of the flow variables. The costs in column L yield the product of the activities in column K and the cost rates in column H. These values are displayed after the optimisation in addition to the objective function value in cell C15 and the activities of `netFlow` constraints of the nodes in column D.

| | A | B | C | D | E | F | G | H | I | J | K | L | M |
|---|---|---|---|---|---|---|---|---|---|---|---|---|---|
| 1 | **Nodes** | | | | | **Arcs** | | | | | | | |
| 2 | | supplies | demands | net flows | | from | to | cost rate | min. cap. | max. cap | flow | costs | marginals |
| 3 | P1 | 400 | 0 | | | P1 | W1a | 50 | 0 | 500 | | 0 | |
| 4 | P2 | 500 | 0 | | | P1 | W2a | 60 | 0 | 500 | | 0 | |
| 5 | P3 | 600 | 0 | | | P2 | W1a | 40 | 0 | 500 | | 0 | |
| 6 | W1a | 0 | 0 | | | P2 | W2a | 50 | 0 | 500 | | 0 | |
| 7 | W2a | 0 | 0 | | | P3 | W1a | 70 | 0 | 500 | | 0 | |
| 8 | W1b | 0 | 0 | | | P3 | W2a | 30 | 0 | 500 | | 0 | |
| 9 | W2b | 0 | 0 | | | W1a | W1b | 0 | 0 | 800 | | 0 | |
| 10 | D1 | 0 | 350 | | | W1b | D1 | 20 | 0 | 500 | | 0 | |
| 11 | D2 | 0 | 450 | | | W1b | D2 | 10 | 0 | 500 | | 0 | |
| 12 | D3 | 0 | 500 | | | W1b | D3 | 30 | 0 | 500 | | 0 | |
| 13 | D4 | 0 | 200 | | | W1b | D4 | 40 | 0 | 500 | | 0 | |
| 14 | | | | | | W2a | W2b | 0 | 0 | 750 | | 0 | |
| 15 | total costs | | | | | W2b | D1 | 70 | 0 | 500 | | 0 | |
| 16 | | | | | | W2b | D2 | 30 | 0 | 500 | | 0 | |
| 17 | | | | | | W2b | D3 | 30 | 0 | 500 | | 0 | |
| 18 | | | | | | W2b | D4 | 50 | 0 | 500 | | 0 | |

Figure 4. Transhipment problem in Excel.

The CmplXlsData `transhipment.xdat` file starts in the `source` section with the entry for the Excel file `transhipment.xlsx` and the sheet `transhipment` from which the data is to be read and into which the results are to be written.

```
01 @source
02   %file < transhipment.xlsx >
03   %sheet < transhipment>
04
05 @input
06   %edges set[2] < F3:G18 >
07   %nodes set < A3:A13 >
08
09   %c[edges] < H3:H18 >
10   %d[nodes] < C3:C13 >
11   %s[nodes] < B3:B13 >
12
13   %minCap[edges] < I3:I18  >
14   %maxCap[edges] < J3:J18 >
15
16 @output
17   %x[edges].activity < K3:K18 >
18   %x[edges].marginal < M3:M18 >
19
20   %netFlow[nodes].activity < D3:D13 >
21
22   %objValue < C15 >
```

Listing 6. CmplXlsData file of the transhipment problem

The following `input` section usually starts with the definition of index sets that will later be used for parameter arrays. In line 06, a 2-tuple set `edges` is defined, to which the IDs of the edges stored in cells `F3:G18` are assigned. The following line defines the set `nodes` and assigns the IDs given in the Excel sheet in the cell range `A3:A13`. These sets are used to define the parameter arrays for the cost rates `c` of the edges (line 09), as well as the supplies `s` and demands `d` of the nodes (lines 10 and 11) and assigns the data stored in the cell ranges indicated in the angle brackets. The minimum and maximum capacities (`minCap` and `maxCap`) of the edges are given in lines 13 and 14.

The `output` section is designed to enable all the requested results of the optimisation to be written into the specified Excel sheet. In lines 17 and 18 it is specified that the activities and marginals of the flow variables `x` must be written in the cell ranges `K3:K18` and `M3:M18`. The activities of the `netFlow` constraints of the nodes should be displayed in `D3:D13` and the objective function value in cell `C15`.

These specifications are connected with the corresponding CMPL model using the CMPL header entry `%xlsdata` in the first line of the model.

```
01 %xlsdata : nodes set, s[nodes],
   d[nodes], edges set[2], c[edges],
   maxCap[edges]
02
03 var:
04   { [i,j] in edges: x[i,j] :
05      real[minCap[i, j]..maxCap[i, j]];
06   }
07
08 obj:
09   sum{ [i,j] in edges:
10         c[i,j]*x[i,j]} ->min;
11
12 con:
13   {i in nodes : netFlow[i]:
14      sum{j in edges *> [i,*]  : x[i,j]}-
15      sum{j in edges *> [*,i]  : x[j,i]}=
16      s[i] - d[i];
17   }
```

Listing 7. CMPL file of the transhipment problem

The variables of the model are organised in an array `x`, which is defined by using the 2-tuple set `edges`. They are all continuous variables with lower and upper bounds defined in the vectors `minCap` and `maxCap`. These variables are the flows of the uniform good on the edges (lines 04–06). The objective function to be minimised is defined in the `obj` section (lines 09–10) as the sum over all edges of the product of the unit transport costs `c[i,j]` and the flow `x[i,j]` on the edge. For all nodes, a flow balance constraint `netFlow[i]` has to be created in which the difference between the outgoing and incoming flow on the left-hand side must be equal to the difference between the supply `s[i]` and the demand `d[i]` of this node on the right-hand side (lines 13–17).

The results can be found after the optimisation in the cells specified in the CmplXlsData file as shown in Figure 5.

The planned quantities on the edges can be seen in column K. A few of the edges are unused, whereby the marginal values in column M show the reduced cost of these non-basic variables. For fully utilised edges, the marginals show the shadow prices. For example, the auxiliary edge for the transhipment node W1 has a shadow price of 20 due to the fully used capacity of 800 units. The activities of the `netFlow` constraints written in column D show that all the supply, demand and flow balance constraints of the nodes are satisfied. This transport plan results in a minimum transport cost of 100,500 which is shown in cell `C15`.

| | A | B | C | D | E | F | G | H | I | J | K | L | M |
|---|---|---|---|---|---|---|---|---|---|---|---|---|---|
| 1 | **Nodes** | | | | | **Arcs** | | | | | | | |
| 2 | | supplies | demands | net flows | | from | to | cost rate | min. cap. | max. cap | flow | costs | marginals |
| 3 | P1 | 400 | 0 | 400 | | P1 | W1a | 50 | 0 | 500 | 200 | 10.000 | 0 |
| 4 | P2 | 500 | 0 | 500 | | P1 | W2a | 60 | 0 | 500 | 200 | 12.000 | 0 |
| 5 | P3 | 600 | 0 | 600 | | P2 | W1a | 40 | 0 | 500 | 500 | 20.000 | 0 |
| 6 | W1a | 0 | 0 | 0 | | P2 | W2a | 50 | 0 | 500 | 0 | 0 | 0 |
| 7 | W2a | 0 | 0 | 0 | | P3 | W1a | 70 | 0 | 500 | 100 | 7.000 | 0 |
| 8 | W1b | 0 | 0 | 0 | | P3 | W2a | 30 | 0 | 500 | 500 | 15.000 | -50 |
| 9 | W2b | 0 | 0 | 0 | | W1a | W1b | 0 | 0 | 800 | 800 | 0 | -20 |
| 10 | D1 | 0 | 350 | -350 | | W1b | D1 | 20 | 0 | 500 | 350 | 7.000 | 0 |
| 11 | D2 | 0 | 450 | -450 | | W1b | D2 | 10 | 0 | 500 | 450 | 4.500 | 0 |
| 12 | D3 | 0 | 500 | -500 | | W1b | D3 | 30 | 0 | 500 | 0 | 0 | 10 |
| 13 | D4 | 0 | 200 | -200 | | W1b | D4 | 40 | 0 | 500 | 0 | 0 | 0 |
| 14 | | | | | | W2a | W2b | 0 | 0 | 750 | 700 | 0 | 0 |
| 15 | total costs | | 100.500 | | | W2b | D1 | 70 | 0 | 500 | 0 | 0 | 40 |
| 16 | | | | | | W2b | D2 | 30 | 0 | 500 | 0 | 0 | 10 |
| 17 | | | | | | W2b | D3 | 30 | 0 | 500 | 500 | 15.000 | 0 |
| 18 | | | | | | W2b | D4 | 50 | 0 | 500 | 200 | 10.000 | 0 |

Figure 5. Results for the transhipment problem in Excel

CMPL's Excel interface CmplXlsData is not an add-in, but it enables interactive working, as both Excel and CMPL's IDE Coliop can be run simultaneously (Figure 6). Each change to the data organised in Excel results in new solutions when CMPL is restarted, which are immediately displayed in the specified cell ranges in Excel. If the Excel file is not open, CMPL opens it automatically.

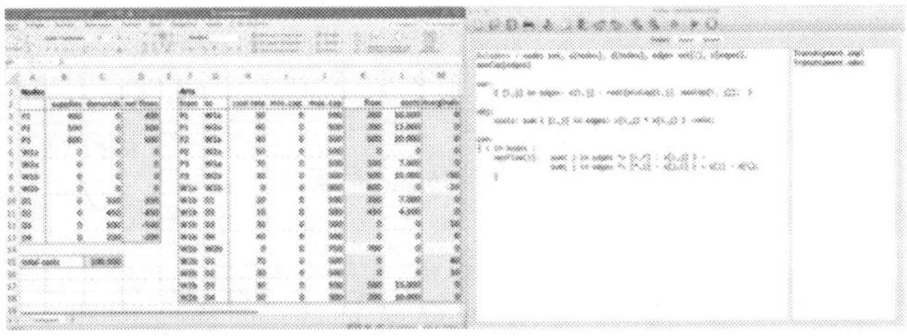

Figure 6. Interactive mode with Excel and Coliop

Unlike the AIMMS Excel add-in and SolverStudio, CmplXlsData is available for Windows and macOS. An additional installation routine to connect Excel and CMPL is not required. A user only needs to install Excel and CMPL. The connection between the two is established automatically by CmplXlsData.

As shown in the example, this interface is easy to use as it provides a simple and structured syntax similar to CmplData, which is another data interface of CMPL.

## V. SUMMARY

This paper deals with the combination of spreadsheet programs and optimisation software.

Spreadsheet programs, which are easy to use and available at most workplaces, are essential for preparing and supporting decisions. It is reasonable to connect spreadsheet programs with optimisation software to combine the modelling capabilities of optimisation software with the data maintained in spreadsheets. Such software solutions can be divided into spreadsheet add-ins and data interfaces, which are investigated in this work. Add-ins in spreadsheet programs such as the Excel solver add-in allow interactive work, although modelling with cell ranges does not seem suitable for complex models. Data interfaces to spreadsheets of algebraic modelling languages, which are excellent for modelling complex problems, do not allow interactive work. In addition, there are some approaches that combine modelling languages with Excel in the form of an Excel add-in and thus combine interactive work with excellent modelling possibilities. Unfortunately, these are only available for Windows and some of them seem to have been discontinued.

The consideration of all the advantages and disadvantages of the available tools led to the motivation to create CmplXlsData, which is CMPL's interface to Excel. It is an easy-to-use interface between this modelling language and Excel, which allows interactive work and is available for Windows and macOS. This paper describes this interface with its main functionalities and an illustrative example.

## REFERENCES


[1] Microsoft, "Define and solve a problem by using Solver," 2021. [Online]. Available: https://support.microsoft.com/en-us/office/define-and-solve-a-problem-by-using-solver-5d1a388f-079d-43ac-a7eb-f63e45925040. [retrieved: July 2021].

[2] Frontline, "Excel Solver – Overview and Example" 2021. [Online]. Available: https://www. solver.com/excel-solver-overview-and-example. [retrieved: July 2021].

[3] LibreOffice, "Solver," 2021. [Online]. Available: https://help.libreoffice.org/7.0/en-US/text/scalc/01/ solver.html?DbPAR=CALC. [retrieved: July 2021].

[4] OpenSolver, "About OpenSolver," 2021. [Online]. Available: https://opensolver.org. [retrieved: July 2021].

[5] A. J. Mason, "OpenSolver – An Open Source Add-in to Solve Linear and Integer Progammes in Excel," in *Operations Research Proceedings 2011*, Berlin and Heidelberg, pp. 401-406, 2012.

[6] Frontline, "Solver - Add-on for Google Sheets," 2021. [Online]. Available: https://workspace.google.com/ marketplace/app/solver/539454054595. [retrieved: July 2021].

[7] Palisade, "Evolver - Innovative Optimization for Spreadsheets," 2021. [Online]. Available: https://www. palisade.com/evolver/default.asp. [retrieved: July 2021].

[8] L. S. Inc., " What'sBest! 17.0 - Excel Add-In for Linear, Nonlinear, and Integer Modeling and Optimization," 2021. [Online]. Available: https://www.lindo.com/index.php/ products/what-sbest-and-excel-optimization. [retrieved: July 2021].

[9] Addinsoft, "The leading Optimization Solver for Microsoft Excel®," 2021. [Online]. Available: https://www.xloptim.com/en. [retrieved: July 2021].

[10] A. J. Mason, "SolverStudio: A New Tool for Better Optimisation and Simulation Modelling in Excel," *INFORMS Transactions on Education*, vol. 14, no. 1, pp. 45-52 , 2013.

[11] AMPL, "AMPL Direct Spreadsheet Interface," 2021. [Online]. Available: https://ampl.com/resources/new-features/spreadsheets/. [retrieved: July 2021].

[12] M. Software, "MPL for Windows Manual - Import Data from Excel Spreadsheet," 2021. [Online]. Available: http://www. maximalsoftware.com/mplman/mpw07060.html. [retrieved: July 2021].

[13] A. B.V., "AIMMS Excel Library - AXLL," 2021. [Online]. Available: https://how-to.aimms.com/Articles/85/85-using-axll-library.html. [retrieved: July 2021].

[14] GAMS, "Data Exchange with Microsoft Excel," 2021. [Online]. Available: https://www.gams.com/latest/docs/UG_DataExchange_Excel.html. [retrieved: July 2021].

[15] IBM, "ILOG CPLEX Optimization Studio/ 20.1.0 / Spreadsheet Input/Output," 2021. [Online]. Available: https://www.ibm.com/docs/en/icos/20.1.0?topic=sources-spreadsheet-inputoutput. [retrieved: July 2021].

[16] FICO, "The Excel interface," 2021. [Online]. Available: https://www.fico.com/fico-xpress-optimization/docs/latest/mosel/mosel_data/dhtml/secsetup_sec_secexcelsetup.html. [retrieved: July 2021].

[17] V. DelGobbo, "Integrating SAS® and Microsoft Excel: Exploring the Many Options Available to You," SAS Institute Inc., https://www.sas.com/content/dam/SAS/support/en/sas-global-forum-proceedings/2019/2991-2019.pdf, 2019 [retrieved: July 2021].

[18] M. Software, "OptiMax Component Library," 2021. [Online]. Available: http://www.maximalsoftware.com/optimax/. [retrieved: July 2021].

[19] FICO, "Launching Mosel from Excel using VBAFICO Xpress Optimization Examples Repository /," 2021. [Online]. Available: https://examples.xpress.fico.com/example.pl?id=excelmosel1. [retrieved: July 2021].

[20] AIMMS B.V., "AIMMS - The Excel Add-In User's Guide," https://download.aimms.com/aimms/download/references/AIMMS_excel.pdf, 2016. [retrieved: July 2021]

[21] A. J. Mason, "SolverStudio," 2021. [Online]. Available: https://solverstudio.org. [retrieved: July 2021].

[22] Microsoft, "Solver Foundation," 2014. [Online]. Available: https://docs.microsoft.com/en-us/previous-versions/msdn10/hh145003(v=msdn.10). [retrieved: July 2021].

[23] .NET Foundation, "IronPython - the Python programming language for .NET," 2021. [Online]. Available: https://ironpython.net. [retrieved: July 2021]

[24] M. Steglich and T. Schleiff, "CMPL," 2021. [Online]. Available: http://coliop.org. [retrieved: July 2021]

[25] M. Steglich and T. Schleiff, "CMPL: Coliop Mathematical Programming Language," *Wildauer Schriftenreihe - Entscheidungsunterstützung und Operations Research,* vol. 1, 2010.

[26] COIN-OR, 2021. [Online]. Available: https://www.coin-or.org. [retrieved: Sep 2021]

[27] M. Steglich, "CMPLServer - An open source approach for distributed and grid optimisation," *AKWI Anwendungen und Konzepte der Wirtschaftsinformatik,* no. 4, pp. 9-21, 2016.

[28] xlwings, "xlwings - Python for Excel," Zoomer Analytics GmbH, 2021. [Online]. Available: https://www.xlwings.org. [retrieved: July 2021]

[29] F. Hillier and G. Lieberman, Introduction to Operations Research (International edition), vol. 10th ed., New York et al.: McGraw-Hill, 2015.

[30] M. Steglich, D. Feige, and P. Klaus, Logistik-Entscheidungen: Modellbasierte Entscheidungsunterstützung in der Logistik mit LogisticsLab, Berlin and Boston: De Gruyter, 2016.

# Can Simulation Prevent Companies from the Bullwhip Trap?

## New Approaches to Model the Bullwhip Effect with the Aid of Excel and High-Level Petri Nets

Carlo Simon, Lara Zakfeld, Cecilie Elizabeth Jensen, Denis Klietsch, and Mario Montag

Hochschule Worms
Erenburgerstr. 19, 67549 Worms, Germany
Email: {simon,zakfeld}@hs-worms.de

***Abstract*—There exist many explications for phenomena in logistics – one of them is the so called bullwhip effect. It explains ups and downs in turnovers in a supply chain if demands and offers of the participants are not synchronized. While previous work on the simulation of the bullwhip effect was intended to explain it in general, surprisingly little research has been conducted with focus on how to make these simulations available for companies. In doing so, simulation based forecasts could reduce storage and production costs significantly, prevent companies from getting stuck in the bullwhip trap, and thus enable significant savings. This paper, in contrast, demonstrates how to develop models of the bullwhip effect for a given scenario with the aid of Excel and with a novel, freely accessible modeling and simulation environment for high-level Petri nets, and compares the findings. Companies can use both approaches and adapt them easily to their specific problem. Hence, this paper has two major outcomes: The models themselves but also an explanation on how to find such models.**

***Keywords*—Logistics; Bullwhip effect; Modeling; Simulation; Excel; Petri nets; Savings.**

## I. Introduction

Many companies strive to reduce their internal costs. But in addition, there is another significant potential for savings through a better understanding of the market and coordinated communication with the other market participants. How high this savings potential is can exemplary be explained using the *bullwhip effect (BWE)*: Strong fluctuations in terms of production and sales of the participants in a supply chain can be observed, which lag behind current market developments.

Although phenomena such as the bullwhip effect are known, this knowledge rarely has any practical impact on business decisions. Appropriate simulation models could change that. But entrepreneurs need both suitable models and software to be able to carry out the corresponding simulations. This enables savings in production and logistics as well as a significant contribution to increasing sustainability in supply chains. For this, however, practitioners need guidance on how to proceed methodically and which tools they can use for this.

This paper answers the question how to develop a simulation for the bullwhip effect in a step-by-step approach in correspondence with the phase model of Figure 1 with commonly available tools. It may therefore serve as a source for practitioners to apply the findings to their own business. A detailed description of an imagined scenario is the starting point where the actual process and the business rules which trigger procurement and production are the most important components.

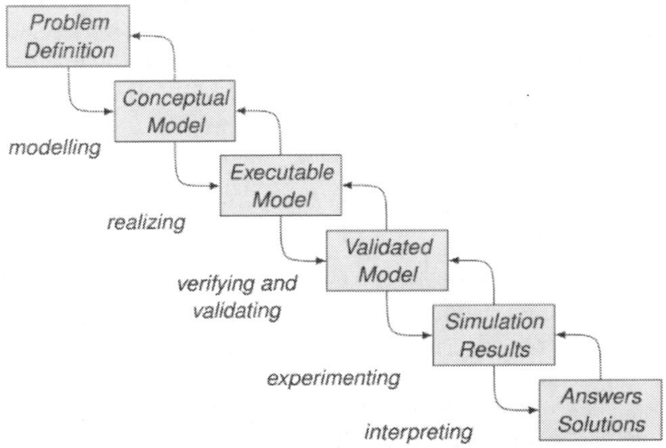


Figure 1. Phases of a Simulation Study adapted from [1].

An Excel based simulation model served as a conceptual model. For each simulation period distinct calculations had to be defined. Although this was a helpful step to understand the problem, this solution does not scale very well. Interested readers are invited to ask for the original Excel file. Afterwards, a Petri net model was developed as an executable model. Also here, interested users are invited to ask for the model and to test it with the aid of the tool which is free to use for academic purposes. Both, Excel and Petri net solutions were used to validate each other. What must not be underestiamated is the need for a meaningful visualization of the simulation results to solve the problem.

This paper is organized as follows: Section II explains the bullwhip effect and discusses former work on its simulation. Section III introduces a supply chain scenario for which simulation models have been developed in Excel as described in Section IV and with the aid of high-level Petri nets as described in Section VI. Since modeling and simulation of Petri nets highly depends on the tool used, Section V is inserted in between, introducing Petri nets and the Process-Simulation.Center (P-S.C). Finally, in Section VII visualization is addressed as a major topic to enable decision making based on the simulation results. A summary and an outlook are given in Section VIII.

## II. Related Work on the Bullwhip Effect

Various definitions of the term BWE exist in literature. In general, the BWE can be described as a volatile gap between a company's orders and its suppliers expectation which increases in the up- and downstream of a supply chain. Typically, the BWE is considered concerning the variables order volume, inventory, lot size, and production capacity [2].

The drivers of the BWE are manifold: An increased demand due to a delayed information is called *Forrester effect*, while order bundling within a player is found as *Burbridge effect*. The *Houlian effect* describes a situation where participants expect a possible bottleneck of their suppliers and therefore declare a higher demand as necessary. Finally, the *promotion effect* results from price fluctuations [3]–[5]. Often behavioral and psychological factors of the decision makers in the supply chain have a major impact on the degree of volatility [6].

There exist several approaches to simulate the BWE. But [7][8] criticize that most authors use rather simple supply chains which consist only of two to four stages with one player on each stage. This means an unacceptable level of abstraction for practical applications.

Other approaches to simulate supply chains are conjoint with high entry barriers for potential users [9]. exemplary, [10] use a genetic algorithm to consider cost and liquidity management of supply chains. [11] use an adaptive network based fuzzy inference system (ANFIS) trained with the production information of a beverage producer. Companies can hardly adopt such methods because their modes of action are in-apprehensible for IT laymen.

Thus, companies use software technologies to accelerate the information flow and production speed in the hope of avoiding or at least reducing the BWE, instead of using the knowledge concerning the bullwhip effect. In 2020, 45% of the asked companies use inventory and network optimization tools and another 44% will adopt these tools within the next five years. Robotics and automation, which can be used to speed up reactions on changing demands, are recognized as the technologies with the highest potential (above 60%) [12].

From the authors' perspective, these technologies result in local and isolated improvements. Their impact on the entire supply chain remains vague. The methods and tools used in this paper to model the BWE, however, enable practitioners to understand the causality within a simulation model, adapt the models to their own needs, and to develop confidence in the simulation results.

## III. Simulation Scenario

The presented simulation of the bullwhip effect is conducted at the example of an imagined scenario (see Figure 2), where consumers' demands pull goods through a supply chain which also consists of retailers, producers and raw material suppliers.

Figure 2. Stages of the supply chain scenario.

The scenario considers production and trading of shampoos called *Aloe*, *Chai*, *Coco* which are kept simple: They consist of bottled soap and odor of various ratio (see Figure 3). The focus is on the flow of the bottles. For other raw materials there would be similar results, hence they are omitted here.

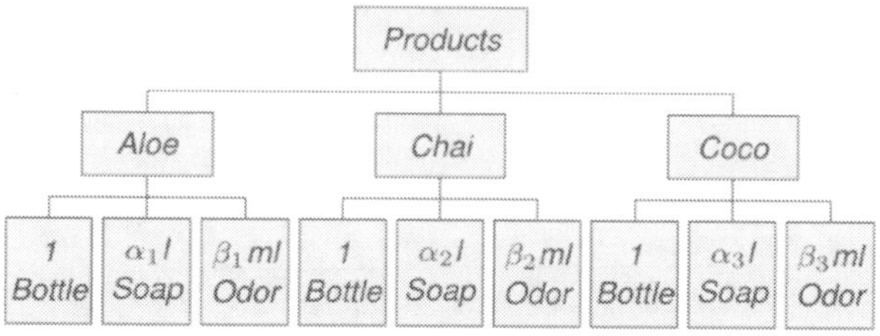


Figure 3. Product Tree.

Products and raw materials are produced on demand. After selling products to the consumers out of their stocks, retailers fill up their stocks when they reach their specific reorder level. For this, the producers have to empty their stocks and eventually order raw material from their suppliers for the production of new products for upcoming requests. Also, the producers use reorder levels to calculate their specific demand.

There exist 8 retailers named *Ali*, *Ede*, *Glo*, *Lid*, *md*, *Pha*, *Rew*, and *Ros*. (and probably German readers assume which real retailers the authors had in mind). Each of them offers all three products and procures them from 6 producers called *Body*, *Head*, *Neck*, *Hand*, *Knee*, and *Foot*. Each producer produces one of the mentioned products and has exclusive contracts with one or more retailers. The sourcing matrix in Table I shows the relations between the different partners.

TABLE I. SOURCING MATRIX: RETAILER, PRODUCER, PRODUCT

| | Ali | Ede | Glo | Lid | md | Pha | Rew | Ros |
|---|---|---|---|---|---|---|---|---|
| Aloe | Body | Head | Neck | Body | Head | Neck | Body | Head |
| Chai | Hand | Knee | Hand | Knee | Hand | Knee | Hand | Knee |
| Coco | Foot | Foot | Foot | Foot | Foot | Foot | Foot | Foot |

All raw material is delivered by one supplier since the focus here is on the bullwhip effect for retailer and producer.

The simulation runs over 12 periods. All stocks of retailers and manufacturers are initialized with 150% of their reorder levels as shown in Table II. Retailers have access to their global storage so local storages are not considered.

TABLE II. INITIAL STOCKS (IS) AND REORDER LEVELS (RL) OF THE RETAILERS FOR THREE PRODUCTS (IN THOUSANDS)

| | | Ali | Ede | Glo | Lid | md | Pha | Rew | Ros |
|---|---|---|---|---|---|---|---|---|---|
| Aloe | IS | 105 | 105 | 90 | 105 | 105 | 90 | 105 | 105 |
| | RL | 70 | 70 | 60 | 70 | 70 | 60 | 70 | 70 |
| Chai | IS | 120 | 90 | 120 | 82.5 | 120 | 90 | 120 | 82.5 |
| | RL | 80 | 60 | 80 | 55 | 80 | 60 | 80 | 55 |
| Coco | IS | 82.5 | 105 | 75 | 90 | 82.5 | 105 | 75 | 82.5 |
| | RL | 55 | 70 | 50 | 60 | 55 | 70 | 50 | 55 |

As summarized in Table III, the total consumption varies seasonally from 700.000 to 1.400.000 bottles over all products and their market share varies from 25% to 60% of the total depending on the success of the marketing campaigns.

TABLE III. MARKET (IN THOUSANDS) AND SHARE PER PERIOD

| Period | Total market | Product distribution | | |
|---|---|---|---|---|
| | | Aloe | Chai | Coco |
| 1 | 1.000 | 60% | 20% | 20% |
| 2 | 1.200 | 25% | 50% | 25% |
| 3 | 800 | 25% | 25% | 50% |
| 4 | 1.000 | 33% | 33% | 34% |
| 5 | 700 | 60% | 20% | 20% |
| 6 | 1.400 | 25% | 25% | 50% |
| 7 | 1.000 | 25% | 25% | 50% |
| 8 | 800 | 33% | 33% | 34% |
| 9 | 1.200 | 60% | 20% | 20% |
| 10 | 700 | 25% | 50% | 25% |
| 11 | 1.300 | 25% | 25% | 50% |
| 12 | 900 | 33% | 33% | 34% |

Table IV shows the fluctuating market shares per Retailer across the 12 phases.

TABLE IV. RETAILERS' MARKET SHARE PER PERIODS

| Period | Retailer distribution | | | | | | | |
|---|---|---|---|---|---|---|---|---|
| | Ali | Ede | Glo | Lid | md | Pha | Rew | Ros |
| 1 | 12% | 12% | 10% | 18% | 15% | 11% | 14% | 8% |
| 2 | 10% | 11% | 11% | 15% | 18% | 11% | 10% | 14% |
| 3 | 9% | 10% | 12% | 13% | 11% | 17% | 14% | 14% |
| 4 | 8% | 8% | 14% | 9% | 19% | 12% | 10% | 20% |
| 5 | 14% | 19% | 8% | 11% | 11% | 19% | 8% | 10% |
| 6 | 12% | 12% | 10% | 18% | 15% | 11% | 10% | 14% |
| 7 | 10% | 11% | 11% | 15% | 18% | 11% | 10% | 14% |
| 8 | 9% | 10% | 12% | 13% | 11% | 17% | 14% | 14% |
| 9 | 8% | 8% | 14% | 9% | 19% | 12% | 10% | 20% |
| 10 | 14% | 19% | 8% | 11% | 11% | 19% | 8% | 10% |
| 11 | 12% | 12% | 10% | 18% | 15% | 11% | 14% | 8% |
| 12 | 10% | 11% | 11% | 15% | 18% | 11% | 10% | 14% |

These assumptions allow to calculate the specific demand of each product for all retailers in every period. Table V shows exemplary the demand for each product in the first period.

TABLE V. RETAILERS' DEMAND FOR THE DIFFERENT PRODUCTS AT THE EXAMPLE OF PERIOD ONE (IN THOUSANDS)

| Retailer | Ali | Ede | Glo | Lid | md | Pha | Rew | Ros |
|---|---|---|---|---|---|---|---|---|
| Aloe | 72 | 72 | 60 | 108 | 90 | 66 | 84 | 48 |
| Chai | 24 | 24 | 20 | 36 | 30 | 22 | 28 | 16 |
| Coco | 24 | 24 | 20 | 36 | 30 | 22 | 28 | 16 |

The supply chain can be simulated period-wise, where each period is divided into the following phases:

1) Retailers fulfill the demands of their consumers if possible. This reduces their stocks. Unfulfilled demands are backlogged and deferred to the next period.
2) Retailers order products from their producers (e.g., *Ali* orders *Aloe* from *Body*) when their stocks decrease below their reorder level. The order amount is the difference between reorder and current level multiplied by a nervousness-factor which is set to 2 in the following. Unfulfilled amounts are deferred to the next period.
3) Producers satisfy the orders out of their stocks in the sequence given by the retailers' names. Unfulfilled demands are backlogged and deferred to the next period. The production is restricted by the amount of bottles in the raw material stocks of the producers.
4) If bottle stocks sink below individual reorder levels, new bottles are ordered as described above.
5) The production of bottles is assumed to be unlimited.

Since this scenario has several and widespread parameters, it can be adapted to many real-world situations.

## IV. Simulation with the Aid of Excel

When developing a conceptual model of the BWE with Excel, it was the aim to keep the calculations technically as simple as possible. Hence, no VBA was used with the consequence that each modification of a stock, the calculation of order amounts and of backorders had to be mapped with the aid of individual data cells.

The challenges of this approach are to keep all calculations of comparable concepts consistent and to chain the calculations of a given period with its previous one. Beside the simplicity with respect to possible modifications of the model, the calculation of the twelve periods occurs instantly.

Several data sheets for products, periods, demands, retailers and producers were built as follows:

**Product** contains product master data to extend calculations for more complex product recipes in the future.

**Period** contains the assumed situation per period described by market share per product and per retailer.

**Demand** uses *Period* data to charge the demand of the consumers for a specific product sold by a retailer per period.

**Retailer** uses *Demand* to change the initial stock of and the demand for a specific product for each retailer. Then, the stock level after fulfilling the consumers' demands and a possible backlog of unfulfilled demands are calculated. The purchase volume equals the difference between current stock and reorder level multiplied with the nervousness factor, if the stock is below the reorder level.
The calculation of the following periods is conducted in a similar way except for the initial stock per period which is derived from the previous one.
Since 12 periods are considered for 8 retailers, the calculation stretches over more than 100 rows and within the rows stand out three column blocks for each product.

**Producer** is set up in a similar way like *Retailer*. Product and retailer data are used to fulfill the initial demands of the retailers. Supply conflicts between retailers are avoided by serving them in alphabetical order.
Also the producers' stocks after delivery are calculated and a possible backlog is build up. If a producer's inventory is below the reported level, it produces enough to replenish the inventory, multiplied by the nervousness factor. This is only restricted by the amount of available bottles.

Finally, bottles are ordered if the bottle amount is below the reorder level, again multiplied by the nervousness factor. It is assumed that the producer of the bottles can always fulfill this demand.

The calculation of the following periods is conducted in a similar way, and complexity of the sheet *Producer* is similar to that of the sheet *Retailer*.

In addition to these calculation sheets, also sheets with graphical dashboards have been established to observe changes concerning the BWE if parameters like the initial stocks, demands, reorder levels, or nervousness factors change. This makes the simulation experimental.

Although it was easy to get started with the Excel model, it became worse with the number of periods, products, and retailers that had to be added to the sheet until the scenario setting had been reached. One reason for this is that it is difficult to include well readable comments to the excel sheets. Also changing delivery policies like the order in which retailers are served by the producers must be implemented cell by cell, since it is difficult to centralize such decisions. Hence, it must be stated that it is almost impossible to develop scalable models for the BWE in Excel. Nonetheless, for the described problem size it is a good alternative and helped to validate the results of the Petri net model explained next.

## V. Petri Nets and the Process-Simulation.Center

Petri net models are used to analyze and simulate dynamic systems. Their main benefit is the ability to describe concurrency in a natural way and concurrent actions are not forced into a schedule. Hence, they are beneficial for the definition of business processes and supply chains [13][14]. One popular and currently widely discussed application of Petri nets in business process management is Process Mining [15][16].

Originally, Petri nets are defined as Place/Transition nets (P/T) with anonymous tokens indicating a system's state [17], but concepts like Predicate/Transition nets (Pr/T) and Colored Petri Nets (CPN) also support the representation of high level information [18]–[20]. Demanding models of high-level Petri nets need appropriate software for modeling and simulation.

The *Process-Simulation.Center (P-S.C)*, which is introduced next, supports P/T and Pr/T nets. The Pr/T net concept is realized in such a way that places have an assigned data type and can be used in analogy to tables in a database. Functions encoded on transitions and edges may process this data. Data which is spread over several places can be joined into a single data record. Own types for date and time are substructures for the simulation of processes in production and logistics and enhance the approaches to timed Petri nets [21].

In contrast to relational algebra and, hence, SQL, in P-S.C the processing of tuples on places is serialized. The reason for this design choice is that in business and production processes work items are also treated one after another. The concrete sequence is decided upon locally by the transitions of the net and its marking [22].

Moreover, the P-S.C can be used to connect the process view on a system with other views. Process maps may combine different processes with each other and express the strategic value of a specific process as a primary, support, or management process. Also, the organizational structure of an institution can be combined with the Petri net view by arranging the process nodes in swim lanes of the corresponding responsible organizational units. Organizational charts complete the functions of the P-S.C [22].

It is worth mentioning that for a better readability the P-S.C draws nodes in such a way that their labels can be presented within. To further strengthen visual clues of their functionality, nodes can be provided with symbols [22].

The dearth of current Petri net tools, the quaint user experience of most of the still working ones and the unique approach of using textual programming instead of drag-and-drop modeling in combination with the added functionality are the main reasons for the implementation of the P-S.C [22].

## VI. Simulation with the Aid of Petri Nets

Figure 4 shows the Petri net model of the described scenario. Swimlanes are used to separate the model into three parts, called *Exchange, Supply Chain and Phases*, that interact in order to simulate a period with the following five phases:

**Phase 1** In the first phase transition *Buy Shampoo* realizes the transfer of goods from retailers to consumers. It is enabled as long as there is unfulfilled demand for the current period, which is coded in the token information on place *1. Phase*. For this place, *Demand* contains the demand information for all periods and place *Retailer Dashboard* encodes the initial stocks at the beginning and later the achieved stocks as the simulation proceeds. Delivered goods are coded on place *Bought*.
Transition *next* below from *1. Phase* initiates the next phase, if transition *Buy Shampoo* is no longer enabled.

**Phase 2** The second phase occurs when the corresponding place is marked with the number of the current period. Now the retailers order shampoo if the stocks are below the reorder level. At the same time, the producers' stocks of finished goods are emptied. For this, the current stocks of the producers are encoded on place *Producer Dashboard*. Delivered goods are coded on place *Delivered*.
When transition *Order Shampoo* is no longer enabled, transition *next* below of *2. Phase* fires and phase 3 begins.

**Phase 3** The third phase simulates the production of new shampoo, restricted only by the number of available bottles. Therefore, only the producer information must be considered. The produced amount is stored on place *Produced*.
When transition *Produce Shampoo* is no longer enabled, transition *next* below of *3. Phase* fires to begin phase 4.

**Phase 4** The fourth phase simulates the re-stocking of the bottles if the current stocks are below the reorder level. It is assumed that the producers of the bottles have infinite supply available.
When transition *Deliver Bottles* is not enabled anymore, transition *next* behind *4. Phase* fires and the last phase of a period begins.

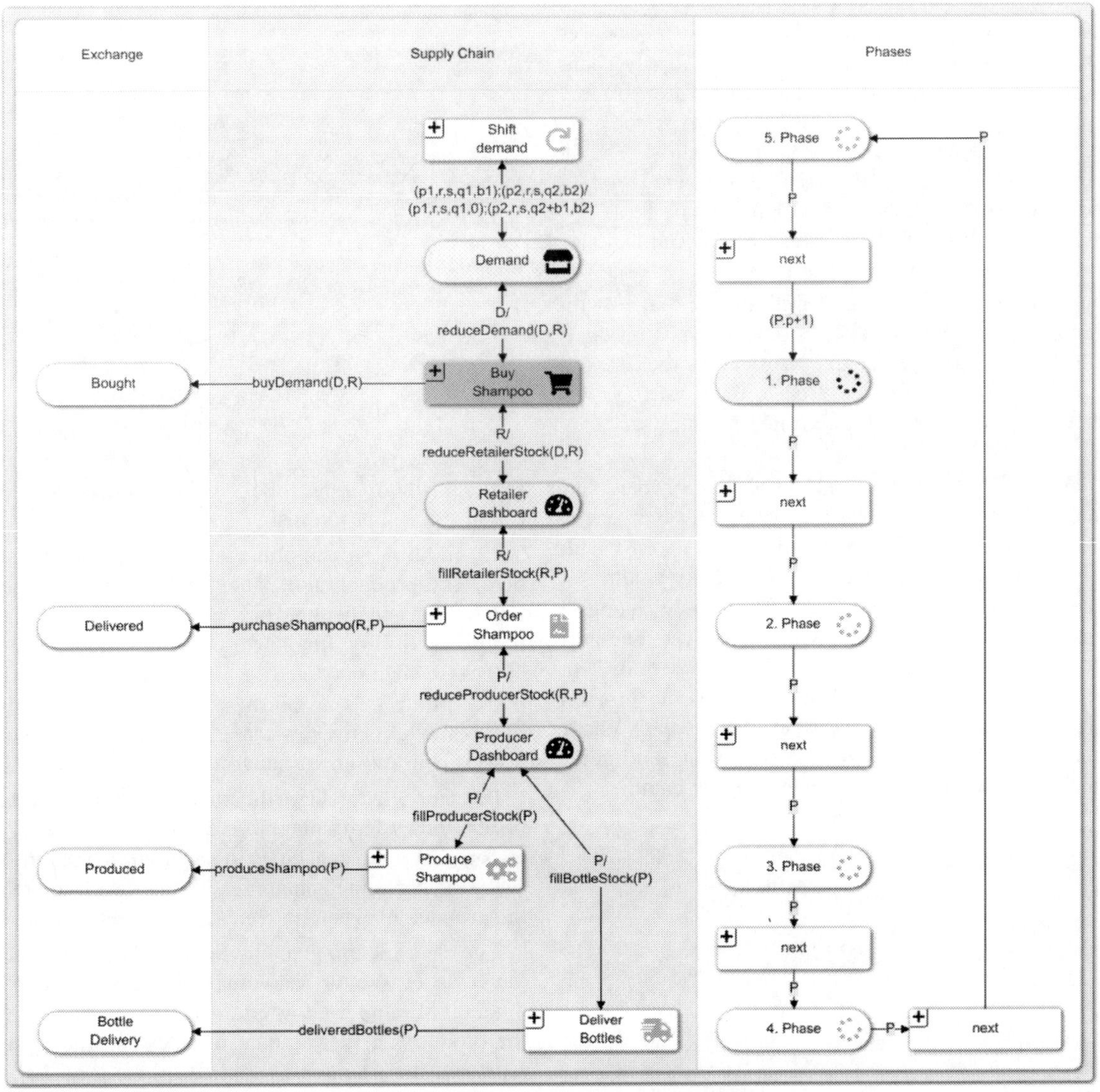


Figure 4. Petri net model of the scenario's supply chain.

**Phase 5** The final phase takes unfulfilled demands of former periods and copies them to the upcoming one. If all backlog information are copied, the transition below *5. Phase* increments the period counter by one and the next period starts with its first phase.

Figure 5 shows exemplary how the (initial) marking of place *Demand* can be operated within the tool.

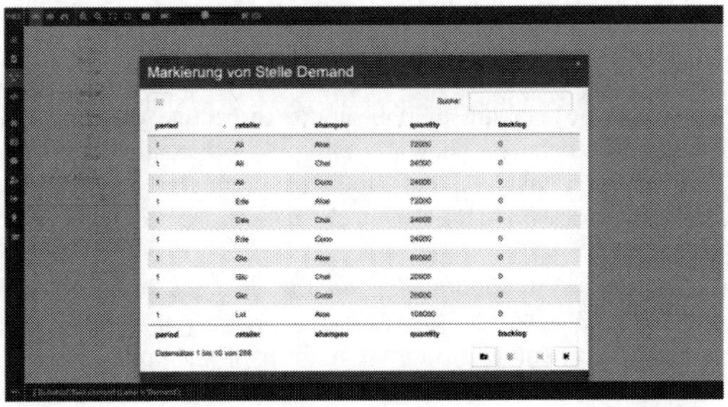


Figure 5. Screenshot showing the initial marking of place *Demand*.

At the end of the simulation run, the P-S.C exports the entire set of reached markings for further analytics.

## VII. Visualization of the Bullwhip Effect

The classic bullwhip effect is manifested by pronounced fluctuations in inventory levels upstream in the supply chain. Besides, different views of what is happening are possible. Visualizations are suitable for addressing different perspectives within or interdependencies across the supply chain. To see the bullwhip effect of a product in the supply chain, viewers look into the participants' warehouses. The data for this is a CSV-export generated by the P-S.C at the end of the simulation.

Figure 6 provides a first view: The four 3D area graphs in the diagram represent the summed inventory per stage of the supply chain: Light green ≙ retailer stock, green ≙ producer stock I (finished goods), dark green ≙ producer stock II (raw material). All eight retailers offer *Aloe* in their portfolio, but this product is manufactured by only three producers.

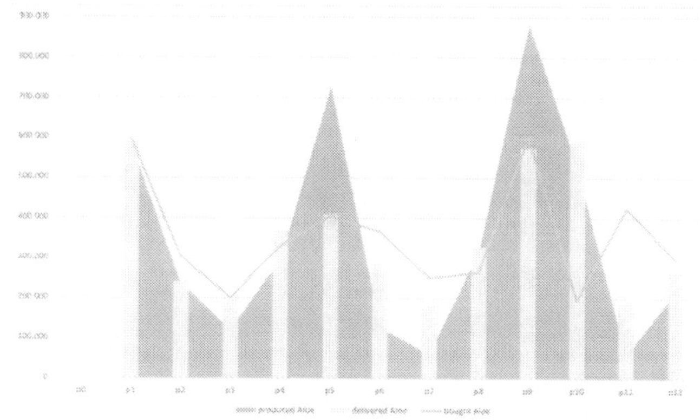

Figure 7. Activity of the product *Aloe*.

The stocks of *Body*, *Head*, and *Neck* and of the eight retailers reach a similar level. Increased sales between periods 3 to 5 (from 200k to 404k shampoos sold) have a well visible impact for the upstream participants in the supply chain.

Period zero represents the initial values in the warehouses when no sales of the products have taken place yet. The gray area chart (≙ bought goods) starts in the first period. This graph also shows the amount of goods actually sold in order to classify the stage-wise inventory level of the supply chain. Further, the bought goods act as an anchor value and could be the benchmark in a customer-oriented supply chain.

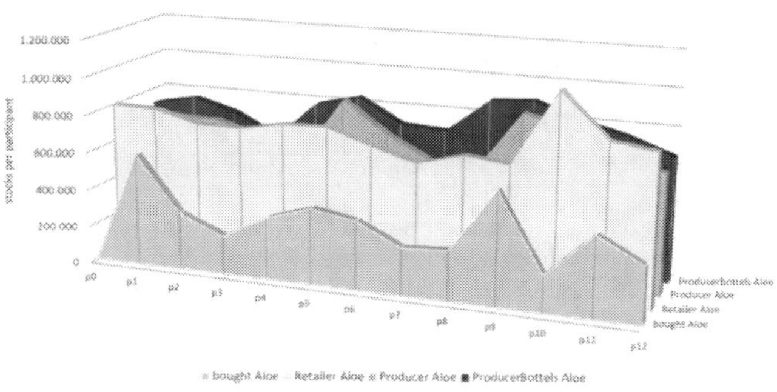


Figure 6. Bullwhip effect for the product *Aloe*.

It is worth taking a look at the respective ordering and production behavior shown in Figure 7. Fluctuations between purchased, delivered, and produced products become more relevant upstream in the supply chain, as described in the BWE literature.

The focus in Figure 7 is on the changes in inventories of the product *Aloe*. Based on the general popularity of the product's consumer group, the number of shampoos supplied and produced is also adjusted here. The gray line shows the actual demand for shampoos. The light green bar reflects the articles delivered to the retailers and the filled dark green line shows the number of shampoos produced. Again, period zero represents the initial stocks: No products are demanded or produced at that moment.

In addition, a simplification of the model is uncovered here: The production capacity of the producers varies greatly. Fluctuations in demand are compensated for almost equally by this flexibility. Imagine a constant production level of e.g., 400-500k shampoos and in a second step imagine the impact on the producer's inventories in Figure 6. The only limitation in this model is the raw material, which must be ordered first, however, in unlimited quantities.

Basically, these large fluctuations cause uncertainty in capacity and quantity planning for the participants. This also has an impact on the capacities to be purchased in terms of loading space or personnel planning. At this level, all movements at the product level can be seen across all retailers and producers.

The clear picture given by Figure 6 becomes confusing from the perspective of an individual. Figure 8 shows an in- and out-diagram of retailer *Glo's* product *Aloe*. The gray bars represent the product's actual amount of sales and the light green bars represent the shampoos supplied by the producer.

The simulation can be considered as an equivalent to a business planning game. Thus, the expired period is analyzed at the same time as the decisions for the coming period are made, e.g., for the delivery volume. So the stock in the warehouse is replenished with the ordered quantity (minus backlog) at the beginning of each period.

Therefore, for example, the inventory at the retailer *Glo* is never empty, because the backlog is never equal to the ordered quantity, but only parts of it.

In this simulation, the demand for the three products *Aloe*, *Chai*, and *Coco* fluctuates, and so does the planning reliability for all involved parties. It becomes clear that at this level the view of the big picture of the market is missing, which is still given above. How would you act as a retailer *Glo* in a 13th period? Would you adjust the order level or perhaps reduce the order quantity? If you would have a simulation as the described one, you could add all available market information to the simulation to soften negative bullwhip effects.

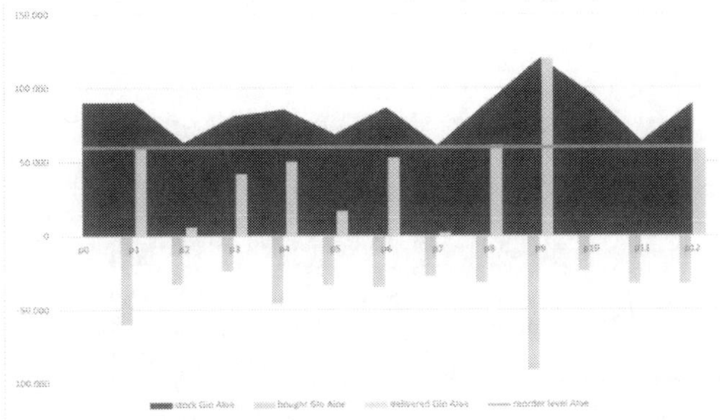


Figure 8. In- and out-diagram of *Aloe* and *Glo*.

## VIII. Summary and Outlook

During the validation phase for this research, the authors found that individual variables such as demand distribution or output data in the market hardly played a role to generate the BWE. Further, the modelers could have imposed much tighter constraints. The simulation model is key. Thus, the models are most applicable to real-world data from enterprise users. Even with the arbitrary numbers, the simulations produce the bullwhip effect, which is clearly visible at the level of an individual participant.

In conclusion, the following lessons can be summarized when running a simulation with Excel:

1) At the beginning, a clear and consistent structure should be developed directly, especially with regard to the interaction between the tables.
2) Calculations with formulas should be kept as simple as possible, because they must be repeated for the various periods, products, retailers and producers.
3) Subsequent changes often lead to errors in the formulas; the four-eyes principle should be applied.

Also for the Petri net simulation lessons could be learned:

1) It took several detours until the clear final structure presented in this paper was found.
2) However, the final solution scales and only the initial data for more periods have to be added. The Petri net structure stays the same.
3) Without a mature tool for modeling and simulation of high-level Petri nets, it is impossible to develop a comparable model and to benefit from this.

Each approach can meet the user at their individual skills and supports the performance of what-if analyses and in running through different scenarios. This is the beauty of these approaches and paves the way for practical use.

But is this enough to protect companies from the bullwhip trap? "Presumably not," because the simulation only takes the user to the heart of the problem: Small changes of the configuration can have a significant impact on the outcome, and incorrect assumptions about the market made by users lead to incorrect predictions regarding the bullwhip effect.

Nonetheless, further research on this topic seems to be reasonable, because this research on bullwhip simulation is only just beginning.

## References

[1] W. M. P. van der Aalst, J. Nakatumba-Nabende, A. Rozinat, and N. Russell, "Business Process Simulation," in *Handbook on Business Process Management 1*, 2010, pp. 313–338.

[2] D. Ivanov, A. Tsipoulanidis, and J. Schönberger, *Operations and Supply Chain Strategy*. Springer International Publishing, 2019.

[3] H. Lee, V. Padmanabhan, and S. Whang, "The Bullwhip Effect in Supply Chains," *Sloan Management Review*, vol. 38, pp. 93–102, 1997.

[4] M. Nakano, *Responsiveness-Oriented Strategy*. Springer Singapore, 2020.

[5] P. McCullen and D. Towill, "Diagnosis and reduction of bullwhip in supply chains," *Supply Chain Management: An International Journal*, vol. 7, pp. 164–179, 2002.

[6] Y. Yang, J. Lin, G. Liu, and L. Zhoul, "The behavioural causes of bullwhip effect in supply chains: A systematic literature review," *International Journal of Production Economics*, vol. 236, 2021.

[7] A. Beer, "The bullwhip effect in a complex production network," in *Information – Organisation – Produktion*, H. Corsten, M. Reiß, C. Steinle, and S. Zelewski, Eds. Springer Gabler, 2013.

[8] S. Umeda and S. Jain, "Integrated supply chain simulation system (isss)," 2004.

[9] F. Campuzano and J. Mula, *Supply Chain Simulation*. Springer, 2011.

[10] E. Badakhshan, P. Humphreys, L. Maguire, and R. McIvor, "Using simulation-based system dynamics and genetic algorithms to reduce the cash flow bullwhip in the supply chain," *International Journal of Production Research*, vol. 58:17, pp. 5253–5279, 2020.

[11] P. Wangphanich, S. Kara, and B. Kayis, "Analysis of the bullwhip effect in multi-product, multi-stage supply chain systems : a simulation approach," *International Journal of Production Research*, vol. 48, pp. 4501–4517, 2010.

[12] MHI, "MHI Annual Industry Report," https://www.mhi.org/publications/report/ (last accessed 04.09.2021), 2020, MHI.

[13] W. M. P. van der Aalst and K. Hee, van, *Workflow Management - Models, Methods, and Systems*. Cambridge, MA: MIT Press, 2002.

[14] W. M. P. van der Aalst and C. Stahl, *Modeling Business Processes - A Petri Net-Oriented Approach*. Cambridge: The MIT Press, 2011.

[15] W. M. P. van der Aalst, *Process Mining*, 2nd ed. Berlin: Springer, 2016.

[16] L. Reinkemeyer, Ed., *Process Mining in Action - Principles, Use Cases and Outlook*. Berlin: Springer, 2020.

[17] W. Reisig, *Understanding Petri Nets*. Berlin: Springer, 2013.

[18] H. J. Genrich and K. Lautenbach, "System Modelling with High-Level Petri Nets," *Theoretical Computer Science*, vol. 13, 1981.

[19] K. Jensen, *Coloured Petri-Nets*, 1st ed. Berlin: Springer, 1992.

[20] M. Montali and A. Rivkin, "From DB-nets to Coloured Petri Nets with Priorities (Extended Version)," *CoRR*, vol. abs/1904.00058, 2019.

[21] C. Simon, "Web-Based Simulation Of Production Schedules With High-Level Petri Nets," in *32rd International ECMS Conference on Modelling and Simulation (ECMS 2018)*, L. Nolle, A. Burger, C. Tholen, J. Werner, and J. Wellhausen, Eds. Wilhelmshaven, Germany: SCS Europe, 2018, pp. 275–281.

[22] C. Simon, S. Haag, and L. Zakfeld, "Clock Pulse Modeling and Simulation of Push and Pull Processes in Logistics," in *SIMMaApp: Special Track at SIMUL 2020: The Twelfth International Conference on Advances in System Simulation*, F. Herrmann, Ed., Porto (Portugal), 2020, pp. 31–36.

# Business Process Simulation Focusing Supply Chain Risk Management Aspects

*Frank Schätter*
Pforzheim University of Applied Sciences
Tiefenbronner Str. 65, 75715 Pforzheim
Germany
email: frank.schaetter@hs-pforzheim.de

*Frank Morelli*
Pforzheim University of Applied Sciences
Tiefenbronner Str. 65, 75715 Pforzheim
Germany
email: frank.morelli@hs-pforzheim.de

*Abstract* - **Decision support systems refer to computable models that assist decision-makers in the identification and/or the estimation of consequences of decision alternatives. In this regard, model-driven decision support systems have been proven successfully, which use simulation models to analyze business processes and respective decision situations based on parameters and a limited amount of data. The focus of this contribution is on the opportunities of using such a business processes simulation in the field of supply chain risk management. Therefore, we present a novel approach that couples a data-based supply chain model with a consequence-driven risk simulation. Our simulation approach reverses the standard risk management cycle by identifying vulnerable parts within the supply chain – in terms of a data-based model – and subsequently backtracking possible triggering risk events instead of predicting such possible events first. The result of our approach is an easy-applicable procedure that allows companies to analyze and to improve the resilience status of their supply chains.**

***Keywords - decision support systems; data-based supply chain model; consequence-driven risk simulation; resilient supply chains.***

## I. Introduction

Simulations can be characterized as descriptions of a real system by a model. They are particularly useful when the system under examination is complex and includes numerous interactions. Simulations offer the opportunity to run through alternative solutions in different scenarios. They make it possible to anticipate the behavior of processes at runtime and thus act as a basis for decision-making without an underlying algorithm for determining an optimal solution. Instead, by incorporating human intuition, insights into characteristics - such as bottlenecks - can be gained. Such dynamic analyses, based on different iterations and multiple variations in inputs (what-if analysis), permit human decision-makers to deepen their knowledge of the real system under study [6] [29] [35]. However, if the complexity, randomness, and variability within the system increase, the corresponding predictability under various conditions becomes more problematic.

Making good decisions depends on the available information describing the relevant aspects of the decision environment. This information can be either deterministic or subject to uncertainty [5]. In a decision situation under uncertainty, the outcome of a decision alternative is probabilistic or even unknown. In this case, the prediction of the consequences is difficult [36] and a computable model in terms of a Decision Support System (DSS) to assist decision-makers are required [8] [18]. A DSS facilitates the structuring of information to make the decision process more productive and agile as uncertainty and complexity of the decision situation can be reduced [17] [34]. Several authors have highlighted the fact that a DSS never aims to replace decision-makers; rather, the support still depends on the decision-makers with the objective of obtaining a good solution in a reduced amount of time [12] [14] [23].

There are typically three management systems included within a DSS: a data management system, a model management system, and a dialogue management system [32]. The first is targeted at structuring internal and external data, processes, information, and knowledge to develop a database as a platform for decision-making. Based on this database, the actual decision problem itself can be solved by implementing a data-based model to identify and test decision alternatives. Finally, interactive queries, reporting, and graphing functions are required to interact with the decision-makers. Particularly systems of data management are highly crucial as decision-makers never had access to more decision-relevant information than today [31]. However, this is not always beneficial as a pre-decision is needed by defining the relevant information to deal with the decision situation [11]. There are various classification schemes of DSSs available in literature. A common possibility is to describe them by their function [23] [28]. In this contribution, the focus is on model-driven DSSs using quantitative simulation models to analyze a decision situation based on parameters and a limited amount of data [28] [31].

Simulation based on a model-driven DSS reveals several opportunities: it enables an integrated view by describing the states of individual system components or even an entire system. Simulation using historical process data can support real-time business operations. From this perspective, complex business processes like supply chains, are of central importance for decision-makers. Adjustments to synchronize process steps of different supply members are often necessary. A corresponding simulation model can support the analysis of various problems for strategic, tactical, and operational questions. The application of simulation in its different methodological shapes is well established in literature of supply chain analysis [15].

In this regard, the supply chain processes must be able to accommodate changes within the environment. A DSS needs to be able to deal both with foreseen and unforeseen changes, even with disruptions to draw the right decisions. This means not only to avoid high costs and loss of profit but also to ensure a sufficient degree of flexibility and resilience. Supply chains are faced by lots of uncertainties, which makes risk management a key factor for success. In this paper, we consider possibilities of business process simulation to be used in supply chain risk management with the objective of creating a resilient supply chain. The rationale of our contribution is organized as follows: Sections 2 and 3 provide a summary of current developments in supply chain risk management and business processes simulation. In Section 4, we present a novel approach that facilitates the analysis of resilient supply chains based on a data-based risk simulation. The key aspects of our research are finally summarized in Section 5.

## II. Supply Chain Risk Management

Supply chains are dynamic networks of interconnected multinational firms, including relationships across a possibly large number of involved entities and integrated value-added processes [9]. Each entity refers to a specific functional stage in the supply chain, such as suppliers (e.g., raw material supplier), manufacturers, customers (e.g., wholesalers), and end customers. From the perspective of a specific entity, functional stages are either located in the upstream (supply side) or in the downstream (demand side) [4] [9] [27]. The supply chain consists of physical flows organizing the spatial-temporal transformation of goods, information flows, and financial flows, such as credits, payment schedules, and consignment arrangements [19].

In recent years, supply chains have become more interconnected and complex and they are – in particular in today's turbulent and uncertain world –predisposed to disruptive events [7]. Every organization somehow depends on further firms, industries, and markets and even the most carefully controlled processes are only as good as the links that support them [10]. Disruptions have the potential to cause heavy short- and long-term losses in stock price, shareholder value, sales, and reputation, as well as to damage relationships between suppliers and customers [16]. The recent COVID-19 pandemic or the interruption of the Suez Channel have highlighted how crucial supply chain disruptions might be. Before a disruption occurs, its potential is described by a supply chain risk threating the movement of physical flows [37]. Basically two kinds of risks can be distinguished in this regard: internal risks, such as late deliveries, excess stock, poor forecasts, financial risks, minor accidents, and human error and external risks in terms of natural and man-made disasters (e.g., extreme weather events, wars, terrorist attacks, outbreaks of diseases, or price rises) [37].

For decades, trends, such as globalization, decentralization, outsourcing and just-in-time, have optimized supply chains mostly in the direction of being highly efficient [13]. The other side of the coin has been an increased vulnerability of supply chains towards shocks as, for example, more nodes (entities) in a logistics network increase the threat of disruptions propagating through the highly interrelated networks. Thus, even a local failure can negatively affect businesses on a global scale. The number of events causing such disruptions is growing. According to a study of McKinsey & Company [24], companies should expect supply chain disruptions lasting a month or longer to occur every 3.7 years. Logistics managers have understood the importance of resilient supply chains and, consequently, Supply Chain Risk Management (SCRM) has increasingly become a topic on their agendas. Basically, resilience is concerned with the supply chain's ability to manage the consequences of an avoidable risk event and return to its original operations [3]. Strategies to increase resilience are related to an increased flexibility, agility, adaptability, and visibility of the supply chain [10] [25]. Examples might be postponement, strategic stock, flexible supply base, validations of make-or-buy decisions, economic supply incentives, flexible transportation, and revenue management.

But how should a SCRM be implemented and specified to improve the resilience of the logistics structures? If you open a standard textbook, you will find that supply chain risk management should follow a cyclic risk management approach in terms of identifying, analyzing, evaluating, and monitoring risks threatening the smooth functioning of the networks [e.g., 21]. Although this is relevant information, it does not translate into a direct plan of action for the managers. How can such a procedure be set into motion? Where is the starting point? What data are required? Approaching these challenges from the practical side, managers could turn to one of many commercial SCRM tools, which typically promise network transparency, provision of global real-time information (e.g., weather data) and assistance in the development of reactive emergency measures. However, they focus on very specific resilience issues like, for example, ad-hoc actions to handle a harbor strike by switching the transportation mode from ship freight to emergency air cargo. The tools do not provide what the managers who are eager to implement SCRM are looking for.

## III. Business Processes Simulation

The simulation approach maps systems with their dynamic processes for analysis purposes. It allows to anticipate the behavior of processes at runtime and to consider alternative solutions in different scenarios. System Dynamics (SD), Discrete Event Simulation (DES) and Agent-Based Modeling (AB) can be distinguished as the main simulation paradigms for modeling complex systems. Simulation tools typically allow visualization of the simulation process.

Business processes represent the backbone of the enterprise. The overarching goal of the Business Process Management (BPM) approach is the achievement of continuous improvement in organizations [30]. BPM analyses business activities and their interactions, identifying potential improvements as a support to decision makers. However, the use of simulation models for controlling business processes and related decisions (decision making) proves to be limited [1]. In practice, BPM rarely captures the dynamic characteristics of business processes, although this would provide a better understanding in the event of rapid changes by decision-makers in execution.

The design of business processes both within a company and across company boarders leads from the as-is analysis to the definition of a to-be model and its implementation, which is increasingly characterized using IT solutions in the context of digital transformation. Business process modeling acts as an essential vehicle in this regard and, thus, Business Process Modeling Notation (BPMN) has emerged as a de facto standard. In principle, an extension of the BPMN modeling language for simulation purposes is possible, as shown by the Business Process Simulation Interchange Standard (BPSim). However, there is still a need for research in this context, for example to develop a fully elaborated resource model [20]. By extending such a solution, simulation can be integrated into the business process management concept.

Simulation has been used in the supply chain sector for a long time. The focus is mostly on efficiency aspects and less on risks and resilience. However, basically triggered by global trends and corresponding uncertainties, it is indispensable that a holistic management of supply chains is required which additionally respects risk aspects [26]. Such a holistic management enables logistics managers to adjust their planning individually by steering and trading-off the degrees of efficiency and resilience within their supply chains.

## IV. Business Process Simulation for Supply Chain Risk Management

The objective of our research is to develop a practical SCRM approach that supports decision-makers in simulating the current (as-is) and future (to-be) resilience status of their strategic supply chain processes.

Our approach suggests combining a data-based supply chain model with a consequence-driven risk simulation. In fact, we translate the data available within a company, which describe the strategic supply chain processes in terms of physical flows of goods into a data-based representation of the supply chain. This data-based model provides a platform for decision-making in resilient supply chain design. Firstly, companies can directly identify and analyze vulnerable parts of the supply chains as well as the consequences of specific risk events. Secondly, the suitability of logistics strategies (decision alternatives) to improve the current resilience status can be simulated within the model. Thereby, the consequence-driven risk simulation reverses the standard risk management cycle by identifying vulnerable parts within the supply chain (model) and subsequently backtracking possible triggering risk events instead of predicting such possible events first.

Our approach switches the focus from an efficient to a resilient supply chain management (see Section 2) and provides decision support for supply chain risk managers. The main rationales behind the two core components – data-based supply chain model and consequence-driven risk simulation – are described in the forthcoming paragraphs. The formulation of the steps included within these components as well as their exemplary application is work-in-progress and not the focus of this paper.

*Data-based supply chain model*

The data-based supply chain model includes all physical flows of the network under consideration for a certain reference time (e.g., 12 months) from the perspective of the company. It is the objective of the company to define the scope of the analysis in terms of geographic regions of entities, material groups, and organizational entities. From an analytical point of view, a supply chain is defined as a network of nodes and edges. Each node refers to each one entity of the supply chain, such as suppliers, customers, or company-specific facilities (e.g., factories, warehouses). An edge defines a single physical flow in terms of a delivery, which arises over time between each one sender (point of origin) and receiver (point of consumption) location.

The necessary company data to develop the model refers to transaction and master data, which can be gathered out of the data warehouse of a company. In this regard, one major benefit of our approach becomes obvious: instead of investing in external tools to analyze and improve the supply chain, we suggest applying the data which is already available. Our approach, thus, ensures that SCRM can be conducted incidentally by the companies themselves, which, in turn, implies low cost, as well as high practicability and acceptance.

The relevant systems defining the data warehouse are widespread and might refer to Enterprise Resource Planning (ERP) systems, excel, or Structured Query Language (SQL) files. Our approach does not focus on the origin of the data but on the necessarily required information (as possible parameters in the consequence-driven risk simulation) within the transaction and master data to represent the physical flows. In fact, the data-based model captures transaction data in terms of delivery positions and master data in terms of material data and entity data:

- Delivery positions: each single physical flow in the network refers to a delivery of a certain material across each one sender and receiver location. Such a material-specific flow is called delivery position; several delivery positions can be part of a shipment (e.g., truck load), which, in turn, includes various materials. Delivery positions provide the basis of the data-based supply chain model as they include all spatial information regarding the entities and temporal information regarding the physical flows. Sender, receiver, and material must be identifiable in an unambiguous manner – which implies that each of them is specified by a unique ID. Via this ID, further in-depth information can be captured out of the entity and material master data (see below). Moreover, delivery positions should provide information regarding the sending date (start of delivery from the sender location), receiving date (end of delivery at the receiver location), material quantity (number of parts to be delivered), and transportation mode (e.g., road transport, air cargo).
- Entity and material data: entities included within the supply chain might be suppliers, customers, or company-specific facilities, such as factories or warehouses. Master data should be used to pull further entity-specific information per delivery position via a sender ID or a receiver ID referring to an entity ID. Such further information refers to the entity type (e.g., supplier), entity country, entity city, and

entity geo-information of latitude and longitude. As the objective of our approach is to analyze resilience from a strategic perspective, the aggregation level of geoformation referring to a city is seen as sufficient. Optionally, further details, such as addresses, can be used to further detail the supply chain. Material-specific information per delivery position should be captured from the material master data. Via the unique material ID, such information might be the material description, material weight [kg], material volume [m$^3$], material price [e.g., EUR] and material product group.

TABLE I. NECESSARY INFORMATION OF THE DATA-BASED MODEL

| Data category (source) | Dataset | Description |
|---|---|---|
| Delivery positions (transaction data) | Sender ID | Unique identification of sending location |
| | Receiver ID | Unique identification of receiving location |
| | Material ID | Unique identification of delivered material |
| | Quantity | Number of materials delivered |
| | Transportation mode | Road transport, air freight etc. |
| | Sending date | Date to which the delivery has started |
| | Receiving date | Date to which the delivery has finished |
| Entity data (master data) | Entity ID | Unique identification of entity |
| | Entity type | Characteristic, e.g., supplier or customer |
| | Entity country | Country of the entity location |
| | Entity city | City of the entity location |
| | Entity latitude | Geo-information of the entity location |
| | Entity longitude | Geo-information of the entity location |
| Material data (master data) | Material ID | Unique identification of material |
| | Material weight | Weight [kg] of one piece of the material |
| | Material volume | Volume [m$^3$] of one piece of the material |
| | Material price | Price [e.g., EUR] of one piece of the material |
| | Product group | Material category |

Table I summarizes the necessary information (parameters) of a single physical delivery to be gathered out of the transaction and master data. The arrows in the table highlight connections between transaction and master data. In fact, entity-specific information of a delivery position can be captured by via a unique entity ID (referencing to the sender ID or receiver ID given in the delivery position); material-specific information can be captured by a unique material ID (referencing to the material ID given in the delivery position).

It becomes obvious that the data-based supply chain model consists of a database where each single dataset refers to a delivery position specifying each one material-specific physical flow in the network. Based on this data, further information can be included to the database, such as information regarding the considered part of the supply chain (e.g., an inbound flow between a supplier and a company-specific entity, an intra-company flow across company-specific entities, or an outbound flow between a company-specific entity and a customer), distance [km], which can be easily included by using open-access web tools (distance calculators), or further calculations, such as the total delivery weight (material weight * quantity), delivery volume (material volume * quantity) and total price (material price * quantity).

In summary, each physical flow in the data-based supply chain model provides sender-specific, receiver-specific, material-specific, and transport-specific information. An exemplary representation of this data is given in Figure 1. For two nodes of the supply chain, A and B, the model includes two datasets with the respective information for the physical flows 1 to n.

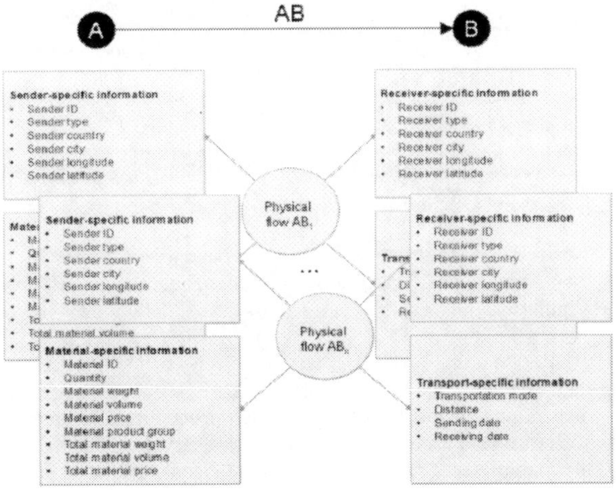


Figure 1. Included data per physical flow

*Consequence-driven risk simulation*

The data-based model provides the ingredients for simulations by changing the values of the parameters, which leads to a modified structure and, thus, performance of the supply chain. It can be used to evaluate the current and future resilience status of the supply chain under consideration. This is because the model allows to directly explore the effects of risk events facing the supply chain as well as logistics strategies to hedge against the negative consequences of such events. In difference to standard approaches of risk management, we propose a procedure that reverses the traditional contents of risk identification, risk analysis and assessment, and risk mitigation (see Figure 2). In fact, we believe that rather than answering to the question "what is happening to the supply chain if a certain risk event enters?", the rationale of SCRM should be: "what are the most vulnerable parts in the network that lead to the highest consequences and how can they be mitigated?".

Therefore, our simulation procedure starts with the identification of the most business-critical and, thus, vulnerable parts of the supply chain, which might be the nodes or edges of the network. For instance, the most vulnerable parts might be the top sending and receiving nodes (e.g., nodes with high frequencies of deliveries, a high value of materials), most exclusive material-specific sender and receiver locations, or top materials (e.g., annual value of deliveries). The data-based model thereby provides a platform to rapidly identify and analyze those vulnerable parts.

Based on the identified vulnerable parts, we suggest simulating effects in the supply chain when the business processes behind the vulnerable parts change (e.g., total weight or value per supplier, outbound flows of warehouses). Therefore, forecasts are implemented, which affect the parameter values, e.g., price increases of certain materials or disruptions of certain regions, sender and/or receiver locations. By modifying the parameter values, worst-case consequences can be revealed when business-critical or vulnerable parts fail.

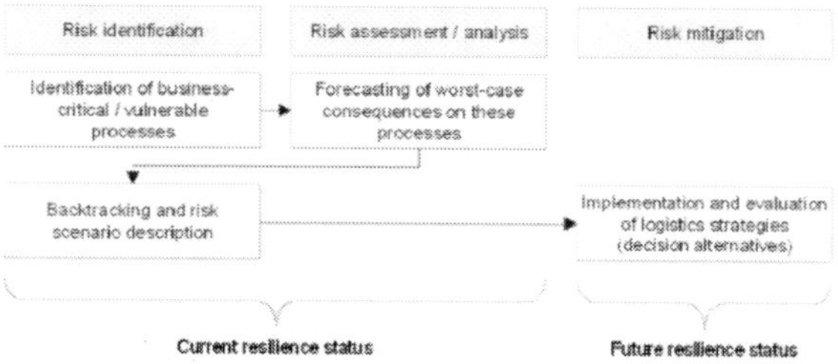


Figure 2. Procedure of consequence-driven risk simulation

Rather than it is the objective of standard risk management, the identification of risk events triggering disruptions is the third step of our procedure. In fact, the scenarios and narrative descriptions are developed leading to the parameter changes, which have been simulated in the previous step. Such scenarios might refer to geographic issues (e.g., natural disasters), political events (e.g., tariffs), drops in demand, or further events, such as disruptions of key entities as warehouses due to strike events.

Finally, the data-based model can be again used to simulate logistics strategies that hedge against the failures of the most crucial parts. These logistics strategies might be, for example, multiple sourcing strategies, additional entities in the network (e.g., further warehouses in certain areas), adapted frequencies in supplies, or further redundancies, such as larger inventories. Again, consequences of the logistics strategies must be translated into several parameters of the data-based model, such as further supplier locations for a previously single-sourcing material. In this way, the effects in the supply chain can be evaluated and the targeted future resilience status can be compared with the previously analyzed current resilience status.

## V. Conclusion

In this paper, we have discussed the relevance of using business processes simulation in supply chain management and, in fact, for the creation of resilient supply chains. Therefore, we have presented the rationale of a novel approach, which consists of two core components: data-based supply chain model and consequence-driven risk simulation. We have outlined the basic rationale behind the two core components and, in fact, how a data-based model and simulation procedure can be used for business processes management in SCRM. The two core components include various steps.

The specific steps of our approach refer to the determination of framework conditions, data gathering, data structuring, data modelling, and the application of standardized key resilience indicators to identify vulnerable parts and to analyze the consequences of risk events. Our future research objective is to develop an easily implementable "cooking recipe" for our SCRM approach by providing in-depth descriptions of those steps for the logistics managers. In this contribution, we have exemplarily outlined the result of the step of data structuring in terms of a clear definition and links of the necessary data to stretch the logistics network (see Table 1). The specification of all further steps is work-in-progress.

Particularly the steps of data modelling and the application of the key resilience indicators include various mathematical formulations (e.g., delivery-specific volumes and weights, percentages of disrupted entities in the network). Those formulations are highly crucial aspects of our "cooking recipe" and will be therefore addressed as the next step of our future research. Moreover, an adequate graphical presentation of the decision support results (e.g., as-is versus to-be scenarios) as well as sensitivity analyses will be highly crucial.

The quality of simulation results strongly depends on the quality of the input data. Business process simulation models are intended to use real-life data sources for gathering relevant data. The process mining approach, which is not discussed further in this article, can make an important contribution to the creation of conceptual models by generating process models from event logs. Process mining enables automated control flow discovery (process model discovery), performance analysis (process bottlenecks), conformance checking (process guidelines vs. actual practices), enhancement (diagnostics), and resource organizational structure (collaboration) [2]. A limitation of contemporary process mining techniques can be seen in the fact that they tend to focus on distinct process instances and not on the multi-case setting of BPS [22]. To utilize a multi-case context in business process Simulation, approaches, such as the Multi-Event-Log from Celonis, can be applied [33].

## References

[1] W. M. P. van der Aalst, "Process Mining and Simulation: A Match made in Heaven!," SpringSim-SCSC, 2018 July 9-12, Bordeaux, 2018.

[2] W. Abhohamad, A. Ramy, and A. Arisha, "A Hybrid Process-Mining Approach for Simulation Modeling," in: Proceedings of the 2017 Winter Simulation Conference, W. Chan, A. D'Ambrogio, G. Zacharewicz, N. Mustafee, G. Wainer, and E. Page (editors), pp. 1527-1538, 2017.

[3] V. Anbumozhi, F. Kimura, and S. M. Thangavelu, Supply Chain Resilience. Singapore: Springer Singapore, 2020.

[4] D. Arnold, H. Isermann, A. Kuhn, H. Tempelmeier, and K. Furmans, Handbuch Logistik, Berlin: Springer, 2008.

[5] V. Bertsch, Uncertainty Handling in Multi-Attribute Decision Support for Industrial Risk Management, Universitätsverlag Karlsruhe, 2008.

[6] S. Bisogno, and A. Calabrese, "Combining modelling and simulation approaches," in: Business Process Management Journal, 22 (1), pp. 56-74, 2015, DOI 10.1108/BPMJ-02-2015-0021.

[7] C. Bode, and S. M. Wagner, "Structural drivers of upstream supply chain complexity and the frequency of supply chain disruptions," in: Journal of Operations Management 36 (1), pp. 215–228, 2015, DOI: 10.1016/j.jom.2014.12.004.

[8] F. Burstein, and C. W. Holsapple, Handbook on Decision Support Systems 1 - Basic themes, Springer-Verlag Berlin Heidelberg, 2008.

[9] M. Christopher, Logistics and Supply Chain Management, Financial Times/ Prentice Hall, 2011.

[10] M. Christopher, H. Peck, "Building the Resilient Supply Chain," in: The International Journal of Logistics Management, 15 (2), pp.1–14, 2004.

[11] S. Djamasbi, "Does positive affect influence the effective usage of a Decision Support System?" Decision Support Systems, 43 (4), pp.1707–1717, 2007.

[12] M. C. Er, "Decision Support Systems: A summary, problems, and future trends," in: Decision Support Systems, 4 (3), pp. 355–363, 1988.

[13] A. Ghadge, S. Dani, M. Chester, and R. Kalawsky, "A systems approach for modelling supply chain risks," in: Supply Chain Management: An International Journal, Vol. 18 (5), pp. 523-538, 2013.

[14] D. J. Hall, "Decision Makers and Their Need for Support," in: F. Burstein, and C. W. Holsapple (editors), Handbook on Decision Support Systems 1, Springer Berlin Heidelberg, pp. 83–102, 2008.

[15] I. Heckmann, Towards Supply Chain Risk Analytics, SpringerGabler, Wiesbaden, 2016.

[16] K. B. Hendricks, and V. R. Singhal, „The effect of supply chain glitches on shareholder wealth," in: Journal of Operations Management 21 (5), pp. 501–522, 2003, DOI: 10.1016/j.jom.2003.02.003.

[17] C. W. Holsapple, "Decisions and Knowledge," in: F. Burstein, and C. W. Holsapple (editors), Handbook on Decision Support Systems 1, Springer Berlin Heidelberg, pp. 21–53, Arnott & Pervan, 2008.

[18] C. A. Hooker, "Introduction to Philosophy of Complex Systems: A: Part A: Towards a framework for complex systems," in: C. A. Hooker et al. (editors), Philosophy of Complex Systems, Volume 10 (Handbook of the Philosophy of Science), Elsevier B.V., pp. 3–90, 2011.

[19] P. R. Kleindorfer, and L. van Wassenhove, "Managing risk in the global supply chain," in: The INSEAD-Wharton Alliance on Globalizing. Cambridge University Press, UK, 2004.

[20] R. Laue, and C. Müller, „The Business Process Simulation Standard (BPSim): Chances and Limits," in: Proceedings 30th European Conference on Modelling and Simulation (ECMS), T. Claus, F. Herrmann, M. Manitz, and O. Rose (editors), pp. 1-6, 2016, ISBN: 978-0-9932440-2-5.

[21] T. Liebetruth, Prozessmanagement in Einkauf und Logistik: Instrumente und Methoden für das Supply Chain Process Management, Springer Gabler, 2020.

[22] N. Martin, B. Depaire, and A. Caris, "The Use of Process Mining in a Business Process Simulation Context: Overview and Challenges," IEEE Symposium on Computational Intelligence and Data Mining (CIDM), Orlando, FL (USA), pp. 1-8, 2014, ISBN: 978-1-4799-4518-4.

[23] A. Mattiussi, M. Rosano, and P. Simeoni, "A decision support system for sustainable energy supply combining multi-objective and multi-attribute analysis: An Australian case study," in: Decision Support Systems, 57, pp.150–159, 2014.

[24] McKinsey & Company. Corona und andere Krisen: Lieferketten werden sich global dramatisch verändern, online: https://www.mckinsey.de/news/presse/2020-08-06-global-value-chains [retrieved: September, 2021]

[25] S. A. Melnyk, C. Zobel, S. E. Griffis, and J. R. Macdonald, Understanding Supply Chain Resilience, Supply Chain Management Review, 2014.

[26] D. Neiger, M. Churilov, M. zur Muehlen, and M. Rosemann, Integrating Risks in Business Process Models with Value Focused Process Engineering, Proc. European Conf. Information Systems (ECIS '06), 2006.

[27] H.-C. Pfohl, „Logistiksysteme - Betriebswirtschaftliche Grundlagen," in: R. Jünemann, and H.-C. Pfohl (editors), Springer-Verlag Berlin Heidelberg, 2010.

[28] D. J. Power, "Decision Support Systems: A Historical Overview," in F. Burstein, and C. W. Holsapple (editors), Handbook on Decision Support System 1. Springer Berlin Heidelberg, pp. 121–140, 2008.

[29] S. Robinson, Simulation: The Practice of Model Development and Use, John Wiley & Sons, 2014.

[30] M. Rosemann, and J. vom Brocke, The Six Core Elements of Business Process Management, Springer, Berlin, Heidelberg, 2015.

[31] F. Schätter, Decision support system for a reactive management of disaster-caused supply chain disturbances., Karlsruhe, Deutschland, 2016.

[32] J. P. Shim, et al., "Past, present, and future of decision support technology," in: Decision Support Systems, 33(2), pp. 111–126, 2002.

[33] B. Shlakeski, Business Process Mining through the lens of "Multi-Event Log" approach. Master Thesis, Pforzheim University of Applied Sciences, 2021.

[34] R. S. Sojda, 2007, "Empirical evaluation of decision support systems: needs, definitions, potential methods, and an example pertaining to waterfowl management," in: Environmental Modelling & Software, 22(2), pp. 269–277, 2007.

[35] C. Vallejo, D. Romero, and A. Molina, "Enterprise integration engineering reference framework and toolbox," in: International Journal of Production Research, Vol. 50 No. 6, pp. 1489-1511, 2012.

[36] R. Vahidov, G. E. Kersten, "Decision station: situation decision support systems," in: Decision Support Systems, 38(2), pp. 283–303, 2004.

[37] C. Waters, and J. Donald, Supply chain risk management. Vulnerability and resilience in logistics, 2nd ed. London, Philadelphia: Kogan Page, 2011.

# Simulating Plug-in Electric Vehicle Charging for AutoML-Based Prediction of Regional Energy Demand

Matthias Schneider and Sören Frey

Daimler TSS GmbH
Wilhelm-Runge-Str. 11, 89081 Ulm, Germany
Email: {matthias.b.schneider, soeren.frey}@daimler.com

***Abstract*—We present a system for simulating home and public charging operations of Plug-in Electric Vehicles (PEVs). We model PEV traffic streams that result in corresponding charging operations. The simulation allows to configure many influential factors, such as the number of PEVs, consumption, charging stations, their locations, charging power, working hour distributions, holiday seasons, and the ratio of regular to irregular rides. In this paper, we demonstrate the applicability of our simulation in the context of predicting the short-term, regional energy demand of PEV charging. The prediction can be used to support energy suppliers and charging infrastructure operation, for instance. We use automated machine learning (AutoML) to train a forecasting model based on the simulation output. This combined workflow, integrating discrete-event simulation and machine learning, allows us to build a prediction pipeline where simulation data can be swapped with real data once available.**

***Index Terms*—Plug-in Electric Vehicle Charging; Simulation; Energy Demand Prediction; Machine Learning; AutoML.**

## I. Introduction

The transportation sector is facing a massive transformation in the upcoming years as the penetration of Plug-in Electric Vehicles (PEVs) is rapidly increasing [1]. This paper describes our work-in-progress Discrete-Event Simulation (DES) that models PEV traffic and emits corresponding charging operations. The simulation can be used in a variety of ways to advance electric mobility, e.g., for analyzing charging patterns and fostering the understanding of PEV owners' charging behavior and their corresponding needs. The simulation incorporates aspects related to driver behavior, e.g., working hour distributions, holiday seasons, and ratio of regular to irregular rides. It also involves equipment and adoption aspects, such as the number of PEVs, charging stations, charging power, battery capacity, and consumption. We demonstrate the usefulness of our simulation with the following application example.

A vital component for the propagation of electric mobility is a reliable and broadly available charging infrastructure. To enable this, it is important to accurately predict the realistic PEV charging operations while taking into account major influencing factors, such as the driver behavior [2]. Connected cars can fuel the underlying data basis for those predictions by providing data points that cover public and home charging operations. However, until connected PEVs will be the prevalent vehicle class, simulation data can be used as a versatile proxy to build up a resilient prediction pipeline. We use the output of our simulation, i.e., charging data, as the basis for training a prediction model with automated machine learning (AutoML, see Section IV) [3]. The model forecasts the short-term (up to a day) energy demand of PEV charging on a regional level. The paper provides the following main contributions:

1) A simulation of PEV charging behavior
2) An application example using the simulation output to train a model for regional energy demand prediction
3) An evaluation of the simulation and prediction model

The remainder of the paper is structured as follows. Section II examines the related work. The simulation is presented in Section III and employed in the application example in Section IV. Then, the evaluation is described in Section V before the conclusions are drawn in Section VI.

## II. Related Work

The simulation of traffic streams was relevant long before electric mobility became more widespread. The traffic simulation SUMO [4] was utilized in traffic management and routing research, for instance. For the analysis of electric vehicle traffic, many different approaches are used, such as Monte Carlo methods [5] or M/M/s queueing theory [6]. In comparison, we use DES and allow for a combination of workday and holiday patterns and incorporate the usually rather slow (private) home charging. Similar to [5] and [6], most other approaches (e.g. [7]) focus only on public charging.

The electric mobility simulators most similar to our system are V2G-Sim [8], ACN-Sim [9], and EVLibSim [10]. V2G-Sim was used to study battery degradation and integration of PEVs in smart grids as power sources, for instance. ACN-Sim and EVLibSim focus on the charging infrastructure perspective and incorporate detailed models for, e.g., pricing or unbalanced three-phase infrastructure. In contrast, we model traffic streams that result in charging operations. There exist several approaches that utilize Machine Learning (ML) for PEV charging load forecasting [11], but our application example is, to the best of our knowledge, the first that uses AutoML.

## III. PEV Charging Simulation

### A. Overview

We utilize the DES framework SimPy [12] for simulating the charging behavior of PEVs. The active components like PEVs or charging stations are modeled as processes, which interact with each other and their environment using events. For example, when a PEV starts to charge, it has to interact with a public or home charging station. This interaction is represented by a triggered charge event, which initiates the recharging of the PEV's battery. The major simulation entities are illustrated in Figure 1. A public or home *ChargingStation* comprises a number of *ChargingPoints*. At a *ChargingPoint*, only one vehicle can charge at a time. *PEV*s and *ChargingStations* are always situated at a specific *Location*. Additionally, *PEV*s have a permanently assigned home *Location*. Furthermore, a PEV is also tied to a regular or irregular *Tour* (see Section III-B), which in turn has exactly two *Locations* (start and destination).

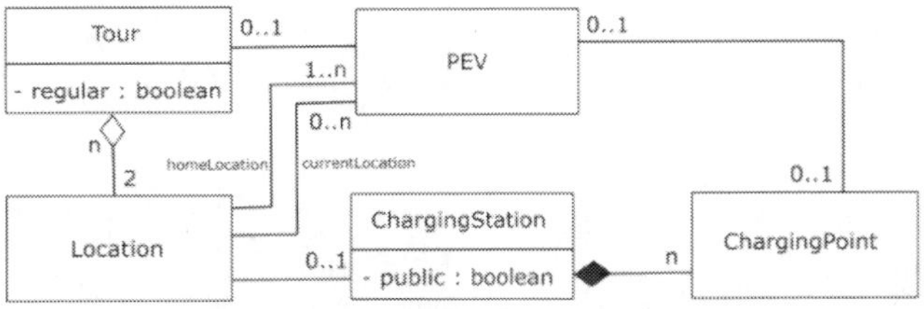


Fig. 1. The most important simulation entities.

### B. Assumptions

The charging behavior of the simulated PEVs underlies some basic assumptions.

1) As soon as a PEV reaches its destination, it charges if it is not capable to perform the next tour with the current State of Charge (SoC). In this case it may have to find a suitable charging station nearby.
2) If a PEV arrives at its home location and the home location has an existing charging station, the PEV always starts to charge regardless of its SoC status.
3) If a vehicle needs to charge during a tour, a suitable charging station is searched along the tour.

The consumption is calculated on the basis of the tours' distance and the average consumption of the PEV.

Public and home charging stations are able to charge multiple PEVs at the same time. This behavior is also reproduced in the simulation. The charging power of the charging points can be configured (see Section III-C).

There are two categories of tours a PEV drives: regular and irregular tours. A regular tour is, for example, the commute to the worksite and back. An irregular tour occurs sometime between the regular tours and represents, for example, a spontaneous trip to drive the children to school because the school bus broke down. When an irregular tour overlaps with a regular tour, the regular tour will be canceled. The times when the PEVs start their regular tours are determined by a normal distribution. Each kind of regular tour has its own normal distribution whose parameters can be configured individually. For example, the simulation initiates tours on weekday mornings and late afternoons, representing rush hour traffic. On weekends the distribution changes and the tours are initiated later than on weekdays. Furthermore, the average amount of tours PEVs drive during weekend days is lower than on weekdays.

In addition to the changing driving behavior between weekdays and weekends, vacation periods are also included in the simulation. During vacation periods, significantly fewer trips are simulated because, for example, the commute to work is omitted. Furthermore, it is assumed that some people are not at home during vacation time and therefore fewer trips and charging events take place. Both the daily number of trips during vacation periods and the vacation periods themselves (start and end times and duration) can be configured (see Section III-C).

### C. Simulation Input

The simulation is configured via a set of files, which are read at the beginning of the simulation. The files contain information regarding charging stations, worksites, and vacation periods, for instance. Moreover, we account for the inherent probabilistic nature of charging behavior by incorporating several distributions in the configuration files. For example, the duration of a vacation period can be configured via a normal distribution, i.e., through defining its corresponding mean ($\mu$) and standard deviation ($\sigma$). An excerpt of the simulation input parameters is shown in Table I. In total, there exist 71 degrees of freedom that can be configured with corresponding simulation parameters.

### D. Simulation Design

As mentioned in Section III-A the simulation contains events, which define the simulation flow. The events are triggered by the processes of the simulation. The event flow for each PEV is depicted in Figure 2.

The simulation of each PEV starts with a *WaitEvent*. This event is triggered when a PEV has currently no tour to drive and/or is sufficiently charged. If a *WaitEvent* ends, a new tour begins by triggering a *DrivingEvent*, which simulates a tour of a PEV by reducing the PEV's SoC. In our work-in-progress implementation the amount of SoC reduction solely depends on the distance the PEV traveled and its average speed. It is always decided in advance which tour (regular or irregular) will be run and when it will start. Moreover, it has to be determined if the PEV's battery has to be recharged. If a charging operation has to be initiated, either a *HomeChargeEvent* or a *PublicChargeEvent* is triggered, depending on the PEV's location. If charging was not necessary or the charging operation finished, a new *WaitEvent* is triggered. The termination condition of the simulation is met as soon as the simulation time is greater than the configured maximum simulation time.

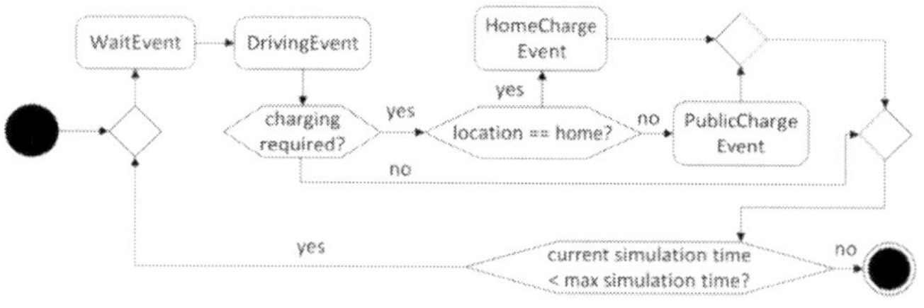


Fig. 2. Event flow for each PEV.

TABLE I
SIMULATION INPUT PARAMETERS (EXCERPT)

| **Name** | **Description** |
|---|---|
| ChargingStation.Location | Location of the charging station |
| ChargingStation.MaxCPower | Max. charging power of charging station |
| ChargingStation.NrCP | Nr. of charging points at charging station |
| Context.NrPEV | Nr. of simulated PEVs |
| Home.Location | Home location of the PEV's owner |
| StartOfWork.NDist.Mean | Mean start time of work |
| StartOfWork.NDist.Sd | Standard deviation start time of work |

TABLE II
SIMULATION OUTPUT DATA (EXCERPT)

| **Name** | **Description** |
|---|---|
| ChargingOperation.Duration | The duration of the charging operation |
| ChargingOperation.Kw | The charged energy amount in kW |
| ChargingOperation.Location | Location of corresponding charging point |
| ChargingOperation.Start | Start time of the charging operation |
| Vacation.Present | Vacation period present during charging? |

### E. *Simulation Output*

The simulation writes the relevant information of the executed charging operations to a CSV file, such as their start time and duration. The most important charging operation data is shown in Table II.

## IV. Application Example

### A. *Overview*

We demonstrate the simulation's applicability with a prediction of regional energy demand on the basis of simulation results. The output of the simulation is utilized to train an AutoML-based model. AutoML creates ML models automatically by using dynamically selected ML techniques. The parameterization of the ML models is also automated. Thus, AutoML only requires a training and test dataset as input, from which an ML model is then generated [3].

In this application example, the presented simulation is used to simulate the charging operations of the city of Stuttgart (Germany) for an entire year. For this purpose, the simulation inputs (e.g., locations of the charging stations or the number of PEVs) are adjusted accordingly. The simulation output is then passed to the AutoML-library auto-sklearn [13], which creates an ML model, predicting the regional energy demands. In order to pass the simulation output to AutoML, the output data must first be transformed. This transformation is also known as Feature Engineering (see Section IV-B) in the context of ML.

### B. *Feature Engineering*

Features are measurable properties of the problem to be solved and are used for training the ML model. We dynamically divide the region Stuttgart into several partitions and create corresponding features by transforming and aggregating the simulation output as follows: (1) All charging operations that occur in a given partition are aggregated. A partition is a rectangle whose height and length are adjustable, i.e., the number of partitions decreases or increases. (2) Charging operations are aggregated by time intervals. (3) All other values describing a charging operation (e.g., charged amount of energy in kW) are aggregated and averaged. In this application example, we use different combinations of one partition size and one time interval at each time to create several AutoML model candidates. The goal is to determine the combination that delivers the AutoML model with the best performance.

Table III shows example input data for a single partition (Id: 6449) and multiple time intervals (with their corresponding start times) and with various derived features. For example, several charging operations might occur in a specific time interval. Hence, we created the feature *MajorityChargingType* that describes, which type of charging operation (public or private) occurred most often. As a consequence, the total charging time (feature *SumChargingTime*) and average charging time (feature *AvgChargingTime*) might also differ if multiple charging operations took place. We used 75% of the data for training and 25% for testing the models.

## V. Evaluation

### A. *Simulation*

The simulation has to comply with the underlying assumptions described in Section III-B. In particular, we analyze and compare the results for simulating weekdays with weekend days. Figure 3 contrasts these two cases and shows the corresponding number of private and public charging operations for examplary days. We find that the total number of charging operations on weekends decreases compared to those on weekdays.

On a weekday, around 5am, private charging operations decrease noticeably, while charging operations at public charging stations increase. This is due to the fact that PEVs are being driven to work sites or other locations. In the evening, the private charging operations then rise considerably, which means that the PEVs are coming home again. This is also supported by the fact that public charging initially decreases during this period. These observations are consistent with findings from [14] and [15]. Chowell et al. and Mucelli Rezende Oliveira et al. report that (1) trips to the worksite usually start around 5am, (2) reach their maximum at 8am, and (3) the workday ends on average between 3-4pm. The renewed increase in public charging operations in the evening suggests that tours take place again (to locations of public life and leisure). This behavior is not seen as strongly on

TABLE III
ML INPUT DATA (EXAMPLE)

| StartTime | DayOfWeek | Partition Id | ChargedKwh | MajorityChargingType | IsVacation | SumChargingTime | AvgChargingTime |
|---|---|---|---|---|---|---|---|
| 1590364800 | monday | 6449 | 39.88 | public | true | 36723.46 | 36723.46 |
| 1590451200 | tuesday | 6449 | 55.18 | private | true | 50814.11 | 25407.05 |
| 1591660800 | tuesday | 6449 | 41.54 | public | false | 38255.0 | 12751.66 |

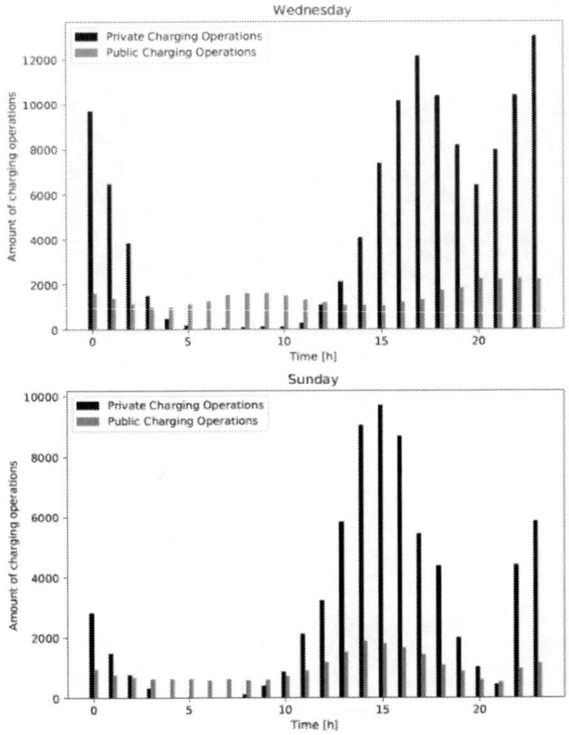


Fig. 3. Amount of charging operations for an exemplary weekday (Wednesday) and weekend day (Sunday).

weekend days. On weekends, it can be observed that there is a strong increase in home charging at around 3pm. This suggests that PEVs are returning from leisure trips (started earlier) at these times. The fact that charging does not increase as much thereafter suggests that many PEVs do not make any more trips on a weekend day. Thus, on average, a PEV drives less tours on weekend days than on weekdays.

The overall behavior of the simulation is plausible and corresponds to the assumptions made in Section III-B.

## B. AutoML

Figure 4 compares the AutoML model candidates created for the combinations of partition sizes (height = length) and time intervals using the metric $R^2$ score (coefficient of determination [16], best 1.0, worst 0.0). This metric is defined as follows:

$$R^2(y, \hat{y}) = 1 - \frac{\sum_{i=1}^{n}(y_i - \hat{y}_i)^2}{\sum_{i=1}^{n}(y_i - \bar{y})^2} \quad (1)$$

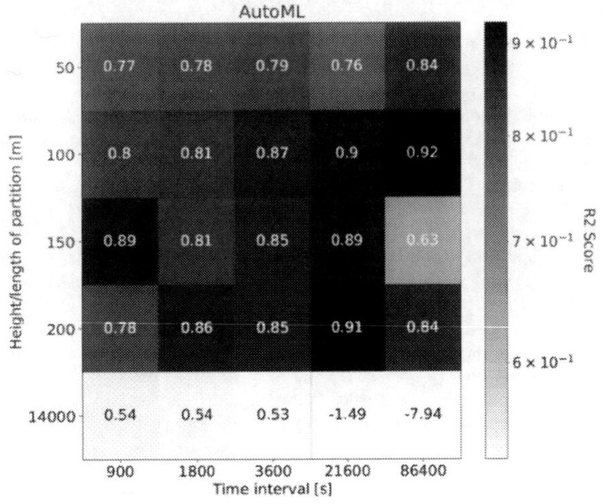


Fig. 4. $R^2$ scores for various AutoML model candidates. Each model was trained with a specific pair of partition- and time interval configuration.

Here, $y_i$ is the true value of the i-th sample, $\hat{y}_i$ is the predicted value for the i-th sample, and $\bar{y}$ is the arithmetic mean [16].

It can be seen that the AutoML models with the greatest height/length of 14,000 meters produce inferior results. All other combinations of edge length and time interval give acceptable results. Apart from the bottom line (partition height/length 14,000), the quality of the models also tend to increase with larger time intervals. In addition, it can be seen that the best models have neither very small nor very large partition sizes. The best result is obtained by the model with partition height/length of 100 meters and a time interval of 86,400 seconds. These observations are also consistent when applying other metrics, such as Mean Squared Error (MSE). Here, the best combination found with $R^2$ also shows a low MSE (799.53) in contrast to the other combinations that exhibit poor $R^2$ results. For example, for the combination of 14,000 meters and 86,000 seconds, the MSE also reaches the overall worst result of 11,320,389.63. In summary, depending on the partition size and time interval, AutoML has created well-performing ML models based on the simulation output.

## VI. CONCLUSION

Simulating PEV charging behavior can support numerous use cases in the context of electric mobility. We presented our corresponding simulation and showed that its results can be applied to train useful ML models. Employing AutoML in our application example yields suitable ML models that can provide very good predictions for the short-term, regional energy demand that is induced by PEV charging operations.

We will further improve the simulation's underlying physical model to take into account additional relevant parameters, such as the outside temperature, battery temperature, and PEVs' charging curves.

## REFERENCES

[1] G. Crabtree, "The coming electric vehicle transformation," *Science*, vol. 366, no. 6464, pp. 422–424, 2019.

[2] K. Chaudhari, N. K. Kandasamy, A. Krishnan, A. Ukil, and H. B. Gooi, "Agent-Based Aggregated Behavior Modeling for Electric Vehicle Charging Load," *IEEE Transactions on Industrial Informatics*, vol. 15, no. 2, pp. 856–868, 2019.

[3] F. Hutter, L. Kotthoff, and J. Vanschoren, Eds., *Automated Machine Learning: Methods, Systems, Challenges*. Springer, 2019.

[4] D. Krajzewicz, J. Erdmann, M. Behrisch, and L. Bieker, "Recent Development and Applications of SUMO - Simulation of Urban MObility," *International Journal On Advances in Systems and Measurements*, vol. 5, no. 3&4, pp. 128 – 138, 2012.

[5] Y. Xiang, Z. Jiang, C. Gu, F. Teng, X. Wei, and Y. Wang, "Electric vehicle charging in smart grid: A spatial-temporal simulation method," *Energy*, vol. 189, p. 116221, 2019.

[6] S. Bae and A. Kwasinski, "Spatial and Temporal Model of Electric Vehicle Charging Demand," *IEEE Transactions on Smart Grid*, vol. 3, no. 1, pp. 394–403, 2012.

[7] Q. Yan, C. Qian, B. Zhang, and M. Kezunovic, "Statistical analysis and modeling of plug-in electric vehicle charging demand in distribution systems," in *2017 19th International Conference on Intelligent System Application to Power Systems (ISAP)*, 2017, pp. 1–6.

[8] "V2G-Sim," http://v2gsim.lbl.gov/, 2021, [Online; accessed 2021-08-24].

[9] Z. J. Lee, D. Johansson, and S. H. Low, "ACN-Sim: An Open-Source Simulator for Data-Driven Electric Vehicle Charging Research," in *2019 IEEE Int'l. Conference on Communications, Control, and Computing Technologies for Smart Grids (SmartGridComm)*, 2019, pp. 1–6.

[10] E. S. Rigas, S. Karapostolakis, N. Bassiliades, and S. D. Ramchurn, "EVLibSim: A tool for the simulation of electric vehicles' charging stations using the EVLib library," *Simulation Modelling Practice and Theory*, vol. 87, pp. 99–119, 2018.

[11] J. Zhu et al., "Electric Vehicle Charging Load Forecasting: A Comparative Study of Deep Learning Approaches," *Energies*, vol. 12, no. 14, 2019.

[12] M. Norman, "Introduction to Discrete-Event Simulation and the SimPy Language," *Davis, CA. Dept of Computer Science*, vol. 2, 01 2008.

[13] "auto-sklearn," https://automl.github.io/auto-sklearn/, 2021, [Online; accessed 2021-08-24].

[14] G. Chowell, J. M. Hyman, S. Eubank, and C. Castillo-Chavez, "Scaling laws for the movement of people between locations in a large city," *Phys. Rev. E*, vol. 68, pp. 661 021–661 027, Dec 2003.

[15] E. Mucelli Rezende Oliveira, A. Carneiro Viana, C. Sarraute, J. Brea, and I. Alvarez-Hamelin, "On the regularity of human mobility," *Pervasive and Mobile Computing*, vol. 33, pp. 73–90, 2016.

[16] J. Devore, *Probability and Statistics for Engineering and the Sciences*. Cengage Learning, 2015.

# A Photorealistic Rendering Infrastructure for Man-in-the-Loop Real-Time Vehicle Simulation

Alessandro Tasora
Dept. of Engineering and Architecture
University of Parma
Parma, Italy
email: alessandro.tasora@unipr.it

Dario Mangoni
Dept. of Engineering and Architecture
University of Parma
Parma, Italy
email: dario.mangoni@unipr.it

***Abstract*— We discuss a software system for high-quality interactive rendering of virtual environments. Such tool embeds a state-of-the-art rendering engine middleware that is capable of rendering environments with high level of detail at interactive frame rates on modern GPUs. The model of the vehicle is defined via a model-based Functional Mock-up Unit that can be generated with an external tool, using the Modelica language.**

***Keywords* – *rendering; real-time; vehicle simulation.***

## I. INTRODUCTION

Thanks to recent advancements in the field of graphics processing unit (GPU) processors, the last generation of 3D rendering engines provides high frame rates even in case of large scenes with high level of detail and complex surface shaders. This allows the adoption of complex effects – such as global illumination and reflections – with a time budget of 20ms per frame, or less; this satisfies the requirement of >50Hz refresh rate for fluid man-in-the-loop interactive simulations, at the same time providing a realistic rendering quality for the best visual cueing [1]. In the past, high refresh rates were achieved at the cost of limiting the complexity of shading and details, hence failing in the so called "suspension of disbelief" effect, that is welcome in fields like virtual reality and vehicle simulators [2]. In detail, the addition of *ray-tracing cores* on the last generation of GPUs can provide unprecedented quality in renderings because ray tracing algorithms can be used, instead of a conventional rasterized rendering [3]. Ray tracing, also evolved as path tracing, can generate physically exact lighting effects, where conventional real-time renderers had to fake effects like reflections or global illumination in sake of performance.

Many applications that require high-performance real-time rendering, such as video games and simulators, are based on extremely powerful third-party middleware such as Unity, CryEngine or Unreal Engine [4][5]. These tools provide ready-to-use rendering algorithms in exchange for some royalties on the final product, or even for free if used in academic projects. In our project, we decided to use Unreal Engine, mostly because it features a well-documented C++ application program interface and because it is renowned for its unparalleled rendering quality.

Although there are many examples of applications that leverage on these rendering technologies for creating car simulations (videogames about racing being a special case of them), in most cases the model of the vehicle is designed directly inside the authoring tools that are provided by the developers of the rendering solutions - in our case it is the Unreal Editor. Doing so, the application could still implement a GUI that allows a user to adjust simple parameters such as the stiffness of a suspension, but if a vehicle designer needs to change some non-trivial property (such as the topology of a suspension or the type of powertrain), the Unreal Editor must be used and the application must be rebuilt again. However, passing through the Unreal Editor all the time that a change is needed, can slow down the design iterations.

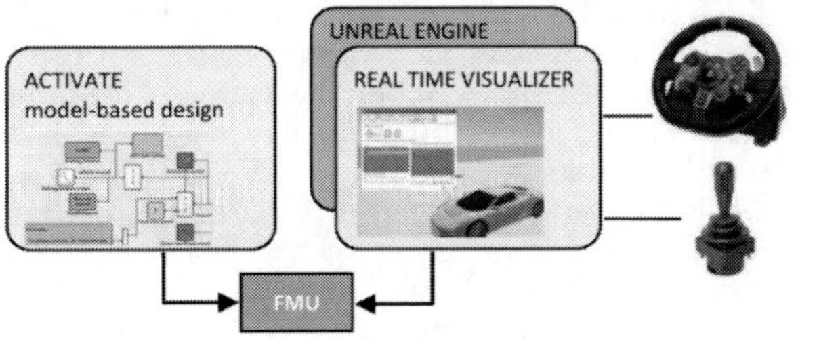


Figure 1. Workflow and software architecture.

In our solution, on the contrary, the user does not need to rebuild the simulator even if radical changes are needed since the vehicle model is separated from the visualization code. In fact, the model of the vehicle is stored into a separated piece of code that always exposes a standardized Application Programming Interface (API), thus allowing for a quick and effective model switching, as shown in Figure 1. This code can be generated by an independent tool – namely an editor for model-based systems – and later loaded in the visualization tool, where the user focuses only on rendering settings and bindings with user inputs.

## II. IMPLEMENTATION

Using the workflow that we designed, the physical model of the vehicle is generated with an external tool (namely, Altair Activate), that is capable of creating a

Functional Mockup Unit (FMU) from a model-based description of the vehicle, by leveraging components from both the Modelica Standard Library, containing basic mechanical and electrical components, and from an in-house vehicle-specific library for dynamical vehicle simulations, written in Modelica language [6]. The model, contained in the FMU, is automatically optimized by the underlying Modelica engine in order to offer best performances while retaining the flexibility of block-based graphical user interfaces. Additionally, also a multi-physics approach can be followed to assemble complex systems at a glance: complex vehicles with electric powertrains can be enriched with thermal and dynamical analysis of the system, together with full multi-body suspension geometries; and this without leaving the common Activate user interface.

Figure 2. Example of a wheeled vehicle in a photorealistic environment, including vegetation and atmospheric effects.

Then, we designed a visualization tool based on the Unreal Engine (UE) rendering technology. The performance-critical part of such tool is written in C++ thanks to the API and build toolchain of UE, whereas the graphical user interface (GUI) is built using the Blueprint visual scripting system of UE. Currently, only the Windows platform is supported.

In detail, the visualization tool parses the FMU and performs a run-time linking of the libraries that are contained in the FMU, and that define the functions for the time integration of the dynamical model. In order to bind visualization shapes to moving objects, the tool parses the XML file that is embedded in the FMU and that describes the name of the variables: a hierarchical structure of classes is constructed from that information, so to detect if the FMU was generated from Modelica blocks that represent 3D shapes (the Modelica standard defines *Visualizer* classes to this end). Once shapes are detected, a GUI shows a dialog that allows the user to pick a 3D mesh from the disk, as saved from a CAD, or to associate it to an asset prepared with the Unreal Editor and packaged in a .pak file. The latter option is meant for advanced users: at the cost of requiring the Unreal Editor, it allows additional effects such as the addition of particle effects and sounds, for instance spinning wheels can generate smoke and scratches at the ground, while engines can produce realistic noise. We also provide a method for bidirectional connectivity between the Unreal Blueprint scripts and the FMU variables.

The user can also attach inputs such as steering wheels, joysticks and buttons to FMU variables. Vice versa, output FMU variables can be exported to plots, CSV file logs, GUI and user-designed head-up displays, so that a full Human Machine Interface (HMI) can be implemented and tested in real-time.

Additional GUI panels allow the control of the level of photorealism, enabling depth of field, lens flares and lens bloom, global illumination, motion blur, color grading, etc.

The user can import scenarios designed with the CAD or with Unreal Editor, for example a vehicle can be tested in a virtual city or in a desert land or off road, as in the example of Figure 2. The sky and weather of the imported scenarios can be modified in run time thanks to a real-time atmospheric subsystem that generates sun, moon, stars, sky scattering, clouds and fog.

## III. Conclusion

We designed a tool that allows the run-time linking of FMU in a visualization framework. This system allows efficient and photorealistic simulations of vehicles of man-in-the-loop type.

## Acknowledgment

This work has been partially sponsored by Altair Engineering Inc. We thank Ewald Fischer, Chrysa Nikopoulou, Georgios Ntaountakis, Pranay Kumar, Michael Hoffmann, Filippo Donida, Livio Mariano, Franck Delcroix and others at Altair for testing the beta release of the tool and for reporting bugs and suggestions.

## References

[1] T. Akenine-Möller, E. Haines, and N. Hoffman, Real-Time Rendering, 4th edition, CRC Press, 2018.

[2] M. Pharr, W. Jakob, and G. Humphreys, Physically Based Rendering: From Theory to Implementation, 3rd edition, Morgan Kaufmann, 2016.

[3] Nvidia RTX platform, https://developer.nvidia.com/rtx [retrieved: July, 2021].

[4] Unity rendering engine, http://www.unity.com [retrieved: July, 2021].

[5] UnrealEngine rendering engine and 3D content creation tool, http://www.unrealengine.com [retrieved: July, 2021].

[6] P. Fritzson, Introduction to Modeling and Simulation of Technical and Physical Systems. Wiley-IEEE Press, 2011.

[7] P. Fritzson, Principles of Object-Oriented Modeling and Simulation with Modelica 3.3, Wiley, 2014.

# Creating a Baseline Scenario for Simulating Travel Demand: A Case Study for Preparing the Region Test Bed Lower Saxony, Germany

Antje von Schmidt, María López Díaz, Alain Schengen
*Institute of Transport Research*
*German Aerospace Center*
Berlin, Germany
e-mail: {antje.vonschmidt, maria.lopezdiaz, alain.schengen}@dlr.de

***Abstract*—Agent-based travel demand models can be used to estimate the impact of possible transportation planning measures and to forecast future development of human mobility. Related transport models and associated simulation results are described often in detail, but explanations of the creation of the required baseline scenario including the necessary data preparation are rarely available and often not shown. Therefore, this paper gives general data requirements for creating a needed virtual representation of a study area. Furthermore, it shows a real example based on the preparation of the region covering the Test Bed Lower Saxony in Germany. Special focus is laid on population, location, and accessibility data within the area. The presented approach can also be used to prepare a different study area. Therefore, possible data sources and recommendations for preparing the data are given.**

***Keywords*—travel demand; synthetic population; locations for activities; accessibility measures.**

## I. Introduction

How, when, where, and why do people move from one location to another? Agent-based travel demand models can give answers to those questions. These models are important tools in transportation planning. They are used to estimate the impact of possible measures, such as the installation of a new public transportation infrastructure. Furthermore, they can provide important insights on various possible future developments in travel demand, like due to an aging population, the use of innovative vehicles, changing fuel prices or new mobility trends.

For simulating the travel demand with agent-based models a baseline scenario is required. It represents the current state and is used as reference. Therefore, a virtual representation of the related study area is an essential input for these models. Recently, recommendations for input data regarding spatial structure and transport offer have been provided [1]. The spatially related structural data often include information about the population and the locations where activities can be performed, whereas accessibility measures and transport network for different modes describe the transport offer. In addition, these models require usually information about travel behavior. Such required detailed information is often not available. Instead, it has to be created from a variety of data sources. In particular, these data are very heterogeneous in terms of format, spatial resolution, and time frame. Such challenges of agent-based models are discussed in [2].

The purpose of this paper is to highlight general data requirements, possible data sources, and appropriate approaches for creating a virtual representation of a study area. It also gives a real example based on the preparation of the region covering the Test Bed Lower Saxony in Germany. Special focus is laid on population, location, and accessibility data within the area.

The paper is organized as follows: Section II gives information on related work and contains an overview about essential input data. The data preparation of the selected study area is outlined in Section III. The results of the virtual representation are presented in Section IV. Finally, Section V includes the conclusions and gives an outlook on future work.

## II. Related Work and Essential Input Data

Travel demand models are often based on the common four-step model [3], which consists of trip generation, trip distribution, mode choice, and traffic assignment. The trip generation includes the estimation of how many trips are generated within a zone whereas the trip distribution covers their destinations. Afterwards, a suitable transport mode is chosen. The exact routes to be selected are determined in the last step. In the case of agent-based models, this traditional approach has been strongly expanded [4]. There is usually no isolated consideration of a single step, but also interactions within and between these steps. Rather than modeling aggregate Origin-Destination (OD) matrices for each zone, these models rely on a non-aggregated approach, where activities are the starting point for representing daily mobility [5].

Detailed descriptions of agent-based models and associated simulation results can be found often, but descriptions about creating the underlying baseline scenario and the data preparation are rarely available. Such models require a variety of different input data for each step. Current research shows that the level of detail of the required input data may differ [6] [7] [8]. This can depend on both the transport model used or the specific research question. In the following, essentially required input data, possible data sources, and further related work for each discussed approach to generate the specific data are given in the subsections below.

### A. Spatial reference units

A subdivision of the study area into smaller units is necessary to reflect spatial differences in travel demand. In travel demand modeling these spatial units are called Traffic Analysis Zones (TAZ). Usually they are homogeneous, for example, containing the same number of households but they can also correspond to administrative boundaries. The spatial reference units are needed within the model, but they are also used for the analysis and visualization of the simulation results [9].

### B. Spatial structure data

For each TAZ, non-aggregated population data are required. Each person of a synthetic population is described by a set of socio-demographic information. In addition, information about available mobility options is required. Household information comprises for example the number of persons, the total household income, and the number of cars that belong to the household. Within the simulation, each tour usually starts and ends at the home location of the person. Therefore, a spatial reference of the address for each household is required. Based on the address, each household can also be assigned to the corresponding TAZ. Such detailed population data are usually not available, but have to be generated on the basis of empirical data and by suitable mathematical methods. The consolidation of all information often remains difficult, as various and heterogeneous data sources have to be used. Therefore, a variety of different approaches have been established for creating a synthetic population. Most of these approaches are sample-based [10]. In order to correspond to both a desired household and person distribution, several methods can be used, for example household weight updating [11], hierarchical fitting [12], or Bayesian networks [13]. Due to limited data availability, alternative approaches that do not require a sample have been developed as well [14]. The synthetic population has a direct impact on the resulting traffic volume, but also on the simulated travel behavior.

Apart from the synthetic population, possible locations where activities can take place at are needed. Location choice depends not only on individuals, but also on location specific characteristics. Frequently used attributes in location and destination choice include type of activity, spatial distribution, accessibility, maximum capacity, as well as destination attractiveness. The main activity types used in agent-based travel demand models are often related to work, education, shopping, and leisure, but further types, such as personal business or accompanying, may be also regarded depending on the model [15] [16]. Information about activity locations usually has to be collected from a variety of sources (e.g., public authorities, surveys, commercial data). Since this process can be time-consuming and expensive, open data is another option, especially OpenStreetMap (OSM). Its suitability and accuracy as a data source for travel demand modeling has been subject of study, with different results depending on the region or activity type, with a possible improvement in data quality over the years [17]. Another possibility is to generate activity locations randomly using complementary data, such as land use [18] or commuter flows [16]. Information about the numbers of workers, students, etc. is used by travel demand models as a capacity constraint to avoid exceeding the location's capacity and is only provided by some data sources. If not available, it can be generated synthetically, for example using building area and number of floors. Another attribute used by some models for destination choice is attractiveness, for example based on store size [18] or using data from a location-based social network [19].

### C. Transport offer data

In an agent-based demand model, each person from the synthetic population acts as an agent. An agent has its own daily plan of activities which need to be simulated. These plans are commonly represented as tours. A tour starts and respectively ends at home and contains a set of trips which connect subsequent activities. Trips are entities that represent the movement between two locations, including the time they should start at, as well as the required time to accomplish them. In order to complete a trip, an agent has to make several choices, such as which location to head to and which mode to use. Since the duration of a trip is known in advance, the choice for a potential destination is, among other things, dependent on mode specific travel times that are structured in OD matrices. To reduce the dimension of these matrices, travel time data between every location is aggregated on TAZ level. There are several possibilities to generate disaggregated travel time data. In the context of motorized individual transport, one can use a graph-based routing algorithm like Dijkstra [20] or A* [21] or acquire raw data from external sources with further processing. In the context of public transport, time table-based data like the General Transit Feed Specification (GTFS) could be used. These accessibility measures play an important role in computing both, destination and mode choice.

### D. Travel behavior data

Information about travel behavior within a study area is required in several steps of the modeling process. Such data can be usually obtained from travel or time-use surveys. Mobility options for the synthetic population can be estimated by related logit models. However, the fundamentals of these microscopic travel demand models are based on activities of each individual. Besides the type of activity, the reported diaries typically include both the start time and the duration of the activity, but also the activity sequence. During a simulation run, the prepared standardized diaries from the survey are used to determine for each person in the synthetic population what activities they undertake, when, and for how long. This also reflects the number of trips to be generated. An appropriate decision model is needed for the choice of the transport mode. For this purpose, a multinomial logit model could be created, for example, based on travel time, trip purpose, and distance obtained from the survey. In addition, the distribution of observed distances per mode, modeshare or trip purpose can be used to calibrate and validate the simulation results.

## III. Preparing the Region Test Bed Lower Saxony

In this section, the study area will be outlined. First, an overview of the data sources is given. Then, the spatial representation of the area. Afterwards, the generation of the synthetic population, followed by the locations including their capacities. Finally, the preparation of accessibility measures for different modes of transport are described. The presented study area will be used within the agent-based travel demand model TAPAS [22] [23]. The software was recently made available as open source and can be found at: https://github.com/DLR-VF/TAPAS.

### A. Overview of data sources

For preparing the study area, various data sets from freely accessible data portals, administrative authorities but also a commercial data provider have been used. The data sources on which the study area are based are listed in Table I and described in more detail in the following subsections B to E.

### B. Study Area

With the Test Bed Lower Saxony [24], a research infrastructure for automated and connected vehicles is currently being created. The test field includes sections of various highways, but also parts of federal and country roads. Furthermore, it also integrates the roads of the Application Platform for Intelligent Mobility (AIM) [25], which is in operation within the city center of Brunswick. In total, the test field will cover more than 280 road kilometers after completion. This road network is located in the federal state of Lower Saxony within the districts of Gifhorn, Helmstedt, Hildesheim, Peine, Hanover region, and Wolfenbüttel, as well as the district-free cities of Brunswick, Salzgitter, and Wolfsburg. Population data for forecast periods are often available at the district level rather than at the municipality level. For this reason, these 6 districts and the 3 independent cities represent the study area which is used in this paper. As mentioned in Section II, it is necessary to subdivide the area into traffic zones. Unfortunately, no small-scale uniform subdivision covering this area was available for free. Therefore, a suitable division by neighborhoods containing approximately 500 households was obtained from Nexiga [26]. As a result, the area is divided into 2807 zones. The region is mainly characterized as urban. Fig. 1 shows the spatial coverage of the study area including the road network of the Test Bed Lower Saxony and the division into traffic zones. The geographical position within Germany is given in the overview image, highlighted in dark gray.

TABLE I. Data sources

| **Data provider** | **Study area** | **Synthetic population** | **Locations for activities** | **Accessibility measures** |
|---|---|---|---|---|
| Connect Fahrplanauskunft GmbH (Connect) | | | | x |
| Federal Agency for Cartography and Geodesy (BKG) | | x | x | |
| Federal and State Statistical Offices | | x | | |
| Kraftfahrt-Bundesamt (KBA) | | x | | |
| Mobility in Germany (MiD2017) | | x | | |
| Nexiga | x | x | x | |
| OpenStreetMap (OSM) | | | x | x |
| Statistics Office of Lower Saxony (LSN) | | x | | |

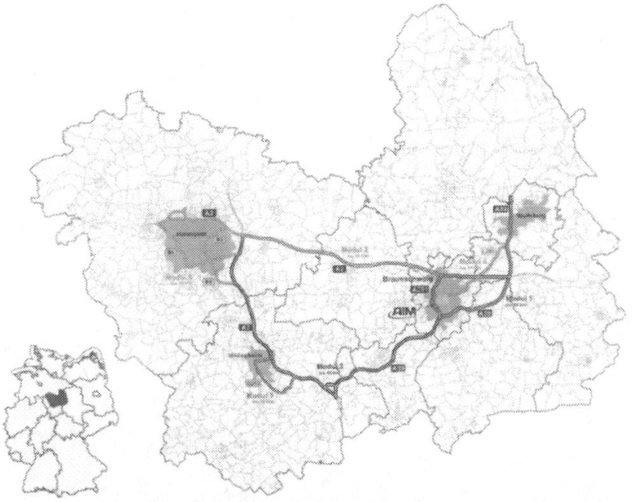


Figure 1. Spatial coverage of the study area including the road network of the Test Bed Lower Saxony and the division into traffic zones. The geographic location within Germany is highlighted in the overview image.

### C. Synthetic population

The required detailed population data are not available in Germany, or if they are, they are not available without charge. Usually, population data for the base year are only available in aggregated form at municipal level. But, this spatial resolution is much too low. For example, a city like Berlin with 3.7 million inhabitants would be a municipality. In order to take spatial differences within the study area into account, the data must, on the one hand, be on a higher spatial resolution and be available in a non-aggregated form. The synthetic population was created using SYNTHESIZER [27]. This in-house application is often used within projects to generate the required non-aggregated population data for TAPAS. Beside the spatial subdivision into traffic zones, aggregated socio-demographic data as marginal totals, and a non-aggregated data set for duplicating the respective households and persons are needed as input. Therefore, aggregated population data on TAZ level from Nexiga were used. This data set includes the number of persons subdivided into various age groups, gender, and labor force. The latter are further subdivided into employed and unemployed persons. In addition, household size and income, as well as number of private cars are included. A person within a synthetic population for TAPAS is mainly described by age, gender, and a status classification like children under 6 years, pupil, trainee, student, both full time and part time employed, unemployed or retired. To get the total number of children under 6 years of age, the corresponding age groups were added. Number of pupils and students in formal education schools, type of employment (part-time or full-time), and number of pensioners come from the LSN [28]. Data on students in higher education were used from the municipal education database [29]. In addition, the scientific use file of the Microcensus [30] was used as non-aggregated sample. Both data sets are taken from the Federal and State Statistical Offices. Since the aggregated data were partly available on different spatial scales, they were proportionally allocated to the corresponding traffic zone in advance. In the SYNTHESIZER application, the respective distributions at household and person level are generated for each TAZ. To ensure that both distributions are included in the target population, a new household weight is generated and used when copying the entries from the sample. The result is a non-aggregated base population.

Section II mentions that an address is needed for each household. So far, only a spatial reference to the associated TAZ is given. Instead of distributing the corresponding households evenly among the associated addresses within a TAZ, the distribution was done by using a weight for each address. This weight is composed of land use, building height, and building area. Depending on the land use in which an address is located, a corresponding factor was assigned to this address, with addresses in residential areas having a higher value. The weight of an address (A) is calculated by the product of the land use factor (LU), the building height (BH), and the building area (BA) as shown in (1).

$$Weight_A = LU_A * BH_A * BA_A \tag{1}$$

Finally, the weighted number of inhabitants was added to each address. It is composed by the product of inhabitants living in a TAZ and the weight of the address (A) divided by the sum of all related address weights located in this TAZ, see (2).

$$Inhabitants_A = \frac{Inhabitants_{TAZ} * Weight_A}{\sum_{A' \in TAZ} Weight_{A'}} \tag{2}$$

Addresses, a digital landscape model, and a three-dimensional building data set with the LoD1 level of detail from the BKG [31] were used to distribute the inhabitants on buildings.

In addition to socio-demographic data, information on available mobility options for each person or, respectively, household are important for the upcoming simulation. The availability of various mobility options was reported in the nationwide household travel behavior survey MiD2017 [32]. Based on the survey data, logit models could be estimated for owning a driver license, a public transport ticket, as well as the ownership and number of cars in the household, and their subdivision into three different size classes. No significant model could be estimated for bicycle ownership. Instead, the respective proportion by gender and age group were used for this purpose. The total number of private cars for each traffic zone from Nexiga was used as the vehicle fleet. Whereas data from the KBA [33] was used for the distribution of the vehicle fleet in regard to the corresponding engine types and their size classes.

### *D. Locations for activities*

Activity locations from different sources were gathered and their format was harmonized for its use in TAPAS. Activity locations in TAPAS can serve different activities and need exact coordinates, activity type, and total capacity as attributes for destination choice. An example for a location serving multiple activities is a school, which can serve for educational and working purposes. All data sets contained spatial information, even if the coordinate reference system may vary. On the contrary, type of activity and capacity were not always available and even if they were, they had to be converted and manually classified.

TAPAS has its own classification of activities with three levels. The first level is based on the main activities work, education, shopping, leisure, and personal matters. Within each category there is a more detailed subdivision with one or two subcategories. This is to address different kinds of locations, especially in matters of size and special use. An example with three levels would be *education-school-primary school*.

From Nexiga came most of work and shopping locations and to a lesser extent locations of other categories. From the BKG forest-related data from the Digital Landscape Model (DLM) and Points of Interest (POI), such as universities, schools, hospitals or embassies, were used. Lastly, different leisure locations, including parks, allotments, playgrounds or places of worship were extracted from OSM. Most of the TAPAS activity categories were mapped onto economic activity codes, which are available for most of the companies in the Nexiga data set. These codes correspond to the German Classification of Economic Activities, which is based on the Statistical Classification of Economic Activities in the European Community. Categories without a link to economic activity codes had to be classified by string-matching or manually, which was the case for the BKG and OSM data, as well as for part of the Nexiga data.

In order to calculate capacities for activity locations, a system based on relating location area to the number of potential users/customers and workers was used and adapted to our needs. These factors can be obtained by planing engineering offices like [34] or from the Trip Generation Handbook [35]. Our system consists of an employee factor as well as a user factor for each activity category. Both factors are interconnected, allowing to determine the number of users per employee and vice versa. We also included a default value (used in case of unavailable capacities), extracted from available data or determined after some visual analysis. Those factors were used to calculate missing capacities for all Nexiga locations as well as for schools and hospitals from BKG, since the number of employees for the former and the number of pupils and beds for the latter were available. For example, for the Nexiga locations the number of users/customers was calculated using the number of employees and the corresponding user factor. From the forest-data the area was used to subtract a possible number of visitors, whereas default values were assign to all OSM locations.

### *E. Accessibility measures*

Since an agent inside a TAPAS simulation has a predefined time frame for a trip, the location choice model is, among other things, based on travel time matrices. Over the course of a simulated day, these matrices have to change because travel time is dependent on factors like current situation on roads and the roads' capacities in the context of individual transport or time table changes when it comes to public transportation systems. As stated in Section II, several techniques exist to compute these for each available mode. Average travel times and travel distances between each TAZ for every mode have been computed using the UrMoAC [36], which is a Dijkstra-based, in-house, and open-source application. Based on the fact that computing all routes between every location in the study area will require a lot of computation time, five location representatives for every TAZ have been chosen at random in advance for all modes. In the context of public transportation, these computations have been done for multiple time frames over three days (Tuesday, Wednesday, and Thursday) in an average week with no special events. Time frames from 7am to 10am and 5pm to 7pm cover the morning and evening rush hour travel times. 10am to 5pm and 7pm to 11pm represent average utilisation. The last time frame from 11pm to 7am contains average travel times for night traffic. A common problem with this approach refers to untrustworthy travel times for trips that start and end in the same zone. The matrix diagonal for the whole area is computed separately, calculating every distance between every location inside the same TAZ and using the median as average travel time [37].

## IV. RESULTS

The study area was prepared for the base year 2017 and the forecast year 2030. The following results refer to the base year.

The synthetic population for this area contains a total of 2.4 million persons grouped into 1.3 million households. Fig. 2 presents the spatial distribution of the population density. The district cities appear quite prominently here. On average, 1.9 people live in each household. The population distribution according to age and gender is shown in Fig. 3. About 51% of all people are female and the remaining are male. Approximately 16% of the inhabitants are younger than 18 years, 62% are of working age and 22% are older than 65 years. 88% people of age 18 or older have a driver license. In addition, about 84% of all people have a bicycle and 23% have a ticket for public transport. 21% of all households do not have a car, whereas 79% own at least one car. All added mobility options correspond almost exactly to the values reported in the MiD2017. Only the value for the public transport ticket is 2% higher than in the survey. This is due to the fact that when adding the public transport ticket, both school as well as semester tickets for students were assumed in the entire study area. The overall level of motorization is about 537 vehicles per 1,000 inhabitants. Fig. 4 shows the spatial distribution of the motorization level. It can be noticed that the level of motorization is lower in the cities of the district. However, if the number of vehicle per km² is taken into account, the vehicle density in the cities is higher than in the surrounding communities.

The preparation of the activity locations resulted in a total of around 220,000 locations, taking into account that some of them correspond to the same location but have different types. For example, a hospital belongs to the categories *work*, but also

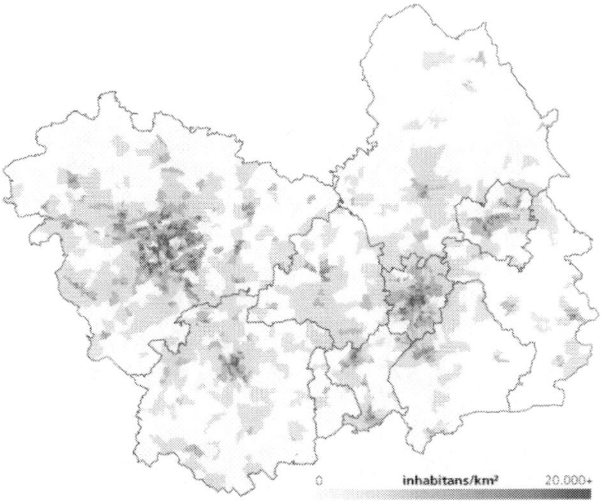


Figure 2. Spatial distribution of the population density.

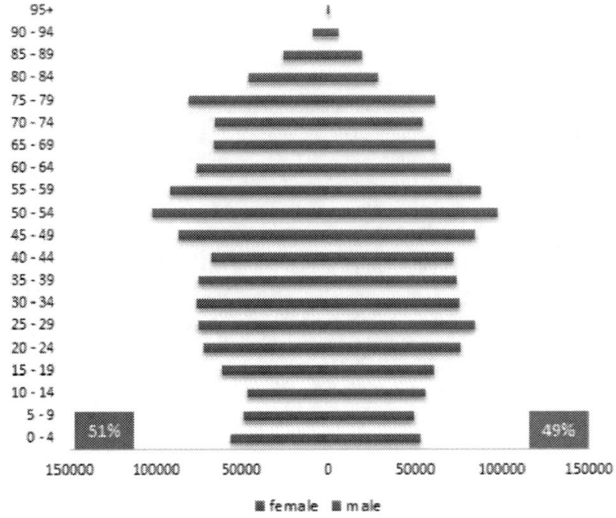


Figure 3. Distribution of individuals by age and gender.

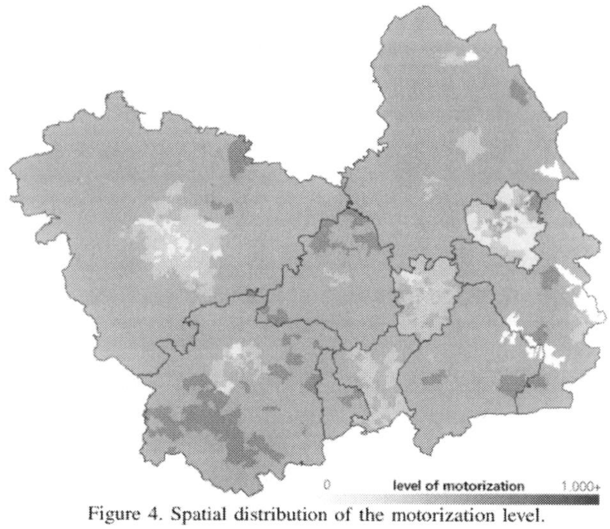

Figure 4. Spatial distribution of the motorization level.

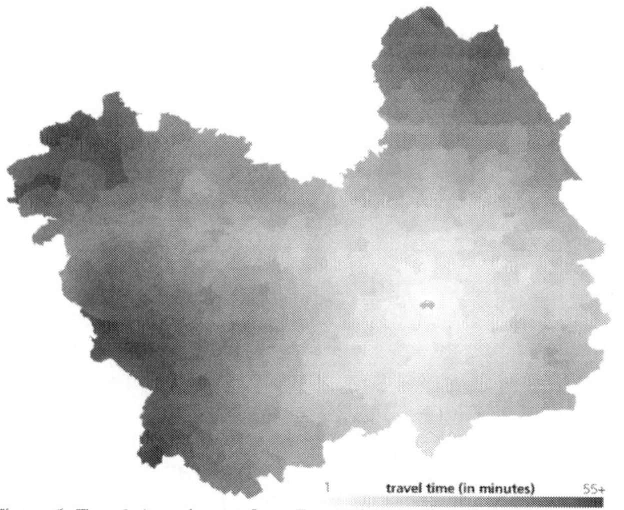

Figure 6. Travel times by car from Brunswick to all traffic analysis zones in the study area.

to *personal matters - health - hospital*, and *personal matters - family - visit*. Approximately half of the locations correspond to workplaces, 4,000 to education, 13,000 to shopping, and 33,000 to personal matters. More than 20% are leisure locations, but this number is misleading, because forests are divided into small areas, of which the centroid represents a location. Furthermore, as with the spatial distribution of the population, most workplaces are concentrated in the main cities, shown in Fig. 5.

Fig. 6 shows the temporal accessibility from the center of Brunswick to all other traffic analysis zones inside the area using a car. One can see that an agent can reach farther regions that are located along highways in a certain amount of time. The main transport network is included in Fig. 1.

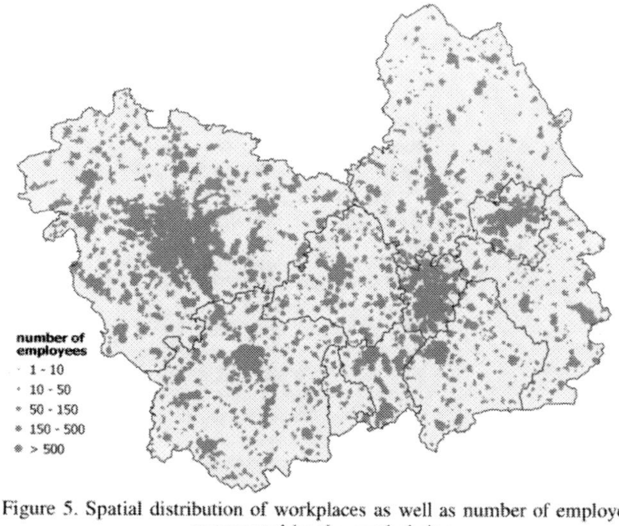

Figure 5. Spatial distribution of workplaces as well as number of employees represented by the symbol size.

## V. Conclusion and Future Work

Agent-based travel demand models are important tools to estimate the impact of possible transportation planning measures and to forecast future development of human mobility. A virtual representation of the related study area is an essential input for these models. This paper gives a real example based on the preparation of the region covering the Test Bed Lower Saxony in Germany for the year 2017. The presented approach can be used to prepare a different study area. Therefore, several recommendations, possible data sources, and approaches to generate the needed data are given. The method for generating the synthetic population could also be used within a different research domain. For this purpose, data on mobility options could be replaced by relevant other information or additional ones could be added.

It should be noted that the quality of the input data has a strong influence on the quality of the simulation results. Therefore, special attention should be paid to the correctness of the data and, if necessary, plausibility checks should be carried out. This ensures that realistic findings and useful conclusions can be derived from the simulation results. Furthermore, data preparation and maintenance can be very time-consuming and expensive, depending on the level of detail and the availability of data for the study area.

Upcoming work will focus on the simulation of different scenarios in the field of autonomous driving. For this purpose, the study area presented in this paper will be used in the travel demand model TAPAS.

## References

[1] FGSV Verlag GmbH, "Recommendations for input data on spatial structure and transport offer for transport demand models", "Empfehlungen für Inputdaten zur Raumstruktur und zum Verkehrsangebot für Verkehrsnachfragemodelle (EIV)" (original title), FGSV 168/3, ISBN 978-3-86446-290-0, 2021.

[2] G. O. Kagho, M. Balac, and K. W. Axhausen, "Agent-Based Models in Transport Planning: Current State, Issues, and Expectations", Procedia Computer Science, vol. 170, pp. 726–732, https://doi.org/10.1016/j.procs.2020.03.164, 2020.

[3] M. G. McNally, "The Four Step Model", UC Irvine: Center for Activity Systems Analysis", 2008, https://escholarship.org/uc/item/0r75311t, retrieved: 2021.09.02.

[4] National Academies of Sciences, Engineering, and Medicine, "Activity-Based Travel Demand Models: A Primer", Washington, DC: The National Academies Press, https://doi.org/10.17226/22357, 2014.

[5] Z. Chu, L. Cheng, and H. Chen, "A Review of Activity-Based Travel Demand Modeling", pp. 48-59, https://doi.org/10.1061/9780784412442.006, 2012.

[6] P. M. Bösch, K. Müller, and F. Ciari, "The IVT 2015 Baseline Scenario", 16th Swiss Transport Research Conference, 2016.

[7] C. Weiss et al., "Assessing the effects of a growing electric vehicle fleet using a microscopic travel demand model", European Journal of Transport and Infrastructure Research, 17 (3), https://doi.org/10.18757/ejtir.2017.17.3.3200, 2017.

[8] D. Ziemke, I. Kaddoura, and K. Nagel, "The MATSim Open Berlin Scenario: A multimodal agent-based transport simulation scenario based on synthetic demand modeling and open data", Procedia Computer Science, Volume 151, pp. 870-877, ISSN 1877-0509, https://doi.org/10.1016/j.procs.2019.04.120, 2019.

[9] M. Loidl et al., "GIS and Transport Modeling—Strengthening the Spatial Perspective," ISPRS International Journal of Geo-Information, vol. 5, no. 6, https://doi.org/10.3390/ijgi5060084, 2016.

[10] J. Y. Guo and C. R. Bhat, "Population synthesis for microsimulating travel behavior", Transportation Research Record, 2014 (12), pp. 92-101, 2007.

[11] X. Ye, K. Konduri, R. M. Pendyala, B. Sana, and P. Waddell, "A methodology to match distributions of both household and person attributes in the generation of synthetic populations", Paper presented at the 88th Annual Meeting of the Transportation Research Board, Washington, D.C., 2009.

[12] K. Müller and K. W. Axhausen, "Hierarchical IPF: Generating a synthetic population for Switzerland", Paper presented at the 51st Congress of the European Regional Science Association, Barcelona, 2011.

[13] L. Sun and A. Erath, "A Bayesian network approach for population synthesis", Transportation Research Part C: Emerging Technologies, 61, pp. 49-62, 2015.

[14] J. Barthelemy and P. L. Toint, "Synthetic Population Generation without a Sample", Transportation Science 47, no. 2, pp. 266-279, 2013.

[15] M. Bradley, J. L. Bowman, and B. Griesenbeck, "SACSIM: An applied activity-based model system with fine-level spatial and temporal resolution", Journal of Choice Modelling, vol. 3, no. 1, pp. 5–31, https://doi.org/10.1016/S1755-5345(13)70027-7, 2010.

[16] K. Meister et al. "Application of an agent-based model of transport demand for Switzerland", "Anwendung eines agentenbasierten Modells der Verkehrsnachfrage auf die Schweiz" (original title), In HEUREKA'08 - Optimierung in Verkehr und Transport, FGSV-Verlag, p. 22, 2008.

[17] L. Briem, M. Heilig, C. Klinkhardt, and P. Vortisch, "Analyzing OpenStreetMap as data source for travel demand models A case study in Karlsruhe", Transportation Research Procedia, vol. 41, pp. 104–112, https://doi.org/10.1016/j.trpro.2019.09.021, 2019.

[18] A. Horni, K. Nagel, and K. W. Axhausen, "The Multi-Agent Transport Simulation MATSim", Ubiquity Press, https://doi.org/10.5334/baw, 2016.

[19] J. Molloy and R. Moeckel, "Improving Destination Choice Modeling Using Location-Based Big Data", ISPRS International Journal of Geo-Information, vol. 6, no. 9, Art. no. 9, https://doi.org/10.3390/ijgi6090291, 2017.

[20] E. W. Dijkstra, "A note on two problems in connexion with graphs", Numerische Mathematik 1, pp. 269–271, https://doi.org/doi:10.1007/BF01386390, 1959.

[21] P. E. Hart, N. J. Nilsson, and B. Raphael, "A Formal Basis for the Heuristic Determination of Minimum Cost Paths", IEEE Transactions on Systems Science and Cybernetics SSC4. 4 (2), pp. 100–107, https://doi.org/10.1109/TSSC.1968.300136, 1968.

[22] M. Heinrichs, D. Krajzewicz, R Cyganski, and A. von Schmidt, "Disaggregated car fleets in microscopic travel demand modelling", 7th International Conference on Ambient Systems, Networks and Technologies, pp. 155-162, https://doi.org/10.1016/j.procs.2016.04.111, 2016.

[23] M. Heinrichs, D. Krajzewicz, R Cyganski, and A. von Schmidt, "Introduction of car sharing into existing car fleets in microscopic travel demand modelling", Personal and Ubiquitous Computing, Springer, pp. 1055-1065, https://doi.org/10.1007/s00779-017-1031-3, 2017.

[24] DLR-Transport, "Test Bed Lower Saxony for automated and connected mobility", https://verkehrsforschung.dlr.de/en/projects/test-bed-lower-saxony-automated-and-connected-mobility, retrieved: 2021.09.02.

[25] Application Platform for Intelligent Mobility, http://www.dlr.de/ts/aim, retrieved: 2021.09.02.

[26] Nexiga GmbH, https://nexiga.com, retrieved: 2021.09.02.

[27] A. von Schmidt, R. Cyganski, and D. Krajzewicz, "Generation of synthetic populations for transport demand models, a comparison of methods using the example of Berlin", "Generierung synthetischer Bevölkerungen für Verkehrsnachfragemodelle, ein Methodenvergleich am Beispiel von Berlin" (original title), In HEUREKA'17 - Optimierung in Verkehr und Transport, FGSV-Verlag, pp. 193-210, 2017.

[28] Statistics Office of Lower Saxony, "LSN-Online - regional database", https://www1.nls.niedersachsen.de/statistik/default.asp, retrieved: 2021.09.02.

[29] Federal and State Statistical Offices, "Municipal education database", https://www.bildungsmonitoring.de, retrieved: 2021.09.02.

[30] Federal and State Statistical Offices, "Microzensus - Scientific Use File", 2015, http://www.forschungsdatenzentrum.de/de/10-21242-12211-2015-00-00-3-1-0, retrieved: 2021.09.02.

[31] Federal Agency for Cartography and Geodesy, https://www.bkg.bund.de, retrieved: 2021.09.02.

[32] infas, DLR, IVT und infas 360, "Mobility in Germany (commissioned by the BMVI)", "Mobilität in Deutschland (im Auftrag des BMVI)" (original title), 2018, http://www.mobilitaet-in-deutschland.de, retrieved: 2021.09.02.

[33] Kraftfahrt-Bundesamt, "Vehicle fleet", 2017, https://www.kba.de, retrieved: 2021.09.02.

[34] D. Bosserhoff, "Program Ver_Bau. Estimation of traffic volume through urban land use planning projects with Excel tables on the PC", "Programm Ver_Bau. Abschätzung des Verkehrsaufkommens durch Vorhaben der Bauleitplanung mit Excel-Tabellen am PC" (original title), 2018, http://www.dietmar-bosserhoff.de/Programm.html, retrieved: 2021.09.02.

[35] K. G. Hooper, "Trip Generation Handbook", ITE, ISBN: 1933452919, 2017.

[36] D. Krajzewicz, D. Heinrichs, and R. Cyganski, "Intermodal Contour Accessibility Measures Computation Using the 'UrMo Accessibility Computer'", International Journal On Advances in Systems and Measurements, ThinkMind, 10 (3/4), pp. 111-123, 2017.

[37] M. Heinrichs, R. Cyganski, and D. Krajzewicz, "Address-based computation of intra-cell distances for travel demand models", Procedia Computer Science, Volume 184, pp. 123-130, https://doi.org/10.1016/j.procs.2021.03.023, 2021.

# Requirements for Highly Integrated Management Systems

## Simulation Expands Past-oriented Documentation to Future-oriented Optimization

Carlo Simon, Stefan Haag and Lara Zakfeld

Hochschule Worms
Erenburgerstr. 19, 67549 Worms, Germany
Email: {simon,haag,zakfeld}@hs-worms.de

***Abstract*—Despite their advantages, Integrated Management Systems mirror the past. Simulation experts, however, can potentially make use of the processes stored therein to predict the future. Based on personal experiences, the authors assume that many practitioners in Business Process Management are unfamiliar with this possibility. To gain insight into this assumption, they examined the relevance of simulation in Business Process Management literature and education, especially in German degree courses on Business Information Systems. Presented in this paper is a summary which serves as the basis to formulate requirements for a new class of Integrated Management Systems called Highly Integrated Management Systems by combining past-oriented documentation and future-oriented forecasts within one system. From the authors perspective, an implementation of a Highly Integrated Management Systems could make use of high-level Petri nets for the realization of the process part since they are well-proven concerning the modeling and simulation of complex processes in administration and production, but can also be used for visualizations needed in a documentation.**

***Keywords*—Highly Integrated Management System; Process Management; Simulation; Petri nets.**

### I. Introduction

Integrative or Integrated Management Systems (IMS) serve two purposes: 1) They facilitate management by process documentation, thus leading to a better comprehension, optimization and implementation of these processes. 2) They provide means that base on these documented processes for establishing systematic management techniques in different fields such as quality, occupational health and safety, environmental protection, or energy utilization, which can be certified after implementation.

However, as the described processes are inherently past-oriented, this is also the case for IMS. Simulation experts, though, can use processes - especially well-documented ones - to examine change along with its possible effects. This makes different courses of action and their consequences manageable and opens room for optimization.

During their work with and visits to several companies of different size, the authors experience a lack of simulation usage. However, nearly all companies implement some form of management system. This begs the question as to whether those practitioners in the field of Business Process Management (BPM) who work with IMS are oblivious to the possibilities of using their documented processes future-oriented.

The authors assume two possible causes for such a non-use: Either, there simply is a knowledge gap, or there is a lack of suitable tools - or both, which seems to be the case. This paper aims at providing support for these assumptions and a solution for practitioners to benefit from simulation possibilities.

Section II outlines the methodology used. Section III provides information about IMS as they are used nowadays while Section IV examines software for IMS. Afterwards, Section V describes the findings of the literature review. Since no related work to extend IMS by simulation could be found, a new class of IMS is introduced in Section VI along with requirements for supporting software. Section VII deals with the necessity of an expanded simulation education. The paper closes with a conclusion and future work in Section VIII.

### II. Methodology

There are two research questions worked on for this contribution: 1) What is the current scope of simulation use regarding processes documented in IMS? 2) What capabilities are missing in today's IMS supporting software - if so - to assist practitioners in conducting such simulations?

The results of this paper base on desk research. They are derived from specifications of IMS, IMS supporting software, and foundational process management literature as processes are the core models of IMS. Also, degree courses in BIS and similar courses at German universities of applied sciences were examined with regards to process management and simulation. The literature reviewed is listed in Sections III, IV, and V.

This work detected remarkable deficits concerning the simulation education in literature and courses. But also for current software for IMS and process management deficits could be observed as these systems are either past- or future-oriented.

In a second step and in a normative manner, requirements for a new class of IMS are derived that combine past and future in one system.

### III. Integrated Management Systems and Process Management

According to ISO 9000, management comprises coordinated activities to guide and direct organizations. Hence, a management system is a set of interrelated functions and elements to conduct these tasks but also to determine a company's policies and objectives and the objectives of its processes [1].

The standardization of management systems by the International Organization for Standardization (ISO) provides companies with a framework to establish such structures. However, this comes along with an extensive documentation obligation if companies seek for a certification. Suitable software can mitigate this effort and the third section gives an overview of corresponding systems. The core of all such documentations is a comprehensive description of the company's processes.

An IMS holistically considers and processes the different elements, functions and perspectives of the organizational structure of a company according to Figure 1 [1][2].

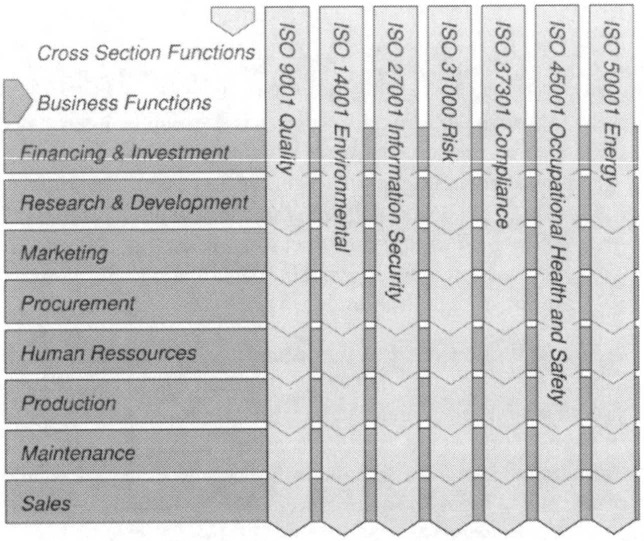


Figure 1. View of companies as network of functions by Integrated Management Systems (based on [2]).

The following overview is intended to show the most important management systems:

**ISO 9001:2015:** Introduced in 1987, this standard for quality management systems today also serves as the basis for the other standards listed in this section, as well as further (quality management) standards like ISO 13485 for medical devices, ISO 29001 for petrochemicals, or ISO 90003 for software engineering.

**ISO 14001:2015:** An environmental management system supports a continuous improvement of environmental performance based on material flow analyses.

**ISO 27001:2013:** Information security management systems are used to assess and address such risks.

**ISO 31000:2018:** Despite the variability of potential risks, ISO attempts to standardize operational risk management.

**ISO 37301:2021:** Compliance management systems aim to identify, prevent, or respond to non-compliant behavior.

**ISO 45001:2018:** This standard for occupational health and safety management systems integrates two formerly independent standards in one.

**ISO 50001:2018:** Energy management systems facilitate an environmentally friendly use of energy sources.

## IV. State of the Art of Software for Integrated Management Systems

This section summarizes the presumably most important characteristics of software for IMS as database-driven systems to collect and link the process documentations for the various management systems.

Table I shows a set of criteria that have been used in [3] to compare the nine modeling software systems for IMS listed in Table II. This catalog extends a former one discussed in [4] by criteria used in students' projects and by criteria considered in evaluation portals. Naturally, the description of processes constitutes an important part. However, it also contains previously unexamined criteria, such as that for executability.

TABLE I. COMPARISON CRITERIA FOR SOFTWARE FOR INTEGRATED MANAGEMENT SYSTEMS (BASED ON [3])

| Group | Criterion | Example characteristics |
|---|---|---|
| Process modeling | Modeling languages | BPMN/EPC/Petri nets/... |
| | Process saving | |
| | Process description | Model integrated/... |
| | Process indicators | |
| | Simulation | |
| | Animation | |
| | Search | Keywording/Full text |
| | Swimlanes | |
| | Subprocesses | |
| | Process adaptability | |
| | Modelint guidelines | |
| | Comments | Model integrated/... |
| | Versioning | |
| Overviews | Process map | |
| | Organigram | |
| Usability | Multi language | English/German/French/... |
| | Individual views | Everyone/Admin only |
| | Individual start page | Everyone/Admin only |
| Role management | User groups | Own/Predefined |
| | Permission release | |
| | Task management | News/Reminders |
| Quality management | Documentation | Online/Offline/Exportable |
| | ISO-Certification | ISO 9001/14001/27001/... |
| | Audit-Organisation | Planing/Feedback |
| | Maturity assessment | |
| | Process qualification | |
| Implementation | Operating systems | Windows/Mac/Linux/... |
| | Availability | On-premise/SaaS |
| | Maintenance/Updates | On-premise/Remote |
| | Interfaces | Graphs/XML/... |
| | Mobile | iOS/Android/Web-App |
| User support | Hotline | Phone/Chat/Email |
| | Training | Seminar/Webinar |
| | Offline manual | Online manual/Videos |
| | Help Assistant | Auto complete/Suggestions |
| Pricing | Fees | |
| | Licensing | |
| Application | Sector specific | Automotive/Financial/... |
| | Department | Purchasing/Logistics/... |
| Real life execution | Indicator evaluation | Yes/No/... |
| | Evaluation in maps | |
| | Release workflow | Approvals/Tasks |
| | Third-party extensions | |
| | Release online | |
| | Process analysis | |

The selected groups, criteria and possible characteristics cover a broad range from various process modeling approaches, integrated quality management, role management, but also usage aspects. Group *real life execution* considers different possibilities to link stored documentations to real world phenomenons.

The tools listed in Table II have been selected for personal reasons or due to being mentioned in other tool comparisons. Their evaluation concerning the mentioned criteria was conducted by evaluating information supplied by the manufacturers' websites and through subsequent interviews with the providers, to which all but two were willing to respond.

TABLE II. SOFTWARE SELECTION FOR TOOL COMPARISON (BASED ON [3])

| Tool | Publisher | IMS |
|---|---|---|
| Aeneis | Intellior AG | Yes |
| ARIS | Software AG | Yes |
| Bflow* Toolbox | Prof. Dr. R. Laue & Team | No |
| BIC Cloud | GBTEC Software + Consulting AG | Yes |
| Business Transformation | iGrafx LLC | Yes |
| Camunda BPM | Camunda Services GmbH | No |
| Process Manager | Signavio GmbH | Yes |
| Prozessdesigner | JobRouter AG | No |
| Smart Process | CWA GmbH | Yes |

The following results are to be highlighted in summary:

- Seven tools offer evaluation of process indicators.
- Four products fully implement release workflows.
- Six manufacturers claim possibilities for process simulation, although in some cases only the actual process flow is represented and a connection with real data is impossible although this would be important for execution.
- Those tools that cannot be classified as software for IMS support according to Table II lack options for linking the models in a process map, the possibility of storing the models in a central database, or the representation of responsibilities with the aid of organizational charts.

Only two of these products support all of these features, namely *Process Manager* by *Signavio* and *Smart Process* by *CWA*. Most simulation solutions only provide means to check the basic feasibility of the processes. In some cases, however, simulations of throughput times, costs or bottlenecks are included. Since real world data such as current stock levels or customers' orders cannot be factored in, the simulation results remain on a primitive level.

(Pro-)active opportunity and risk management and the support of a culture of continuous improvement are two subtasks of IMS [5]–[7]. Still, they are not sufficiently implemented by the systems' past-orientation thus far. At the same time, they testify to the need for a stronger future-orientation.

This aspect is also evident in the High Level Structure (HLS), a meta standard according to which ISO has organized the structure of its management system standards since 2012. The common requirements for management systems - or their standards - can be summarized in a basic management system and extended by sector-specific properties [5].

The HLS is described in a document called Annex SL, consisting of ten chapters according to which a management system should be implemented and documented [8]. Annex SL establishes uniform terms and definitions, an overarching architecture for all new ISO management system standards and revisions, and guaranteed identical text modules in the clauses of all standards [9]. Using the same outline for different management systems simplifies their integration.

## V. Process Management from a Business Information Systems Perspective

As this article is partially derived from German education in BIS, several German sources are quoted in this section. However, also comparable literature in English is referred to where applicable. For an introduction to BIS the authors recommend [10] and for one to BPM [11]. According to [10],

> *A business information system is a group of interrelated components that work collectively to carry out input, processing, output, storage and control actions in order to convert data into information products that can be used to support forecasting, planning, control, coordination, decision making and operational activities in an organisation.*

This definition clarifies the future-oriented character of the subject. The role of BPM in this task is shown by the structure of [12], which starts with this topic in advance of an introduction to enterprise resource planning systems or information systems for specific industries. Also, considerations concerning a digital transformation of organizations begin with a process perspective [13].

A similar view is found in the relevant literature to BPM itself. [14] points out that the hierarchical order of an organization should follow its processes. [15] and [16] also emphasize the formative role of BPM, with the latter also clarifying the relation to IMS. The envisioned complex applications of BPM developed by these authors cannot be imagined without suitable software to support this management approach.

BPM is also of central importance for process enactment in Workflow Management Systems (WfMS) [17]. This is further accentuated [18]–[20], who consider the influence of digitalization on process optimization. The considerations of [21], who see processes as the key to digital transformation, go even further and are an important contribution to BIS research.

The German Informatics Society's framework recommendations for teaching BIS also see the design-oriented construction of information systems as a key objective [22]. Again, process management sits at the core with topics as strategic process management, enterprise and process modeling, process mining, analysis, mining and optimization, and domain-specific reference models. IMS, though, only play a marginal role.

This view can also be confirmed after an analysis of a selection of process management modules in courses of study in BIS or in computer science with a corresponding specialization.

For this purpose, the authors examined 46 study programs at 34 German universities of applied sciences and classified the characteristics of the modules. A total of 96 modules were identified in the context of process management, 35 of which were included in the evaluation because at least 5 topics of BPM were clearly named. Table III shows an overview of the examined module descriptions. The modules' titles have been translated to English equivalents; for reference, the original German titles can be found as an appendix.

TABLE III. SAMPLE OF PROCESS MANAGEMENT MODULES IN GERMAN BUSINESS INFORMATION SYSTEMS DEGREE PROGRAMS

| University | Level | Module |
|---|---|---|
| FH Aachen | Bachelor | Business Information Systems |
| | Bachelor | Business Process Management |
| | Bachelor | ERP Systems Implementation and Extension |
| HS Augsburg | Bachelor | Business Process Modeling |
| | Master | Business Process Modeling |
| HTW Berlin | Bachelor | Business Processes and Operational Applications |
| | Master | Applications in Business Administration 2 |
| TH Brandenburg | Bachelor | Fundamentals of Process Modeling |
| | Master | Process Modeling and Analysis |
| | Master | Process Implementation |
| HTW Dresden | Bachelor | Business Process Modeling |
| HS Flensburg | Bachelor | Business Process Management |
| HS Furtwangen | Bachelor | Business Process Design |
| HS Kaiserslautern | Bachelor | Operational Business Process Modeling |
| HS Karlsruhe | Bachelor | Modeling IT Systems |
| | Bachelor | IT Systems Planing |
| | Master | Process Integration and Organizational Development |
| | Master | Processes Design & Implementation |
| HS Mainz | Bachelor | Business Process Management |
| HS Mannheim | Bachelor | Advanced Business Process Management |
| TH Mittelhessen | Bachelor | Digital Business Processes |
| HS Niederrhein | Bachelor | Business Process Management |
| HS Pforzheim | Bachelor | Business Process and Project Management |
| | Master | Enterprise Information Systems |
| OTH Regensburg | Bachelor | Business Process Analysis and Design |
| HS RheinMain | Bachelor | Business Process Management |
| | Bachelor | Process Digitalization |
| HS Stralsund | Bachelor | Business Processes |
| HS Trier | Bachelor | Strategic Enterprise Process Management |
| | Master | Business Process Management |
| FH Wedel | Bachelor | System Modeling |
| | Bachelor | Process Model Implementation |
| TH Wildau | Bachelor | Business Process Management |
| HS Worms | Bachelor | Business Process Management |
| | Master | Process Management |

The content shown in Table IV was derived from the subject-specific module descriptions. Due to varying degrees of detail in the module manuals, this overview is still incomplete but reflects the relevant tendencies.

TABLE IV. PROCESS MANAGEMENT TOPIC AREAS OF THE MODULES EXAMINED

| Topic | Occurrences | |
|---|---|---|
| Requirement analysis | 7 | |
| Automation / RPA | BPMS & WfMS: 13 | RPA: 1<br>Other: 7 |
| Documentation | 4 | |
| Implementierung | SAP: 2 | Other: 11 |
| Integration | 5 | |
| Process indicators / Controlling | 8 | |
| Lifecycle | 5 | |
| Mathematical basics | Graph theory: 2 | Other: 1 |
| Modeling | 25 | |
| Modeling languages | BPMN: 23<br>BPEL: 3 | EPC: 12<br>Petri nets: 2<br>Other: 17 |
| Modeling tools | ARIS: 5<br>Signavio: 1 | Camunda: 4<br>Other: 10 |
| Process Mining | 5 | |
| Process analysis & tools | 17 | |
| Reengineering / Optimization | 17 | |
| SCOR | 2 | |
| Views | ARIS house: 6 | Other: 3 |
| Simulation | 3 | |
| Strategic tools | Process maps: 7<br>Strategy development: 1 | Culture: 1 |
| Others | Cost Accounting: 5 | Other: 9 |

In 17 modules, the analysis of process models is addressed, the same applies to reengineering and optimization. 13 modules cite implementation in connection with business process or workflow management systems.

Focusing on more rarely mentioned topics, strategic aspects are stated nine times, key indicators or process controlling are only included eight times, and process documentation (beyond the actual modeling) is mentioned only four times.

Of major importance to the SIMUL conference series is the observation that simulation is only considered three times. This is possibly related to the low use of Petri nets, which are taught seldom and - if at all - only with regard to their basic concepts. The exciting possibilities for innovating software for IMS with high-level Petri nets are almost not considered.

Standards and certifications that are of major importance for many industries and for operational practice are not included in any of the module descriptions.

## VI. Requirements for Software for Highly Integrated Management Systems

While the previous part of this article was descriptive, it is continued with a normative definition of a new kind of IMS, which combines the contrary contributions discussed so far. Simulation, being the core theme of the SIMUL conferences, is also the key concept for this entirely new approach:

> *A Highly Integrated Management System combines a holistic documentation with multi-perspective simulations across different management systems.*

While management and control are comprehensively reflected in IMS and their supporting software, other topics like planning, change and transformation are still underrepresented.

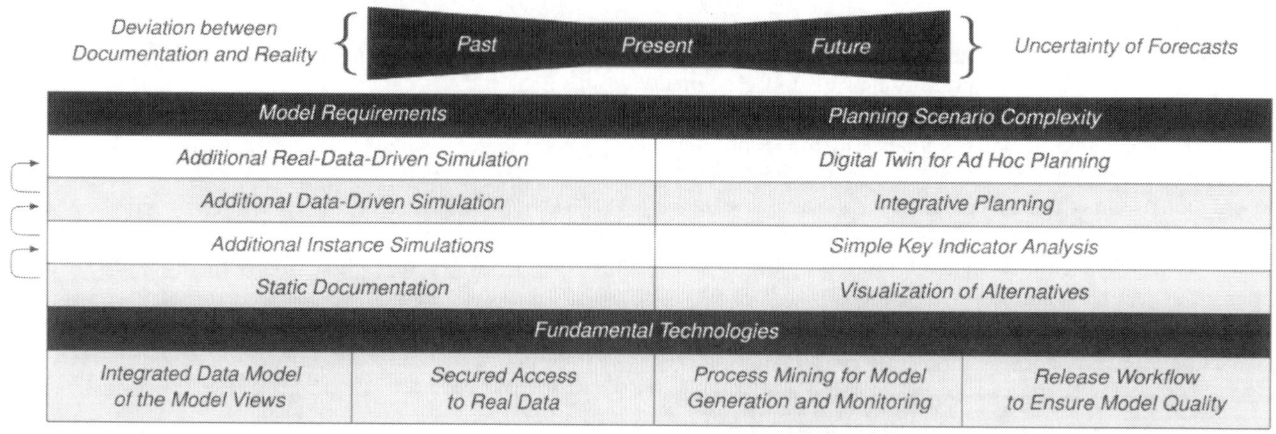


Figure 2. Characteristics of a Highly Integrated Management System (own illustration).

The disadvantage of this deficit can be illustrated by a problem many companies may face in the near future:

*Due to regulatory requirements, a company strives to decarbonize its production and, for this purpose, stores the expected costs for emission certificates in the environmental management system. At the same time, customers inquire about the carbon footprint of products, which leads to corresponding entries in the quality management system. An emergent simulative planning could show the interactions between these two systems, but also provide information of the effects on other connected systems such as energy management or even production itself. To this end, it would be necessary to link this simulation extensively with current production data.*

A comparable scenario can neither be described by means of current IMS nor are these systems suitable to support the transformation processes to develop a company in the described manner. One major reason for this is that in current IMS software processes are described with BPMN, flow chart diagrams or EPCs that have their strengths in rapid process visualization but their weaknesses concerning simulation. At best, instance simulations can provide information regarding the correct executability of processes [23][24]. However, since no formal mathematical semantics are defined for the mentioned modeling languages even these instance simulations may vary depending on the tool used [23][25][26].

For the described problem, however, it rather would be necessary to consider the different views in a holistic, multi-perspective simulation. Against this background, a return to Petri nets seems to be helpful for two reasons:

**1.** As theoretical underpinning of process mining, Petri nets can be used to automatically generate process models from transaction data of operational information systems, which simplifies the modeling task significantly and ensures a better match between reality and model [27].

**2.** With high-level Petri nets, in which places can be interpreted as tables in a database, complex production processes can be modeled and the consequences of strategic changes such as one from push to pull production can be estimated in advance [28][29].

In both application areas of Petri nets, powerful modeling, analysis and simulation tools are needed. Such tools are available and they have contemporary user interfaces. However, a fusion with the requirements for software to support IMS is still pending.

Figure 2 visualizes these requirements for an HIMS and for software to support it. The goal is an optimal supply of information in the present by mapping the current situation and at the same time enabling forecasts into the future. The further back in time the model representing the current situation was created, the greater the deviation between reality and documentation becomes. Likewise, the occurrence probability of forecasts decreases the further they are projected into the future. This is accompanied by the desire for new functionalities that go beyond the possibilities of current IMS software.

These functionalities are shown in the middle part of the figure. The demands on the models and their analysis and execution increase with the complexity of the planning scenarios that can be expressed with them. A simulation environment that is able to simulate processes parallel to reality on the basis of fed-in real data, may be regarded as a digital twin.

In addition, there are requirements regarding the fundamental technologies that make model integration and operational use possible in the first place. These range from data storage and secure access to release workflows that ensure the necessary model quality.

There are probably two options for the development of corresponding systems: Either the simulation features of software for the support of IMS are extended, for example following the capabilities of higher Petri nets, or simulation tools are extended by functionalities such as a management of shared documents, monitoring of key performance indicators and release workflows.

## VII. Simulation Education

Supplying companies with simulation capabilities by means of HIMS is one part of the challenge. The other one is providing them with competent workforce as modeling and domain expertise often only exist separately (cf. [30]).

Opportunities, methods, limitations, and applications of simulation should play a more integral part in the education of BPM, of BIS, and also of IMS. The simulation community should engage intensively in this field.

The first field of possible engagement is the development of appropriate tools. Domain experts need HIMS that make modeling easy and simulation experts have to learn how to adopt specific domain knowledge and especially, how to produce visualizations of the simulation results that are understood by the domain experts, i.e. an HIMS also must provide visualization components.

This, however, requires personnel who are able to work in an interdisciplinary manner. Therefore, university education must provide students with factual and interdisciplinary knowledge but also - and probably more important - with the skills to gain cross-disciplinary insights themselves.

## VIII. Conclusion and Future Work

This paper provides support for two assumptions regarding the use of simulation in the context of IMS: The first one is a lack of IMS software suited for process simulation and, therefore, optimization. However, the examined tools supposedly are but a fraction of available software. The second assumption is the missing simulation competencies many practitioners show in the authors' anecdotal experience. This is supported by literature both for practice and education. Both points, though, base on German sources, possibly illustrating a country-specific phenomenon. Thus, international inquiries seem beneficial - if only to improve the situation in Germany.

The authors see two paths for research to follow from here on. The first is the creation of an HIMS suitable for practical use. Since this idea is completely new and contradicts existing assumptions on how an IMS should work and look like, a fast commercial implementation cannot be expected. An experimental research environment at a university or research department seems to be better suited for this task. Further, since conferences like SIMUL show that the development of novel simulation techniques often takes place in a research context, adding IMS capabilities to an existing process simulation environment would be reasonable. As a Petri net-based modeling and simulation tool is in active development by the authors, it seems obvious to use this as a starting point to proof the concept.

The second path refers to simulation education: How differ other countries' degree courses in BIS from the ones examined so far? What are the implications of such differences on HIMS? What can be learned from simulation in other fields of study, for example physics, social science, but also business management games?

We cordially invite the interested community to reach out for an exchange on different - or missing - points of view, established handling, best practices or planned changes - both in education and in implementing suitable software for (Highly) Integrated Management Systems.

## Appendix

TABLE V. ORIGINAL GERMAN MODULE TITLES OF TABLE III

| University | Level | Module |
|---|---|---|
| FH Aachen | Bachelor | Business Information Systems |
| | Bachelor | Geschäftsprozessmanagement |
| | Bachelor | ERP Systeme implementieren und erweitern |
| HS Augsburg | Bachelor | Geschäftsprozess-Modellierung |
| | Master | Geschäftsprozess-Modellierung |
| HTW Berlin | Bachelor | Geschäftsprozesse und betriebliche Anwendungen |
| | Master | Betriebswirtschaftliche Anwendungen 2 |
| TH Brandenburg | Bachelor | Grundlagen der Prozessmodellierung |
| | Master | Modellierung und Analyse von Prozessen |
| | Master | Implementierung von Prozessen |
| HTW Dresden | Bachelor | Geschäftsprozessmodellierung |
| HS Flensburg | Bachelor | Business Process Management |
| HS Furtwangen | Bachelor | Geschäftsprozessdesign |
| HS Kaiserslautern | Bachelor | Modellierung Betrieblicher Leistungsprozesse |
| HS Karlsruhe | Bachelor | Modellierung von IT-Systemen |
| | Bachelor | Planung von Informationssystemen |
| | Master | Process Integration and Organizational Development |
| | Master | Processes Design & Implementation |
| HS Mainz | Bachelor | Business Process Management |
| HS Mannheim | Bachelor | Advanced Business Process Management |
| TH Mittelhessen | Bachelor | Digitale Geschäftsprozesse |
| HS Niederrhein | Bachelor | Geschäftsprozess-Management |
| HS Pforzheim | Bachelor | Geschäftsprozess- und Projektmanagement |
| | Master | Unternehmensinformationssysteme |
| OTH Regensburg | Bachelor | Geschäftsprozessanalyse und -design |
| HS RheinMain | Bachelor | Geschäftsprozessmanagement |
| | Bachelor | Digitalisierung von Prozessen |
| HS Stralsund | Bachelor | Geschäftsprozesse |
| HS Trier | Bachelor | Strategisches Unternehmensprozessmanagement |
| | Master | Geschäftsprozessmanagement |
| FH Wedel | Bachelor | Systemmodellierung |
| | Bachelor | Prozessmodellimplementation |
| TH Wildau | Bachelor | Geschäftsprozessmanagement |
| HS Worms | Bachelor | Geschäftsprozessmanagement |
| | Master | Prozessmanagement |

## References


[1] *ISO 9000:2015: Quality management systems — Fundamentals and vocabulary*, Geneva, 2015.

[2] A. Neumann, *Integrative Managementsysteme*, 3rd ed. Berlin: Springer Gabler, 2017, German, transl. *Integrative Management Systems*.

[3] J. Foos, "Marktüberblick für Software zum Prozessmanagement," Master's thesis, Hochschule Worms, 2020, German, transl. *Market Overview for Process Management Software*.

[4] D. Adam, N. Riegel, T. Jeswein, M. Koch, and S. Imal, "Studie BPM Suites," Fraunhofer IESE, Kaiserslautern, Tech. Rep., 2013, German, transl. *BPM Suites Study*.

[5] A. Badreddine, T. B. Romdhane, and N. B. Amor, "A multi-objective risk management approach to implement an integrated management system: Quality, security, environment," in *IEEE International Conference*

*on Systems, Man and Cybernetics*. San Antonio, TX, USA: IEEE, 2009, pp. 4728–4733.

[6] S. Salah, J. A. Carretero, and A. Rahim, "The integration of quality management and continuous improvement methodologies with management systems," *IJPQM*, vol. 6, no. 3, pp. 269–288, 2010.

[7] S. Vulanović, M. Delić, B. Kamberović, I. Beker, and B. Lalić, "Integrated management systems based on risk assessment: Methodology development and case studies," *APEM*, vol. 15, no. 1, pp. 93–106, 2020.

[8] *High-Level Structure: Management System Standards - Annex SL*, https://www.iso.org/management-system-standards.html (last accessed 25.08.2021), Geneva, 2012.

[9] R. Tricker, *Quality Management Systems - A Practival Guide to Standards Implementation*. Abingdon-on-Thames: Taylor & Francis, 2019, ch. What is Annex SL all about?, pp. 114–131.

[10] P. Bocij, A. Greasley, and S. Hickie, *Business Information Systems*. London, UK: Pearson, 2008.

[11] J. Jeston, *Business Process Management*. Abingdon-on-Thames: Taylor & Francis, 2018.

[12] H. R. Hansen, J. Mendling, and G. Neumann, *Wirtschaftsinformatik*, 12th ed. Berlin: De Gruyter - Oldenbourg, 2019, German, transl. *Business Information Systems*.

[13] A. Fleischmann, S. Oppl, W. Schmidt, and C. Stary, *Contextual Process Digitalization*. Cham: Springer Nature, 2020.

[14] M. Gaitanides, "Strategic Planning and Structuring of Organization," in *European Approaches to International Management*, K. M. und W. H. Staehle, Ed. Berlin: de Gruyter, 1986.

[15] G. Fischermanns, *Praxishandbuch Prozessmanagement*, 11th ed., ser. ibo-Schriftenreihe. Gießen: Verlag Dr. Götz Schmidt, 2013, vol. 9, German, transl. *Handbook Project Management*.

[16] H. J. Schmelzer and W. Sesselmann, *Geschäftsprozessmanagement in der Praxis*, 8th ed. München: Hanser, 2013, German, transl. *Business Processs Management in Practice*.

[17] W. M. P. van der Aalst, A. H. M. ter Hofstede, and M. Weske, "Business process management: a survey," in *Proceedings of the 2003 International Conference on Business Process Management*. Springer, Berlin, 2003, pp. 1–12.

[18] T. H. Davenport, *Process Innovation: Reengineering Work through Information Technology*. Boston, MA: Harvard Business institution Press, 1993.

[19] M. Hammer and J. Champy, *Reengineering the Cooperation*. New York: Harper Business, 1993.

[20] M. Hofmann, *Prozessoptimierung als ganzheitlicher Ansatz*. Wiesbaden: Springer Gabler, 2020, German, transl. *Process Optimisation as a Holistic Approach*.

[21] G. Bontinck, Ö. Isik, J. van den Bergh, and S. Viaene, "Unlocking the Potential of the Process Perspective in Business Transformation," in *Int. Conf.on BPM*. Springer, 2016, pp. 161–176.

[22] Gesellschaft für Informatik, "Rahmenempfehlungen für die Ausbildung in Wirtschaftsinformatik an Hochschulen," GI, Bonn, Tech. Rep., 2017, German, transl. *Recommendation Framework for the Education in Business Information Systems at Universities*.

[23] K. Rosenthal, B. Ternes, and S. Strecker, "Business Process Simulation: A Systematic Literature Review," in *ECIS 2018 Proceedings*. Portsmouth, UK: AIS, 2018, pp. 199–216.

[24] G. Wagner, O. Nicolae, and J. Werner, "Extending Discrete Event Simulation by Adding an Activity Concept for Business Process Modeling and Simulation," in *Proceedings of the 2009 Winter Simulation Conference*, 2009, pp. 2951 – 2962.

[25] P. Bocciarelli, A. D'Ambrogio, A. Giglio, and E. Paglia, "Empowering Business Process Simulation Through Automated Model Transformations," in *Proceedings of the Symposium on Theory of Modeling and Simulation*. Tampa, FL, USA: SpringSim, 2014, paper 39, pp. 1–9.

[26] T. Berger and W. Gleissner, "Integrated management systems: linking risk management and management control systems," *IJRAM*, vol. 21, no. 3, pp. 215–231, 2018.

[27] W. M. P. van der Aalst, *Process Mining*, 2nd ed. Berlin: Springer, 2016.

[28] C. Simon and S. Haag, "Simulatable Reference Models To Transform Enterprises For The Digital Age – A Case Study," in *ECMS 2020: 34th International ECMS Conference on Modelling and Simulation*, M. Steglich, C. Müller, G. Neumann, and M. Walther, Eds., 2020, pp. 294 – 300.

[29] C. Simon, S. Haag, and L. Zakfeld, "Showing the Advantages of Pull over Push Production with the Aid of Petri Nets," *EMISA Forum: Proceedings of the SIG Enterprise Modelling and Information Systems Architectures of the German Informatics Society*, vol. 41, pp. 9–10, 2021.

[30] ——, "Research-Agenda for Process Simulation Dashboards," in *ECMS 2021: 35th International ECMS Conference on Modelling and Simulation*, 2021, pp. 243–249.

# An Agent-Based Modeling Approach for Informing the U.S. Plastic Waste Management Process

Yuanhui Huang
Computer and Information Technology
Purdue University
West Lafayette, USA
Email: huan1275@purdue.edu

Tugba Karabiyik
Purdue Systems Collaboratory
Purdue University
West Lafayette, USA
Email: tugba@purdue.edu

Aasakiran Madamanchi
Computer and Information Technology
Purdue University
West Lafayette, USA
Email: amadaman@umich.edu

Alejandra J. Magana
Computer and Information Technology
Purdue University
West Lafayette, USA
Email: admagana@purdue.edu

*Abstract*— **Recycling is one of the most significant issues in the waste management system. As the use and demand for plastics increase every year, finding efficient and environment-friendly solutions to handle the plastics in the plastic waste management system gets more challenging. There are economic, environmental, and educational factors affecting plastic waste management. This paper investigates the effects of educational campaigns and system-wide improvement. For this, we used an Agent-Based Modeling and Simulation approach in the NetLogo environment. We provided various scenarios in the current plastics waste life cycle using a real dataset to validate our model, which was from the American Chemistry Council and the National Association for PET Container Resources from 2018. We found that education, technology, and infrastructure changes should be considered holistically to overcome this problem at a system level.**

***Keywords-Agent-Based Modeling; NetLogo; Recycling; Plastic Waste Management***

## I. INTRODUCTION

The demand for plastics increases every year, and over 300 million tons of plastics were produced in 2018. All of these plastics meet one of three fates within the plastic waste system: (1) recycling and reproduction, (2) thermal destruction (combustion with energy recovery), and (3) landfill deposition. Recent estimates of the fates of all plastics ever made indicate that only 9% was recycled, 12% was incinerated, and 79% was deposited in landfills or discarded in natural environments, such as the oceans [1][2].

The plastics recycling process faces three significant challenges. First, dealing with plastic waste is hugely expensive. Simply removing plastic litter from the United States' west coast costs taxpayers $520 million each year [3]. Effective regeneration techniques are still lacking in current plastic management systems. While the plastics generation increases every year, it leads to an imbalance between input and output. Secondly, combustion and discarding have severe negative impacts on the environment. The degrading process is slow, and toxic greenhouse gases are produced. Plastics waste breaking into smaller pieces, known as microplastics, can adhere to waterborne organic pollutants and infiltrate food webs [4]. Thirdly, due to the outbreak of COVID-19, the consumption and demand for plastics have increased sharply [5]. One hundred twenty-nine billion face masks and 65 billion gloves are used with a monthly estimate [6]. The increasing demand and use of plastics cause significant problems in the plastic waste management system [2]. Many recycling facilities' safety-related suspensions further exacerbate this trend. Without proper public waste management, there is a risk of widespread environmental contamination [6].

The current plastic waste management system needs better approaches to deal with these large numbers of post-consumer plastics. However, it remains unclear what interventions will best support plastic waste management. This paper presents an agent-based model that simulates the plastics waste management lifecycle at multiple scales. Agent-based modeling is a simulation technique that can be used to analyze complex social systems. It is a computational approach that agents with specific variables, behaviors, and characteristics interact with each other [7]. This modeling and simulation provide a direct and visual approach to modeling different scenarios in the current plastics waste lifecycle. Our research question for this study is the following:

R.Q.: How do strategies, such as an education campaign and a system-wide improvement, influence the behavior of plastics waste management?

The paper is structured as follows: Section 2 reviews related background in plastics waste management. Section 3 outlines the research methodology. The research results and recommendations are shown in section 4, followed by a conclusion in Section 5.

## II. Background

In this section, we will review tthe plastics waste management framework, the classification of recyclable plastics and non-recyclable plastics, and the introduction of Agent-Based Modeling.

### A. *Plastics Waste Management Framework*

Plastics' low cost, lightweight, and versatility have a vast area of use in industries. Furthermore, plastic materials usually have ecological and economic advantages over conventional materials throughout their life cycle, with or without considering the End-of-Life stage [8]. Unfortunately, more than half of all plastics end up in landfills, and only 9% of used plastic can be recycled [9]. Additionally, a given plastic piece can only be recycled 2 to 3 times on average [10]. Despite its limitations, recycling remains the best solution for processing plastic waste due to its beneficial economic and environmental impacts. The requirements for successful plastic recycling include proper infrastructure to collect the waste, available technology to reprocess the waste into secondary products economically, and develop markets for the cost-effective use of recycled products [11].

### B. *Recyclable Plastics and non-recyclable plastics*

Recycling is the process of converting waste materials into new materials. However, research shows that impurities take up to 28% of plastic waste and that around 75% of plastics waste is considered as Low-Quality applications [12]. The study indicates that although varying between polymer types, the recyclability of "Low-Quality" plastic waste is 12% to 35% lower than those categorized as "high-quality" plastics waste. Therefore, plastics have different recyclability depending on polymer types, legislative requirements, product lifetime, and other variables. Recyclable plastics are clean bottles and containers, bags, etc. As contamination in recycling has many negative effects, such as recycling becomes more expensive as money and time are required to separate contaminants [13][14]. In addition, the quality of recyclable by-products decreases if contaminated, reducing the market value [15]. In other words, if the plastic wastes are contaminated, they will not be considered 'recyclable' anymore. Therefore, the recycling systems are in need of cleaner recycling.

### C. *Agent-Based Modeling and its Applications in Recycling*

Agent-Based Modeling and Simulation (ABMS) is the approach used for the development of the model. ABMS is a computational modeling approach centered around the concept of to the term "agent" to describe complex processes, behavior, and phenomena [23]. Unlike other conventional modeling tools, agent-based modeling responds to the environment actively [24]. Certain properties and attributes are autonomous and self-directed, modular, social and interactable, living in an environment capable of learning and adapting, and having explicit goals and resource variables [25].

A popular ABMS technology extensively used in education and research on human behavior is NetLogo [26][27]. NetLogo, a multi-agent and modeling environment, can simulate natural and social phenomena. It allows users to alter the agents and environment to observe the differences directly. It is also well suited for modeling a system that needs a few years to evolve and change [28]. Four types of agents existed in NetLogo are turtles, patches, links, and observer [26]. Turtles are active agents that can move inside the environment. It can perform the programmed functions during the 'turtles' movement and reflect correlative interactions between other turtles and agents. The patch is the square ground where turtles can move on, the links connect two turtles, and the observer is the agent who observes the simulated world and acts as the interface between it and the researcher [29].

ABMS has also been used to study recycling behaviors. For instance, a study conducted in 2018 discovered behavior changes in post-consumer recycling through an agent-based modeling approach [30]. The simulation was applied to analyze the impact of critical factors in recycling behavior changes in Beijing's residential community. The experiment showed that the provision of recycling facilities could cause little change in 'residents' behavior. However, face-to-face interactions between the experiment team and participating households increased awareness of plastic recycling.

## III. Research Method

As the plastic waste lifecycle's detailed investigation can be time-consuming and expensive, NetLogo may be an efficient tool to estimate one action's outcomes. Once an ABMS has been built, the user can change multiple parameters manually to simulate a given environment's plastics recycling process through an open user interface. The proposed system zooms in the life cycle of the general plastics waste. Three kinds of turtles were created: Plastics (plastics wastes), Center (recycling centers), and Houses (the number of households in a community).

### A. *Definition of the Variables*

Variables shown in Table 1 were created in order to record the interaction of different turtles and the value changes, some variables were created to keep track of the progress and trigger different behaviors. Table I demonstrates the simulation variables with corresponding explanations and justifications for use.

TABLE I. Variables Used in the NetLogo Model

| **Variables** | ***Data type*** | ***Explanation*** |
|---|---|---|
| initial-houses | Integer [0, n] | The number of households created in the environment |
| recycle-approach | String: Chemical or Mechanical | The most common approach that the recycling facility uses in the simulated environment |
| RecyclingParticipatio n | Integer [0, 1000] | The percentage of households that recycle. The variable is internally expressed as an integer |

| Variables | *Data type* | *Explanation* |
|---|---|---|
| | | from 0 to 1000 in the program, and then divided by 10 to show the percentage with 1 decimal place |
| contamination_rate | Float [0, 1] | The percentage of plastic waste that is contaminated |
| recyclability | Float [0, 1] | The possibility of plastic waste to be considered as recyclable |
| Demand | Integer [0, n] | The average number of plastic wastes (in kg) generated by the houses weekly |
| ptime | Integer [0, n] | The number of times the plastic waste has been recycled in the system |
| landfill | Integer [0, n] | The amount of plastic waste (in kg) is ended up in a landfill. |
| finish_recycle | Integer [0, n] | The amount of plastic waste (in kg) has been sent to the recycling center and has been recycled in the system |
| totalplastics | Integer [0, n] | The total amount of plastic waste (in kg) that are generated in the system |
| collect | Integer [0, n] | The amount of plastic waste (in kg) has been sent to the recycling center |
| new | Integer [0, n] | The amount of plastic waste (in kg) becomes secondary products |

### *B. The Simulation Workflow*

The process starts when the houses use plastics based on their weekly demand (variable demand). Then, the system checks the household's recycling participation percentage (variable RecyclingParticipation) to see if the house will decide to recycle the plastic waste. If the household does not plan to do the recycling action, all plastic waste generated from the house will go into landfills. In contrast, the households that choose to perform the recycling action send the plastics to the recycling center. When the plastic wastes arrive at the recycling center, the center will check for the contamination rate (variable contamination_rate) of the collected plastics (variable collect). Only the plastics that are considered as uncontaminated can continue the process and check for their plastics recyclability (variable recyclability), while the "dirty" plastics will be sent to landfills. If the plastic waste is non-recyclable plastic, it will go into a landfill. The recycling center checks its recycling approach (variable recycle-approach) for the rest of the plastics. If the center applies a chemical recycling approach, the plastic waste will be converted to secondary products (variable new). In the case the center uses the mechanical recycling process, the plastic waste will be recycled with an increment in the number of times the plastics have been recycled in the system (variable ptime). Plastic waste that exceeds the recycled time will be downcycled and will disappear in the system. Eventually, the recycled plastics that are shipped back to the community will satisfy households' needs and reduce their next cycle consumption. The user interface is shown in Figure 1.

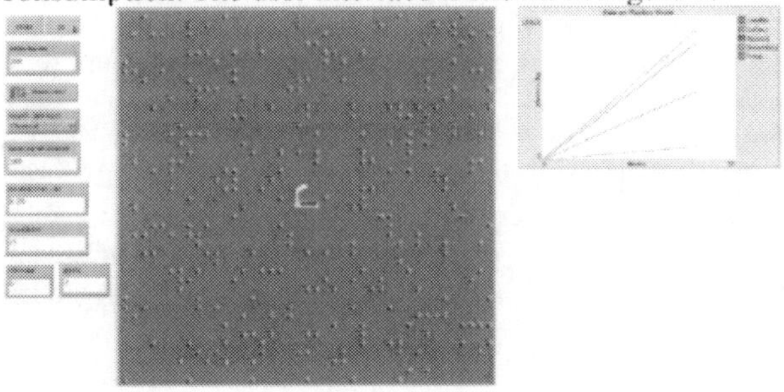

Figure 1. The Screenshot of the simulation interface.

During the simulation running, graphic charts track the variables to support the calculations, named "Data on Plastics Waste." Figure 2 provides the methodological framework used in the simulation.

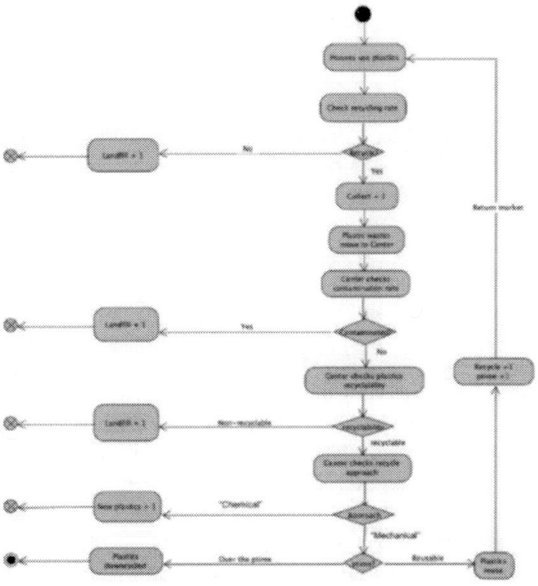

Figure 2. Simulator methodology framework.

A software tool named BehaviorSpace, which is part of NetLogo, allows us to test each scenario for ten repetitions and calculate the overall mean and standard deviation.

## IV. Simulation Experiments and Results

To test the feasibility of the simulator, we applies real-world paramenters to the simulation. A baseline scenario is constructed to demonstrate the effect of the education campaign and system-wide improvement. All the results are collected from 10 repetition run simulating the activities in 25 weeks.

### A. *Feasibility Testing*

According to the American Chemistry Council and the National Association for PET Container Resources, in 2018, (1) 35,680 thousand tons of plastics waste were generated, (2) 5,620 thousand tons of plastics waste were combusted with energy recovery, (3) 3,090 thousand tons of plastics waste were recycled, and (4) the rest of 26,970 thousand tons of plastics waste ended up in landfills. Then, the recycling rate of 2018 plastics waste was 8.66%. On average, 25% of collected wastes are contaminated to be recycled [22]. If we assumed that all non-recyclable plastics would be incinerated, and 25% of the collected plastics went to landfill. Also, the sum of collected plastics in 2018 would be 11613 thousand tons, with a 32.55% recycling participation rate (collected plastics/total generated plastics) and 35.48% of recyclable plastics rate (recycled plastics/non-recyclable plastics). Based on The Guardian, the U.S. produces about 106.2 kg of plastics waste per person per year [32]. The weekly consumption per person would be 2.04 kg (106.2 kg/52 weeks). Applying these parameters in the simulation, the average recycling rate is 8.97% for ten weeks run, and this result has less than 0.5% difference with the PET Container Resources data in 2018.

### B. *Baseline Scenario*

Based on the nationwide parameters and literature review, we constructed a baseline situation in our model. The baseline Scenario simulates 500 households, with the recycling participation of 25%, plastics recyclability of 25%, and uses a mechanical approach. The maximum time that plastic waste could be reused was set to 2, and the average plastics consumption per household was 6 kg/week. Therefore, a fixed 25 percent contamination rate is applied in the baseline scenario and the rest of the experiments. Because the number of turtles needs to be positive integers, the parameters used to generate turtles were rounded up to whole numbers. This simulation scenario was acted as a 'baseline' to evaluate the effect of customer behavior changes or system-level improvements. The results of the baseline scenario are included in Figure 3.

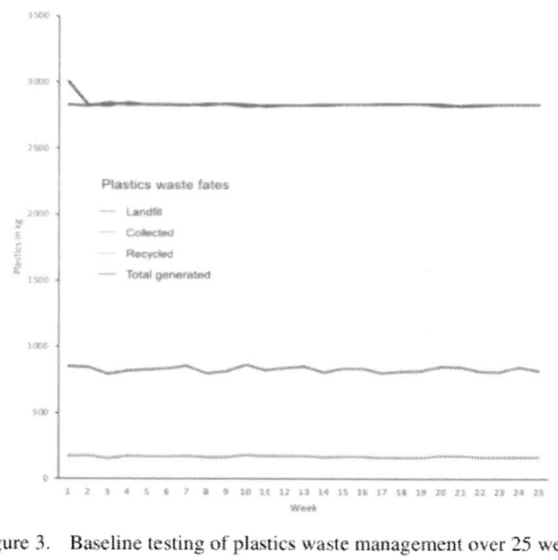


Figure 3. Baseline testing of plastics waste management over 25 weeks.

### C. *Effect of an Education Campaign*

Plastics Recyclability is the percentage of plastics considered "recyclable" when they arrive at the recycling center. Recycling participation refers to the tendency of each household to recycle weekly. Two possible reasons that cause the plastics waste unrecyclable are: there are no facilities supporting recycling for the specific type of plastics, and the plastics are contaminated during transportation or without improper recycling procedures. In this paper, we have a fixed contamination rate of 25% applied to all collected plastics, so the recyclability of the plastic here will only examine the plastic types.

Education can make more people decide to recycle, or it can make them recycle more effectively and adequately. In this experiment, we tested the effect of an education campaign that produces individual improvement in recycling participation or plastics recyclability. We looked at the effect of 5%, 10%, 25%, and 50% improvements on plastics recyclability and recycling participation from our baseline, reflecting the increased sorting and recycling behaviors. The results, which are compared to the baseline testing, are shown in Figure 4.

### D. *Experiment 2: Effect of System-wide Improvement*

This experiment examined potential system-wide improvement based on technological changes, infrastructure investments, or policy implementation that may boost recycling participation and plastics recyclability. Unlike education campaigns, system-wide improvements significantly improve waste management, such as California's single-use plastic bags ban [35]. Improved recycling infrastructure can handle a broader set of plastics. We tested the plastics recyclability and recycling participation scenarios when they were 50%, 75%, and 100% (Hypothetical maximum), and the results are shown in Figure 5.

Similar to the education campaign, higher plastics recyclability and higher recycling participation can lead to larger recycled plastics amounts, lower landfill deposits, and lower total plastics. Compared to plastics recyclability, recycling participation creates a slightly stable percentage increase in recycled plastics and percentage deduction in landfill deposits and total plastics. Especially in boosting the recycling participation, recycled plastics follow a similar increase proportion every week as the percentage increases. Therefore, we could predict that if the government considers investing in the system-wide development in its plastics waste to raise its recycling rate, increasing recycling participation may lead to a stable boosting in the recycling rate over weeks while increasing the recyclable plastics have more variations each week. Moreover, in this experiment, 100% improvement is a test of hypothetical boundary conditions. The result shows that there remains a significant landfill problem even in a hypothetical scenario with recycling participation.

## V. CONCLUSION

The results of the feasibility testing of nationwide data support that the simulator developed in this paper can be a way to predict the plastic waste trend. This study's main conclusion was that approaching this system-level problem in a one-dimensional way is insufficient. Simply altering individual behaviors through education has limited effects on the system. Similarly, solely examining the technology development in both system-wide improvements has limited effects. Education, technology, and infrastructure changes should all be carried out to ameliorate the plastics waste management problem. Nevertheless, promulgating a policy or developing an advanced technology is not easy; before a system-wide improvement takes place, individual behavior change still affects the recycling rate to a certain degree.

There are still some limitations and shortcomings in the present study. First, the plastics recycling approach was mainly based on plastic types. The simulation assumes all plastics categorized as recyclable can undergo both mechanical and chemical processes. Second, recycle participation can be a subjective factor and hard to record. Third, household amount limitation restricted the simulation's scope, which can only simulate a community's small region. Fourth, the incineration process was not considered in the simulator. Despite its limitations, the study combined the plastics waste management life cycle and computer technology to test various scenarios and predict possible outcomes. Further research is needed to consider the plastic types and test out the effect of the combination of education, technology, and infrastructure improvements in the system.

## REFERENCES


[1] J. R. Jambeck et al., "Plastic waste inputs from land into the ocean," *Science*, vol. 347, no. 6223, pp. 768–771, Feb. 2015, doi: 10.1126/science.1260352.

[2] R. Geyer, J. R. Jambeck, and K. L. Law, "Production, use, and fate of all plastics ever made," *Sci. Adv.*, vol. 3, no. 7, p. e1700782, Jul. 2017, doi: 10.1126/sciadv.1700782.

[3] C. M. Rochman et al., "Classify plastic waste as hazardous," *Nature*, vol. 494, no. 7436, pp. 169–171, Feb. 2013, doi: 10.1038/494169a.

[4] M. Cole, P. Lindeque, C. Halsband, and T. S. Galloway, "Microplastics as contaminants in the marine environment: A review," *Marine Pollution Bulletin*, vol. 62, no. 12, pp. 2588–2597, 2011, doi: https://doi.org/10.1016/j.marpolbul.2011.09.025.

[5] A. L. P. Silva et al., "Increased plastic pollution due to COVID-19 pandemic: Challenges and recommendations," *Chemical Engineering Journal*, vol. 405, p. 126683, 2021, doi: https://doi.org/10.1016/j.cej.2020.126683.

[6] J. C. Prata, A. L. P. Silva, T. R. Walker, A. C. Duarte, and T. Rocha-Santos, "COVID-19 Pandemic Repercussions on the Use and Management of Plastics," *Environ. Sci. Technol.*, vol. 54, no. 13, pp. 7760–7765, Jul. 2020, doi: 10.1021/acs.est.0c02178.

[7] M. Tracy, M. Cerdá, and K. M. Keyes, "Agent-Based Modeling in Public Health: Current Applications and Future Directions," *Annu. Rev. Public Health*, vol. 39, no. 1, pp. 77–94, Apr. 2018, doi: 10.1146/annurev-publhealth-040617-014317.

[8] C. A. Bernardo, C. L. Simões, and L. M. C. Pinto, "Environmental and economic life cycle analysis of plastic waste management options. A review," *AIP Conference Proceedings*, vol. 1779, no. 1, p. 140001, 2016, doi: 10.1063/1.4965581.

[9] W. d'Ambrières, "Plastics recycling worldwide: current overview and desirable changes.," *The journal of field actions*, no. Special Issue 19, pp. 12–21, 2019.

[10] L. Sedaghat, "7 Things You Didn't Know About Plastic (and Recycling)," *National Geographic Society Newsroom*, 13-Apr-2018. [Online]. Available: https://blog.nationalgeographic.org/2018/04/04/7-things-you-didnt-know-about-plastic-and-recycling/. [Accessed: 23-Aug-2021].

[11] K. S. Rebeiz and A. P. Craft, "Plastic waste management in construction: technological and institutional issues," *Resources, Conservation and Recycling*, vol. 15, no. 3, pp. 245–257, 1995, doi: https://doi.org/10.1016/0921-3449(95)00034-8.

[12] G. Faraca and T. Astrup, "Plastic waste from recycling centres: Characterisation and evaluation of plastic recyclability," *Waste Management*, vol. 95, pp. 388–398, 2019, doi: https://doi.org/10.1016/j.wasman.2019.06.038.

[13] S. Rosenthal and N. Linder, "Effects of bin proximity and informational prompts on recycling and contamination," *Resources, Conservation and Recycling*, vol. 168, p. 105430, 2021, doi: https://doi.org/10.1016/j.resconrec.2021.105430.

[14] M. D. Meng and R. B. Leary, "It might be ethical, but I won't buy it: Perceived contamination of, and disgust towards, clothing made from recycled plastic bottles," *Psychol Mark*, vol. 38, no. 2, pp. 298–312, Feb. 2021, doi: 10.1002/mar.21323.

[15] D. Rachelson, "14 Recycling Contamination Facts That Will Blow Your Mind," *Rubicon*, 22-Jul-2021. [Online]. Available: https://www.rubicon.com/blog/recycling-contamination-facts/. [Accessed: 23-Aug-2021].

[16] "How to Divert Plastics from Landfills," *Plastics Make It Possible*, 24-Oct-2018. [Online]. Available: https://www.plasticsmakeitpossible.com/whats-new-cool/technology-science/plastics-to-energy/how-to-divert-plastics-from-landfills/. [Accessed: 23-Aug-2021].

[17] "Reducing and Reusing Basics," *US EPA*. [Online]. Available: https://www.epa.gov/recycle/reducing-and-reusing-basics. [Accessed: 23-Aug-2021].

[18] J. Lienig and H. Bruemmer, "Recycling Requirements and Design for Environmental Compliance," in *Fundamentals of Electronic Systems Design*, Cham: Springer International Publishing, 2017, pp. 193–218.

[19] "Facts and Figures about Materials, Waste and Recycling," *US EPA*, 2020. [Online]. Available: https://www.epa.gov/facts-and-figures-about-materials-waste-and-recycling/plastics-material-specific-data.

[20] E. Bonabeau, "Agent-based modeling: Methods and techniques for simulating human systems," *National Academy of Sciences*, vol. 99, pp. 7280–7287, 2001.

[21] K. Nguyen-Trong, A. Nguyen-Thi-Ngoc, D. Nguyen-Ngoc, and V. Dinh-Thi-Hai, "Optimization of municipal solid waste transportation by integrating GIS analysis, equation-based, and agent-based model," *Waste Management*, vol. 59, pp. 14–22, 2017, doi: https://doi.org/10.1016/j.wasman.2016.10.048.

[22] C. Macal and M. North, "Agent-based modeling and simulation," 2009, doi: 10.1109/WSC.2009.5429318.

[23] U. Wilensky and W. Rand, *An Introduction to Agent-Based Modeling*. The MIT Press, 2015.

[24] U. Wilensky, *NetLogo*. Center for Connected Learning and Computer-Based Modeling, Northwestern University, Evanston, IL., 1999.

[25] S. Tisue and U. Wilensky, "NetLogo: Design and implementation of a multi-agent modeling environment," in *Proceedings of agent*, 2004, vol. 2004, pp. 7–9.

[26] U. Wilensky, "Programming Guide," *The Center for Connected Learning and Computer-Based Modeling*, 2019. [Online]. Available: http://ccl.northwestern.edu/netlogo/docs/programming.html#agents. [Accessed: 23-Aug-2021].

[27] X. Tong et al., "Behaviour change in post-consumer recycling: Applying agent-based modelling in social experiment," *Journal of Cleaner Production*, vol. 187, pp. 1006–1013, Jun. 2018, doi: 10.1016/j.jclepro.2018.03.261.

[28] X. Shi, A. E. Thanos, and N. Celik, "Multi-objective agent-based modeling of single-stream recycling programs," *Resources, Conservation and Recycling*, vol. 92, pp. 190–205, Nov. 2014, doi: 10.1016/j.resconrec.2014.07.002.

[29] E. Holden, "U.S. produces far more waste and recycles far less of it than other developed countries," *The Guardian*, 03-Jul-2019. [Online]. Available: https://www.theguardian.com/us-news/2019/jul/02/us-plastic-waste-recycling. [Accessed: 23-Aug-2021].

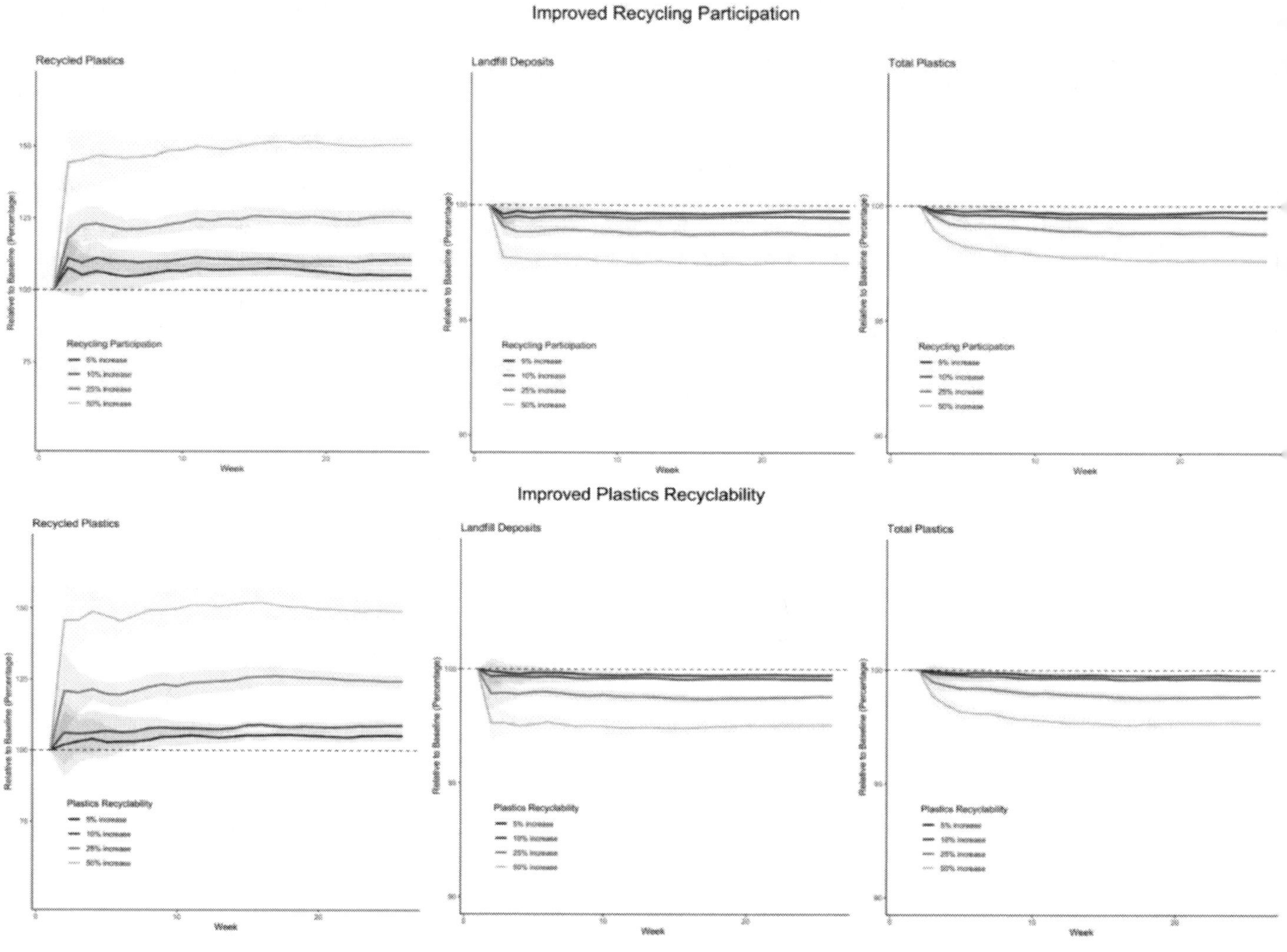


Figure 4. The effect of education campaign over 25 weeks.

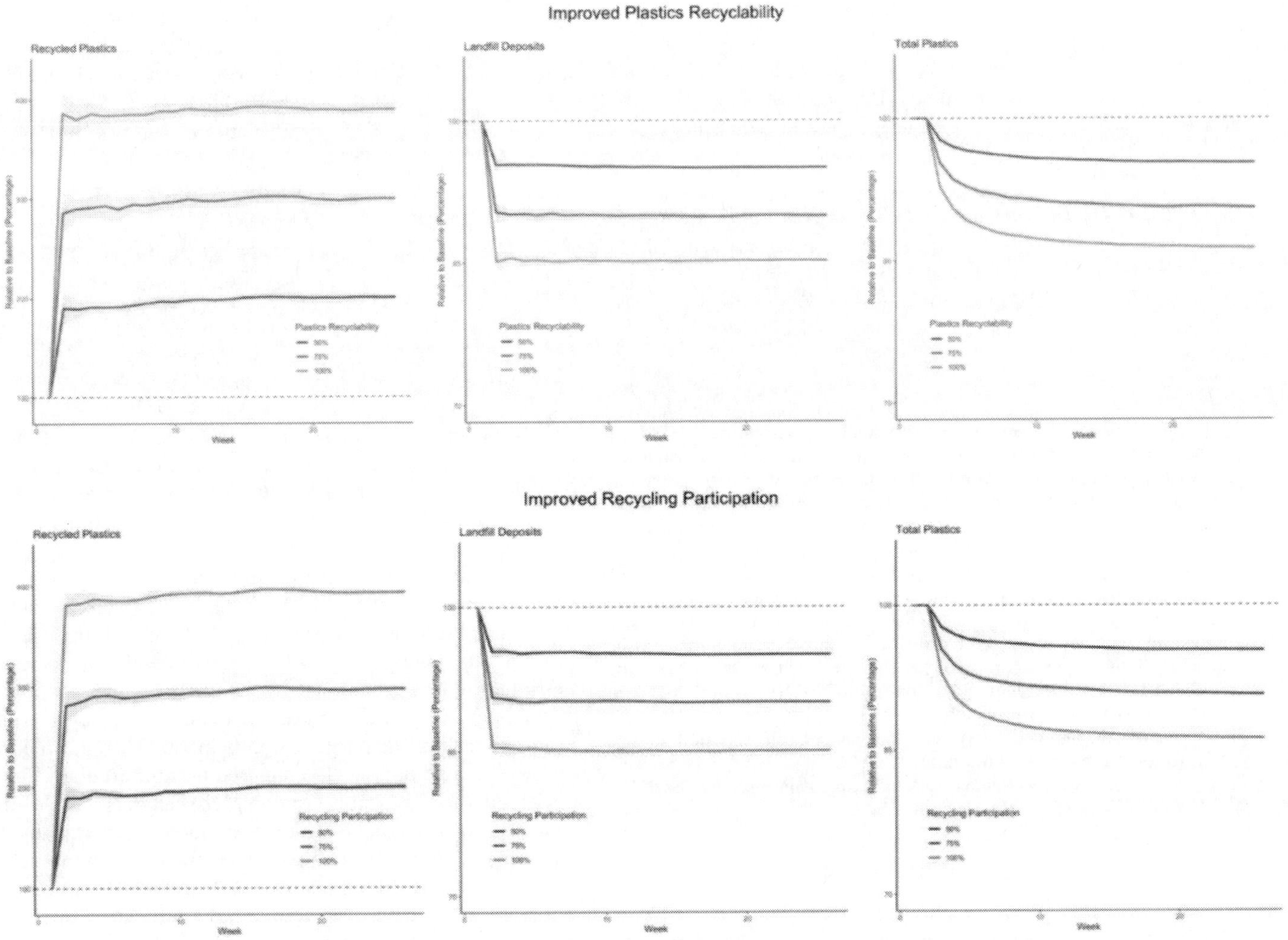


Figure 5. The effect of system-wide improvement over 25 weeks.

# A Mixed-Reality Simulator for an Autonomous Delivery System Using Platooning

Prem Chand Pavani
*CIAD (UMR 7533)*
*Univ. de Technologie de Belfort-Montbéliard*
Belfort, France
email: prem-chand_pavani@etu.u-bourgogne.fr

Pierre Romet
*CIAD (UMR 7533)*
*Univ. de Technologie de Belfort-Montbéliard*
Belfort, France
email: pierre.romet@utbm.fr

Franck Gechter
*CIAD (UMR 7533) and MOSEL LORIA (UMR CNRS 7503)*
*Univ. de Technologie de Belfort-Montbéliard and Univ. de Lorraine*
Belfort and Vandoeuvre, France
email: franck.gechter@utbm.fr

El-Hassane Aglzim
*ISAT-DRIVE*
*Univ. Bourgogne Franche-Comté*
Nevers, France
email: el-hassane.aglzim@u-bourgogne.fr

***Abstract*—Developments in the field of autonomous vehicles have encouraged research to innovate technology to solve everyday problems. E-commerce has been on the rise and, freight transportation is considered an environmental nuisance, especially in the city centers. Electric vehicles have been proposed to reduce the environmental impact of transit vehicles. A package delivery system using a platoon of autonomous electric delivery vehicles and established public transport networks in cities can be employed to solve these problems. But autonomous vehicle testing is a point of concern for authorities and the public alike. This paper acknowledges this problem of validating the algorithms used to create an autonomous delivery system using an innovative solution. A Mixed-Reality simulator based on Unity3D and Robotic Operating System was successfully created to test autonomous vehicle platooning.**

***Keywords*—*Mixed-Reality; Platooning; Autonomous Vehicles; Vehicle-Hardware-in-the-Loop (VeHiL).***

## I. INTRODUCTION

For several years, a significant effort has been made to optimize the transport of goods in urban and peri-urban centers. These improvements are aimed at reduction of the secondary effects of transportation, such as congestion, noise pollution due to the dense traffic flow, or air pollution due to conventional vehicles. Current legislative regulations limit the size and weight of transport vehicles, delivery hours during the day, and suggestions to construct central distribution units close to the city. Other changes include the addition of distribution circuits for tricycles or compact electric vehicles. Nevertheless, these new guidelines and distribution routes are far from reducing the negative impact of transit vehicles circulating in space dedicated to the public. Gechter et al. [1] discusses the solutions available to improve the fright transportation in the city center and proposes a comprehensive model to use the public transportation system and autonomous subnormal-sized electric transits by forming a platoon. Gechter et al. [1] clearly defines the advantages of using platoons of autonomous vehicles that serve as the base for this paper which is part of the project SURATRAM (Système Urbain et Rural Autonome de TRAnsport de Marchandises).

Electric freight vehicles have been at the forefront of combating climate change due to excess production of carbon dioxide. Electrification makes the most sense in an urban environment for short commutes where the combustion engine is the most inefficient. Most cities have separate lanes for public transport that trace the entire city perimeters. Large freight vehicles, which are not nimble on narrow city roads, can use these routes to reduce the congestion. Programming a fleet of autonomous robots to follow the existing public transport entities on these less-used routes by using platooning is a concept that can prove advantageous. Autonomous vehicles require extensive testing and, current simulation tools cannot replicate real-world conditions with a hundred percent accuracy and do not account for few critical or complex scenarios. On the other hand, on-road testing is either forbidden or limited by law in most countries. To address issues of autonomous vehicle testing, we are developing a Mixed-Reality (MR) simulator to validate the use-case of platooning and the algorithms.

Kalra et al. [2] demonstrates that autonomous vehicles would need tests over 14 billion kilometers of on-road testing that could take over 400 years with a fleet of 100 agents running every single hour of the year with a supervisor in the vehicle. Hussein et al. [4] introduces the framework used in simulation using Robotic Operating Software (ROS) and Unity3D to optimize experimentation using smart vehicles. A MR platform based on UDP communication was built using the AIM simulator and an autonomous vehicle to test scenarios at an intersection [5]. AIM does not provide a realistic image of the natural world and has limited application. Another MR simulator was created in [7] using Gazebo and ROS to achieve interaction between simulated and real objects while updating the simulation according to the movement of the robot in the real world. The usage of many commercially available robots is simplified using Gazebo as they are integrated into the simulator. But Unity3D has a more complex and adaptable physics engine compared to Gazebo, giving better realism during testing. Simulation of other elements like traffic can be easily programmed to recreate real-life scenarios. Unity3D also allows training of our driving models using Machine Learning algorithms which is not possible using Gazebo.

Analyzing the convenience of use and the verisimilitude of the simulation to the real world, we propose an MR simulator for our autonomous delivery solution using platooning based on Unity3D and ROS to test our autonomous driving algorithms. The paper is organized as follows: Section II consists of the present technology of simulators used in the literature, while Section III details the MR simulator framework. Section IV provides the results and analysis of our proposal, and Section V concludes the presentation with improvements and the future scope of the project.

## II. State of the Art

As we climb up the various levels of driving automation for on-road vehicles defined by the Society of Automotive (SAE), the complexity of the systems keeps growing. Complex systems include dozens of Electronic Control Units and sensors [8]. Integration of these components becomes challenging, and the necessity of alternative methods to on-road testing becomes evident. Currently, automotive manufacturers are working extensively with XiL in the system development cycle to increase productivity [3].

The first step is to develop the actual model of the plant or hardware in a simulation environment that represents the influential features of the system [9]. A controller is conceived to alter the output of the plant as per the application. This method is known as Model-in-the-Loop (MiL) testing. The behavior of the simulated plant model is governed by the controller logic. MiL is a good starting step to perform controlled tests of the system in a virtual world. When a MiL produces satisfactory results, a code generated from only the controller model replaces the controller block. We simulate using the controller block made of the code with the software model from the previous step [10]. This process is known as Software-in-the-Loop (SiL) testing. The outcome of the test is compared with those obtained in the MiL testing. We alternate these two steps until a reliable algorithm is produced. It is still important to test the controller on the real hardware as the simulated model is based on certain important parameters. Hence in the last step, the simulation model is replaced, entirely or partially, by the actual hardware to test the accuracy of the controller logic, hence the name Hardware-in-the-Loop (HiL) testing [11]. Another class of testing depends on the use of a prototype in the development cycle. The prototype is examined in real-life conditions (like test tracks or on-road) to have the best results. A prerequisite to this is the need for extensive infrastructure. There are several limitations to the on-road testing from the government due to safety concerns. A hybrid that combines the HiL and prototype testing is Vehicle-Hardware-in-the-Loop (VeHiL) that allows manufacturers to test their approach in the initial stages of the development. The method is flexible and convenient as we can moderate all the environmental conditions. The tests are conducted on a chassis dynamometer which is usually heavy and requires plenty of space [3].

User interactive maps using Augmented Reality (AR) (projection of virtual elements in the real world [6]) gives us an immersive experience during navigation through streets. Another impressive technological advancement is the ability to explore the world in Virtual Reality (VR), where we can interface with the virtual elements or create a virtual world. A composite of these technologies is MR, where the physical entities can interact with elements in the virtual world [6]. Integration of MR in autonomous vehicle testing provides versatility, increasing the duplicability of real-world conditions in confined spaces. MR has been used previously to provide driving assistance of welfare vehicles using a virtual platoon control method allowing novice users to control the kart with ease [12].

Given the state-of-the-art, we understand that VeHiL testing is advantageous but requires an actual vehicle or prototype in the testing loop alongside a simulation, as defined in [3]. We built our VeHiL around a Radio Controlled (RC) car to reduce the infrastructure requirement and allow flexible testing of our platooning application using the MR simulator. Developing algorithms using a 1:1 model of the bus and vehicle is financially inconvenient due to costs of fuel and renting a bus. Large vehicles require space for testing. The nearest testing ground is 30kms away from the laboratory. Travelling to the site to validate small changes in the algorithms or ideas is logistically cumbersome and not time efficient. A detailed explanation is provided in the next section.

## III. Mixed Reality Simulator

Evaluating the advantages and disadvantages of the available testing methods, we propose a VeHiL test using an MR simulator using Unity3D and ROS. We will use Unity3D to create a platoon simulation using a bus (representing the public transport) and a Hyundai Kona (representing an electric transit van). Simulation test cases include the car following the bus, parking the vehicle on the side of the road at bus stops to avoid congestion, and dynamically attaching to a bus on a different route to the present one at an intersection to deliver at a specific location. Using the schedule data provided by the public transport provider in Belfort, Optymo, we can synchronize this change of route fluidly. In this paper, we discuss only the platooning test case. We will start our VeHIL tests using a scaled model of the car, in the form of an RC robot equipped with sensors like LiDAR, Ultrasonic Distance Sensor (UDS), Inertial Measurement Unit (IMU). We use ROS to manage data and control the robot. A schematic with the framework of the MR simulator is presented in Figure 1. A comprehensive description of each component is provided in the upcoming few subsections.

### *A. Smart Robot*

The MR simulator is based on an electric Kona, which would act as our autonomous delivery vehicle. During the VeHIL test phase, we did not have the Kona at our disposal. To proceed with the development of the simulator, we used an RC car to replicate the characteristics of the Kona. Hence, the

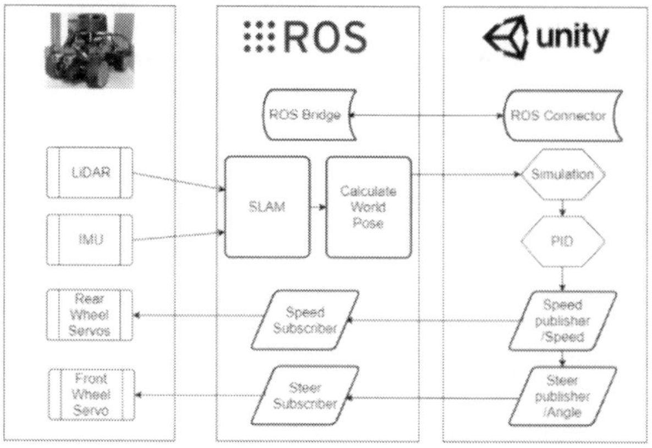


Figure 1. Mixed-Reality simulator framework.

results obtained are not entirely homologous to experiments performed with a Kona due to a mismatch of the physics model of the robot and simulation. We normalized the parameters of the Kona, like torque and turning radius, in the simulation to suit the handling of the robot. Using the PiCar-S kit V2.0 from the robotics company SunFounder, we were able to customize the robot by adding a LiDAR and an IMU, in addition to the UDS to replicate the functionality of the actual vehicle (Figure 2).

Out of the box, the PiCar depends on a Raspberry Pi (RPi) 4B for its computational power running Ubuntu (based on Linux; officially supported by ROS). The propulsion system constitutes of two pulse width modulation (PWM) motors. A 2D LiDAR from SLAMTEC (RPLIDAR A2) used in the project produces up to 8000 samples/second and has a range of 12m with a resolution of 0.15m. A MEMS-based IMU (MPU6050) fuses the programmable 3-axis accelerometer (2g-16g), and 3-axis gyroscope (250°/sec-2000°/sec). An UDS with a range of 0.02m-4m works in the frequency range of 40kHz. The manufacturer provides a library for the RC car, coded in Python that allows users to easily set up the robot.

Figure 2. Smart robot equipped with a LiDAR, an IMU and an UDS.

## B. Unity3D Simulation

To perform the MiL test, we chose Unity3D to run our initial experiments. The simulation primarily consists of two objects, a bus, and a car. The simulation aims to reproduce a platoon that includes a public transport entity (in our case, the bus) and an electric delivery van (Figure 3). The bus will act as the leader of the platoon, with the car behaving as the follower. The bus follows a predefined path, and the car can autonomously follow the bus based on the telemetry data of the leader. The data collected from the follower vehicle is transmitted to the robot. A feedback loop updates the location of the car in the simulation per the real world. The bus is a representative model of Lion's city hybrid buses used in the city of Belfort, manufactured by MAN. The car is comparable to a Kona electric, produced by the Korean manufacturer, Hyundai. We modeled a Kona electric in the simulation as we have the actual vehicle, fitted with a RADAR, two LiDAR's (one frontal, one on the roof), and a Global Navigation Satellite System with an integrated IMU. Unity3D has a configurable physics engine that can adapt to the vehicle using parameters like mass, the center of gravity, or the drag coefficient. Unity3D also allows users to incorporate the tire model by providing the forward friction and sideways friction values (extremum slip, asymptote slip). The simulation also accounts for the unsprung mass and suspension system (damping rate, suspension distance, force application point distance). The maximum torque values and speed limits of both vehicles are programmed. These features can help program physics of most vehicles in Unity3D, making the simulation versatile to test other platooning projects.

Using waypoints, we set the path for the bus to follow. At the beginning of the simulation, we congregate all the waypoints and store them in an array to keep track of the number of points. To steer the bus, we calculate a relative vector to the upcoming waypoint from the current position of the bus; this returns a value between [-1, 1], indicating the direction (negative value implies that the point is to the left of the heading of the bus and on the contrary, a positive value indicates a point on the right). To determine the steering angle, we multiply the relative vector with the maximum steering angle. When the bus is within 5m of the current waypoint, we calculate the steer value to the next waypoint in the array. To control the speed of the bus, we apply a torque to the rear wheels of the bus corresponding to the distance to the next waypoint and reduce this value as we approach the waypoint or if we must navigate a sharp turn. We update our steering and torque values at a fixed period of 20ms or at a frequency of 50Hz. A similar method is deployed on the follower (Kona) to allow the car to move relative to the leader. Analogous to the bus, we use a tracker point placed on the rear axle of the bus to determine the angle of steering required on the car. A Proportional-Integral-Differential (PID) controller ( Gain values P: 80, I: 30, D: 35) adjusts the speed of the Kona proportionately to the distance between the two vehicles. The distance is measured from the front of the Kona to the tracker point. The aim is to maintain a safe distance of 10m which accounts for emergency braking. The PID controller gain values can be updated during the simulation. The PID controller recalculates the speed of the Kona every 100ms (10Hz) by adjusting the error at the rate of 50Hz increases the data queue to be transmitted significantly. As the simulation does not emulate the physics of the robot, a novel PID controller (Gain values P:10, I:7, D:6) and a separate code for steering were adapted to the pace and the turning radius of the robot.

The company Siemens, developed an open-source library in C# to communicate with ROS from .NET applications like Unity using TCP/IP sockets (available on GitHub as ros_sharp). The library includes standard message publishers, subscribers, and Action servers. We created a new object that contains a ros_connector, two data publishers, and a Pose stamped subscriber. The ros_connector script helps us connect to the ROS server running on the robot. We modified two 32-bit float (std_msgs ROS) publishers to transmit the speed and steering angle. We adopted a pose stamped subscriber from the ros_sharp library to receive the coordinates of the robot generated by the Simultaneous Localization and Mapping (SLAM) algorithm.

Figure 3. Simulation of the platoon in Unity3D.

## C. ROS

ROS acts as a middleware to manage the data generated by different sensors and helps various programs running on the robot communicate. It also behaves like a control mechanism for the robot by collecting the data from the simulation. We used ROS Noetic Ninjemys that has good community support and compatibility with the packages required for this project. The first package that is vital is the rosbridge_suite library. The library contains a rosbridge_server package with rosbridge_websocket launch file that creates a server with the IP address of the RPi. A simple listener coded in Python can subscribe to the /speed and /steer topics and receive the 32-bit float messages from Unity3D over the server. Using a modified library provided by SunFounder, we can manipulate the robot according to the received data. The LiDAR point-cloud data is visualized in RVIZ using the package provided by SLAMTEC. This point cloud is accessible from the topic /slam. We used a Python script to decode data from the MPU6050. The linear acceleration and angular velocity values are published using the topic /imu. Next, to fuse the data from the IMU and the LiDAR to form a 2D map of the environment, three SLAM packages are currently available: gmapping [9], Cartographer [10], and Hector SLAM [11]. In our case, we are fusing data from LiDAR and IMU, so hector_slam seems to be the best choice. The SLAM module, based on an Extended Kalman Filter (EKF), generates coordinates of the robot's location in the real world, published using the topic /slam_out_pose. We relay the position to Unity3D via the ROS server, where a Pose Stamped (geometry_msgs ROS) subscriber node converts the data into Unity3D coordinates.

# IV. Experiments & Results

An oval path (L1: 30 units, L2: 20units) is drawn for the bus to trace using waypoints in Unity3D. Each experiment corresponds to the bus completing one full revolution (unless specified) of the oval while being followed closely (10m distance) by the car in the simulation. This section will provide details regarding the analysis and results of the performance of our MR simulator, based on three main criteria: time delay, deviation of simulation from the real-world position, and analysis of the SLAM algorithm.

## A. Time Delay

As we are working on a real-time system, it is crucial to determine the time delay between the transmission of data, the actuation of the system, and the feedback. Anticipating the delay can improve the efficiency of control strategies. A ping of 20ms is commonly observed in wireless connections working at 2.4GHz but, the delay varies for each query. ROS is known to have delays in communication between nodes, which can influence the delay in the system. We identified three components that make up the total delay in our system include: messages to reach ROS from Unity; the time necessary to process the data; update world pose data from ROS to Unity.

*1) From Unity to ROS:* The pose stamped messages (geometry_msgs ROS) were sent from Unity using the ros_sharp library to understand the delay during transmission of data from Unity to ROS. The data is converted to suit the coordinate system in ROS (right-handed, with X forward, Y left, and Z up) as Unity uses a left-handed, Y-Up, Z-forward, and X-left convention. The pose message header contains the time at which the data was generated during the simulation. When the data reaches the ROS subscriber node, the information is parsed, and the output is printed on the command window with time in the Unix format (nanoseconds). The session gets recorded into a rosbag file and saved in a CSV file format. Using a python script, timestamps of the sent and received messages are separated from the CSV file and converted into readable date and time format. Matlab is used to import the data and construct a graph describing the delay for each packet of data to reach ROS from Unity over the number of frames. For each frame, we generate one message.

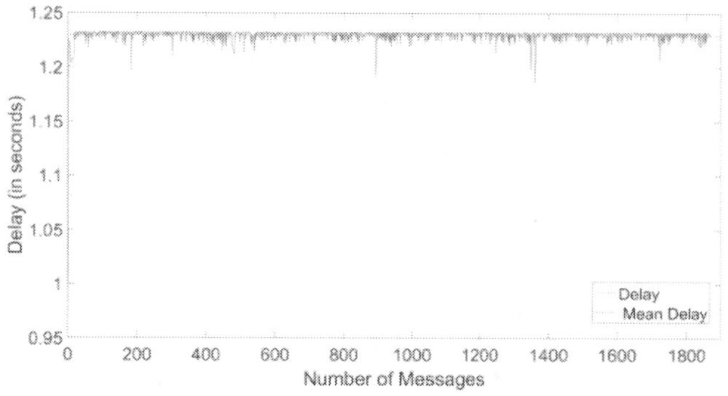


Figure 4. Delay of each message received in ROS from Unity3D.

Tested over 1870 messages (at 50Hz Frame rate), we observe that the first message arrives in ROS after 0.98 seconds, after which the delay for each consecutive packet of data fluctuates between 10ms-20ms (Figure 4). So, the robot is lagging the simulation by 1.3 seconds. The rosbridge socket server is CPU intensive and takes time to process substantial amounts of inbound data. Since the ROS server and simulation are running on different machines, the latency increases significantly. The variation in delay between messages is known as jitter. This is an issue of using the 2.4GHz band as most appliances use the same frequency range along with other people living in the neighborhood, causing significant variations in delay between queries.

*2) Processing Delay:* Every processor takes time to make sense of the received data. We would like to measure the delay between the time when the message is received in ROS to when the robot starts moving. This is measured to show the worst-case delay observed in the system moving from complete rest. Two separate loops are used to process the speed and steering angle data received in ROS, increasing the processing time of the data. When a message is received, the content of the message and the time get printed on the command window. The IMU is sensitive enough to detect every movement. A message with the current time is printed on the command window once there is a change in acceleration in the X-axis above a threshold value of 0.2g. The difference between the timestamp of the first message received from Unity and the timestamp when there is motion provides the time required for processing.

Over nine trials performed to determine the delay between the reception of command and actuation of the servo motor - we observe a mean delay of 1.5 seconds (Figure 5). This loss in time can be attributed to the time delay for the first message to be received in ROS, which is around 0.98 seconds, as mentioned in the previous experiment. So we can deduce that the processing delay is approximately 0.5 seconds which can be due to the sensitivity of the motors to low-speed inputs at the start.

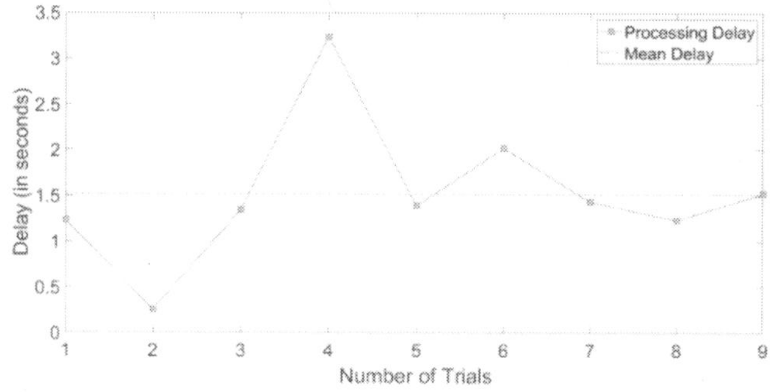


Figure 5. Delay between the reception of message and the robot moving.

*3) From ROS to Unity:* Similar to the delay observed during the relay of data from Unity to ROS, there is a delay during the transmission of data from ROS to Unity3D over the wireless network. We would expect the delay to be around 0.02seconds. To estimate this delay, we generate a Pose Stamped message after the world position of the robot is calculated by the SLAM module and relay this data to Unity. The pose-stamped data from ROS is converted to suit the coordinate system in Unity by the subscriber node in Unity3D. The pose stamped messages contain the timestamp representing the time when they were generated in ROS. Once the message is received in Unity3D, we log the current time. These logs can be accessed from the player log editor. The timestamps are imported into Matlab, and we create a graph between the number of frames and delay in seconds.

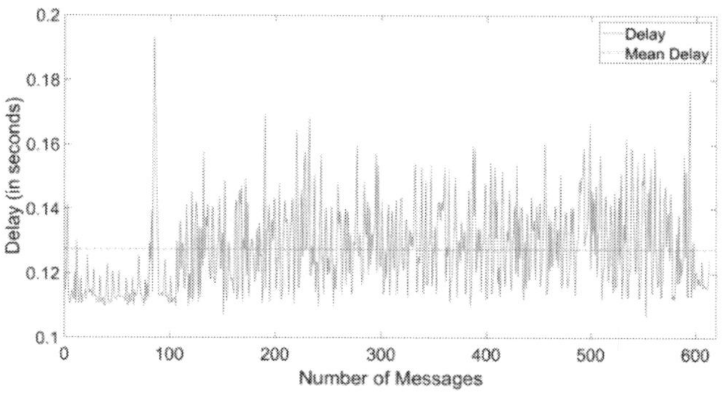


Figure 6. Delay of each message received in Unity3D from ROS.

A comparison between the timestamps of the data reveals that - on average, there is a delay of 0.13 seconds. It varies between 0.11-0.19 seconds (Figure 6). The obtained delay is significantly higher than expected. In addition to the jitter observed while using the 2.4GHz frequency band, we have a delay during the exchange of data between the node responsible to publish the pose stamped messages and the WebSocket server in ROS. Since the server is running on the RPi and the subscriber on the computer, we have a latency between the two host machines and is a factor in the high delay values observed.

*B. Deviation from actual World Pose*

Since the physics model of the simulated entity and the robot are different, it is interesting to see how this difference affects our simulation. We will be able to judge if there is a need to mimic the physics of the actual vehicle in the simulation. The coordinates produced by SLAM module are used to update the simulation. Another object that contains a pose stamped subscriber is created in Unity3D. This object represents the path traced by the robot in the real world. A vector between the path taken by the virtual car and the path traced by the robot is recorded every second in the simulation.

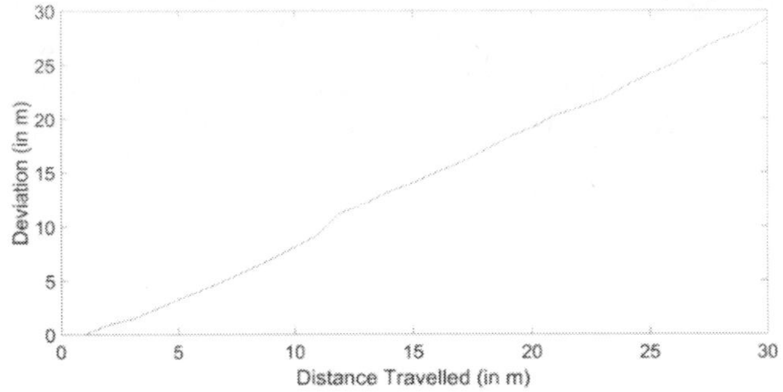


Figure 7. Deviation of simulation from actual world position of the robot.

A comparison between the simulated position and the coordinates of the robot shows a deviation of one meter per every meter of movement in the simulation (Figure 7). At the start of the simulation, the deviation is relatively less as the speed of the vehicles is low. As proven earlier, the RC car lags the simulation by more than a second. Combined with the fact that Unity currently uses a physics model of a car, there is a significant deviation of the path reproduced by the robot in comparison to the virtual car. This result proves the need for an accurate physics model of the virtual vehicle with respect to the real vehicle.

*C. Accuracy of SLAM*

The closeness of the location provided by the SLAM algorithm to the ground truth will increase our confidence in our measurements, enabling us to safely navigate in densely populated urban environments. To test the accuracy of SLAM, a grid (1 $cm^2$) paper is laid out on the floor. The RC car is positioned on one of the edges of the grid cell. We run one cycle of the simulation while filming the robot from a bird's eye view. The position data from the SLAM is recorded into a rosbag file. We note the position of the robot from the video by counting the number of cells traveled on the grid at a period of three seconds and the coordinates given by SLAM in ROS.

We plot the two points to recreate the path followed by the robot in the real world and according to SLAM (Figure 8). The SLAM can localize the robot with good accuracy fusing the LiDAR and IMU data. The robot is not able to recreate the oval circuit drawn in Unity3D due to the difference in physics model. Optimizing speed and angle of steer produces a semicircular movement over three revolutions

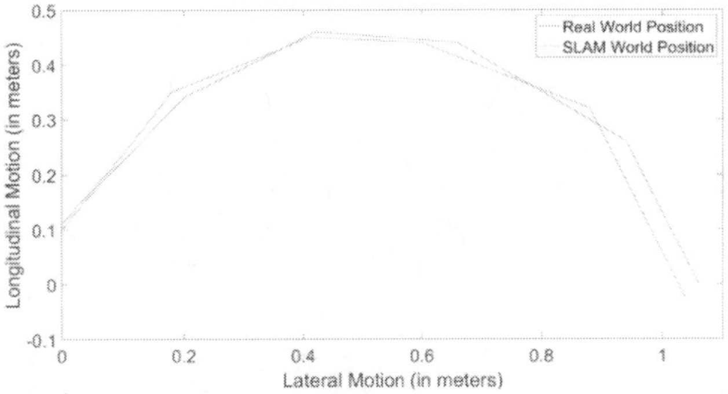


Figure 8. Comparison of position provided by SLAM to actual position.

in Unity, contrary to the other experiments. We could not achieve enough points to evaluate the SLAM with a single revolution of the vehicle in the simulation.

Another graph to depict the deviation over time is plotted by calculating a resultant vector between the two points (Figure 9). We see a mean error of 0.03m between both measurements. The error does not accumulate with time due to the presence of an EKF in the SLAM algorithm, which can predict the trajectory of the robot, reducing the deviation from the actual position. The error can be further reduced by fusing data from an odometer.

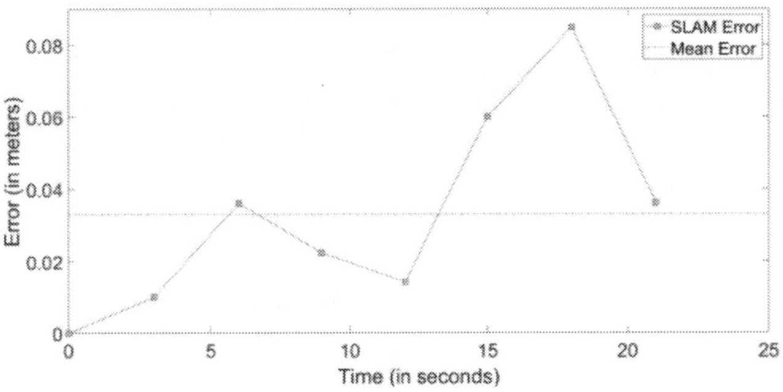


Figure 9. Error between SLAM and actual position.

## V. Conclusion and Future Work

As the use of autonomous vehicles becomes more prominent, innovations in the field of testing become critical. This paper evaluated the adoption of an MR simulator with a VeHiL testing to validate algorithms for an autonomous freight delivery system using the public network system proposed in [1]. We can address a few issues to improve the precision of the simulator. First, the use of a 5GHz wireless communication can reduce jitter during data transmission. To reduce the deviation between the virtual and real-world, we can introduce a Kalman filter in Unity3D. Extending the project to support ROS2 can lower the delay caused due to communication between different nodes, as nodes can communicate directly with each other without the need of a ROS Master. The PID controller can be replaced with more robust controllers to improve follower's capability to keep up with the leader. The fusion of odometer data from the real vehicle can increase the accuracy of the SLAM algorithm. Future research to implement the simulator with the Kona in the VeHiL phase instead of the robot is envisioned, along with testing of other test cases mentioned in Section III. This will avoid issues due to the contrast of the simulation model with the robot. The simulator can be extended to other platooning projects where, researchers can model their vehicles (using the physics model parameters as indicated in Section III: C) in Unity3D along with 3D maps of cities to test their self-driving robots in small spaces, reducing risk of on-road testing and cost of expensive testbeds.

## ACKNOWLEDGMENT

This work is done with the support of the Région Bourgogne-Franche-comté, through the SURATRAM Project.

## REFERENCES

[1] F. Gechter,et al. "Transportation of Goods in Inner-City Centers: Can Autonomous Vehicles in Platoon Be a Suitable Solution?" in 2017 IEEE Vehicle Power and Propulsion Conference (VPPC), pp. 1–5.

[2] N. Kalra, and S. M. Paddock, "Driving to safety: How many miles of driving would it take to demonstrate autonomous vehicle reliability?" in 2016 Transportation Research Part A: Policy and Practice , pp. 94, 182–193.

[3] C. Galko, R. Rossi, and X. Savatier, "Vehicle-Hardware-In-The-Loop system for ADAS prototyping and validation", in 2014 International Conference on Embedded Computer Systems: Architectures, Modeling, and Simulation (SAMOS XIV), pp. 329–334.

[4] A. Hussein, F. Garcia, and C. Olaverri-Monreal, "ROS and Unity Based Framework for Intelligent Vehicles Control and Simulation," in 2018 IEEE International Conference on Vehicular Electronics and Safety, pp. 1–6.

[5] M. Quinlan, Tsz-Chiu Au, J. Zhu, N. Stiurca, and P. Stone, "Bringing simulation to life: A mixed reality autonomous intersection," in 2010 IEEE/RSJ International Conference on Intelligent Robots and Systems, pp. 6083–6088.

[6] W. Honig, et al. "Mixed reality for robotics," in 2015 IEEE/RSJ International Conference on Intelligent Robots and Systems (IROS), pp. 5382–5387.

[7] I. Y.-H. Chen, B. MacDonald, and B. Wunsche, "Mixed reality simulation for mobile robots," in 2009 IEEE International Conference on Robotics and Automation, pp. 232–237.

[8] S. Moten, F. Celiberti, M. Grottoli, A. van der Heide, and Y. Lemmens, "X-in-the-loop advanced driving simulation platform for the design,development, testing and validation of ADAS," in 2018 IEEE Intelligent Vehicles Symposium (IV), Changshu, Jun. 2018, pp. 1–6.

[9] A. R. Plummer, "Model-in-the-Loop Testing" Institution of Mechanical Engineers, Part I: Journal of Systems and Control Engineering in 2006;220(3): pp. 183-199.

[10] S. Demers, P. Gopalakrishnan and L. Kant, "A Generic Solution to Software-in-the-Loop," MILCOM 2007 - IEEE Military Communications Conference, 2007, pp. 1-6.

[11] W. Deng, Y. H. Lee and A. Zhao, "Hardware-in-the-loop simulation for autonomous driving," 2008 34th Annual Conference of IEEE Industrial Electronics, 2008, pp. 1742-1747.

[12] N. Matsunaga, R. Kimura, H. Ishiguro, and H. Okajima, "Driving Assistance of Welfare Vehicle with Virtual Platoon Control Method which has Collision Avoidance Function Using Mixed Reality," in 2018 IEEE International Conference on Systems, Man, and Cybernetics, pp. 1915–1920.

[13] G. Grisetti, C. Stachniss, and W. Burgard, "Improved Techniques for Grid Mapping with Rao-Blackwellized Particle Filters," IEEE Transactions on Robotics, pp. 34-46.

[14] W. Hess, D. Kohler, H. Rapp, and D. Andor, "Real-Time Loop Closure in 2D LIDAR SLAM," in Robotics and Automation (ICRA), 2016 IEEE International Conference on. IEEE, pp. 1271–1278.

[15] S. Kohlbrecher, et al. (2014) "Hector Open Source Modules for Autonomous Mapping and Navigation with Rescue Robots". RoboCup 2013: Robot World Cup.

# Surrogate Predictive and Multi-domain Modelling of Complex Systems by Fusion of Agent-based Simulation, Cellular Automata, and Machine Learning

Stefan Bosse
Dept. Mathematics and Computer Science
University of Bremen
28359 Bremen, Germany
sbosse@uni-bremen.de

*Abstract*— **Modelling of complex dynamic systems like pandemic outbreaks or traffic flows in cities on macro-level is difficult due to a high variance on entity micro-level and unknown or incomplete interaction models. Agent-based and Cellular Automata (CA) simulations based on micro-level modelling can be used to investigate the outcome of system observables in a sandbox. For a reasonable accuracy a high number of agents, sufficient behaviour variance, high computational times, and calibrated model parameters are required. Surrogate predictive modelling of the multi-agent system can be used to replace time-consuming simulations. In this work we present a hybrid approach combining Agent-based Simulation, probabilistic contextual CA, and Machine Learning (ML). We investigate the replacement of the ABS-CA by surrogate ML models trained by simulation data. The predictive model is state-based and applied to time-series data to predict future development of aggregated system observables. We discuss and show the negative impact of uncalibrated real-world sensor data on time-series prediction and an improvement by surrogate modelling of simulation. A use-case of pandemic simulation using real-world statistical data is used to investigate and evaluate the suitability and accuracy of the proposed methods and to show the high sensitivity of surrogate modelling on distorted and biased data.**

***Keywords- Large-scale simulation; Multi-Agent Systems; Cellular Automata; Surrotgae Machine Learning; Data Augmentation.***

## I. INTRODUCTION

The typical goal of a simulation is the prediction of the behaviour of a complex system by aggregate observables for a particular situation. A simulation can be composed of a set of interacting entities on micro-level, like humans in social sciences, to investigate and predict the outcome of system-level aggregate observables. Machine Learning as well as simulation are used to predict the response of a system to a stimulus that is hard to be studied in the real world and to get macro-level from micro-level observables (aggregates). Both techniques use data analysis and mathematical modelling [1]. In most cases a simulation is composed from elementary cells (holonomic approach). Each cell is defined by a micro-level model and by a set of interaction functions. Agent-based modelling (ABM) and simulation (ABS), and Cellular Automata (CA) are prominent examples of this decomposition approach for large-scale dynamic systems. CA can be considered as a simplified sub-class of ABM/ABS with strictly bounded interaction ranges, better suited and scaling for large-scale problems with a very high number of entities typically required to strength statistical quality. A simulation model is typically a simplification and abstraction of the complex real world that is characterised by the behaviour modelling of single entities (core cell elements of the simulation, e.g., an agent or a cell), the interaction between the elements, the number of elements relative to real world systems, and the variance of behaviour and interaction models. Mostly only an ensemble averaged model is used that is derived from real world observations and sensor data; individualism cannot be covered properly.

The combination of Machine Learning and simulation can improve model and simulation quality, i.e., there is according to:

1. Machine Learning assisted simulation improving the simulation model and quality [1];
2. Simulation assisted Machine Learning improving the prediction or classification model [1];
3. Emulation of the multi-agent behaviour model by an ML derived macro model (surrogate modelling) [2][3];
4. Model calibration using ML [1].

The central concept and novelty of this work is a ML-based ensemble estimator for aggregate observables learned from an incremental hybrid and domain-hierarchical MAS/CA simulation with the aim to improve real-word system time-series data prediction. The CA extension was chosen for efficiency and scaling reasons. A tight coupling of the simulation to real-world entities is an additional feature that ensures real-time updates of the simulation and incremental calibration of the simulation at simulation time, supporting crowd sensing and digital twin methodologies (but not stressed in this work). The work utilises and combines:

1. Hierarchical MAS-CA simulation incorporating real-world data for the parametrisation of the simulation world and agent modelling (digital twin concept) to predict future developments of system state observables from past data;
2. Hierarchical domain-specific modelling and decomposition (with respect to longitudinal and spatial scale);

3. Predictive modelling of time-series data using state-based ML models trained on real-world and simulation data;

The major issue with real-world coupled simulations and predictive machine modelling from simulation is the discrepancy of sensor data (input and output observables) collected in real and simulation domains. Typically, the simulation is almost inaccurate (and wrong) with respect to real world, but the sensor measuring is accurate and exact (all population entities can be accessed and measured directly). In contrast, to the real world domain where measurements are inaccurate and in many cases biased and distorted (or at least not representative), especially on the longitudinal scale. For example, considering traffic simulation, the sensors (counting and tracing traffic flows) are relatively accurate and representative in both domains. But in contrast, observations and simulation of pandemic situations disperse significantly in real and virtual world domains. Therefore, we have chosen the COVID19 pandemic use-case to demonstrate the issues with real-world coupled and data-based simulation and the deployment of predictive machine models derived from inaccurate and biased data.

The surrogate ML models should be able to predict future developments of aggregated macro-level observables from past data, e.g., the accumulative incidence rate of a pandemic situation. ML modelling is already applied in social science and ecological modelling [4]. The application of such learned surrogate models on inaccurate and distorted real-world sensor data will still result in inaccurate prediction results. To solve this issue, a sensor correction and calibration model must be derived by using correct simulation sensor data that is acquired by real-world measuring principles resulting in strongly biased and distorted data. To overcome the computational scaling problem due to a required high number of agents (beyond 100000) a hierarchical hybrid model of agents and contextual cellular automata simulating a lattice gas model is proposed. Fine-grained simulation is performed by spatial and temporal partitioning adapting models and simulations in consecutive time intervals based on changing environmental parameter space. As well simulation as prediction models can be updated incrementally by new measured data (longitudinal extension), e.g., by agent-based crowd sensing [5]. The following sections introduce the hybrid and hierarchical modelling and simulation model, showing results of time-series prediction on real-world data, and finally showing in comparison prelimenary results of time-series prediction from simulation data.

## II. The Hybrid and Hierarchical Concept

The hybrid and hierarchical methodology addressed in this work combines MAS-ABS with supervised ML, and the ABS combines two levels of agent behaviour model complexity, state-based reactive agents with complex long-range interaction and CA cells with simple short-range interaction.

The CA is a sub-domain model of the agent model. The simulation framework consists of an agent simulator [6] that is capable to process computational and physical agents (first-level class agents) as well as CA worlds seamlessly. The domain-hierarchical MAS-CA modelling decomposes complex real worlds in simplified organised cell networks on micro-level, the ML methods are used to estimate system-level (ensemble) observables from sensors.

Computational agents are mobile software that can migrate between real- and virtual worlds and they are used for real-world data collection (including mobile crowd sensing) and for creating digital twins in the simulation, whereas physical agents are pure simulation objects that represent physical entities in the simulation world. To reflect spatial variance, the simulation world $\mathbb{S}$ is partitioned into spatial sub-domains $\mathbb{S}=\{S_{di}\}$, associated with a MAS. Each domain is handled by an agent $ag_{di}$ from the MAS that is a spatial and organisational representation of a large set of simple agents situated in a simplified CA world. Each CA represents a spatial region with a high number of interacting entities (e.g., humans). The MAS reflects the coarse-grained, the CA the fine-grained simulation model. The simulation model is composed basically of mobility, behaviour, and interaction of the observed entities.

First-level domain agents represent larger spatial domains (e.g., terrestrial units or entire cities) and interact with each other to simulate crowd flows, organisation, and networking across spatial domains. Each rectangular CA world *CW* connected to one domain agent consists of cells arranged on a regular two-dimensional grid that is partitioned into logical sub-domains (regions) *ld* associated with specific interaction behaviour and environmental constraints, e.g., living and working areas, $CW=\{ld_j\}$, $ld_j=\{cell \in A_j\}$. The second-level class cell agents within the CA are modelled by a "mobile" data structure bound to one current cell in the CA world and processed by a cell activity function. The mobility of agents within the CA world is modelled with a randomised lattice-gas model by shifting the agent state spatially. A CA cell is occupied by one or no agent. Agents can access neighbouring cells (Moore neighbourhood) and can move to neighbour cells. The hybrid and hierarchical architecture is shown in Fig. 1. The main difference between first- and second level agents is the behaviour function. First-level agents bind each their own behaviour function, whereas second-level agents are represented by on shared behaviour function.

The aggregated data collected from simulation is used to train a surrogate machine model for time-series prediction. A state-based Long-Short Term Memory (LSTM) artificial neural network architecture was chosen for time-series prediction [7]. A LSTM network is able to predict a variable $\boldsymbol{x}$ for a future sample point $n+\Delta$ with past data $\{\boldsymbol{x}_1,..,\boldsymbol{x}_n\}$.

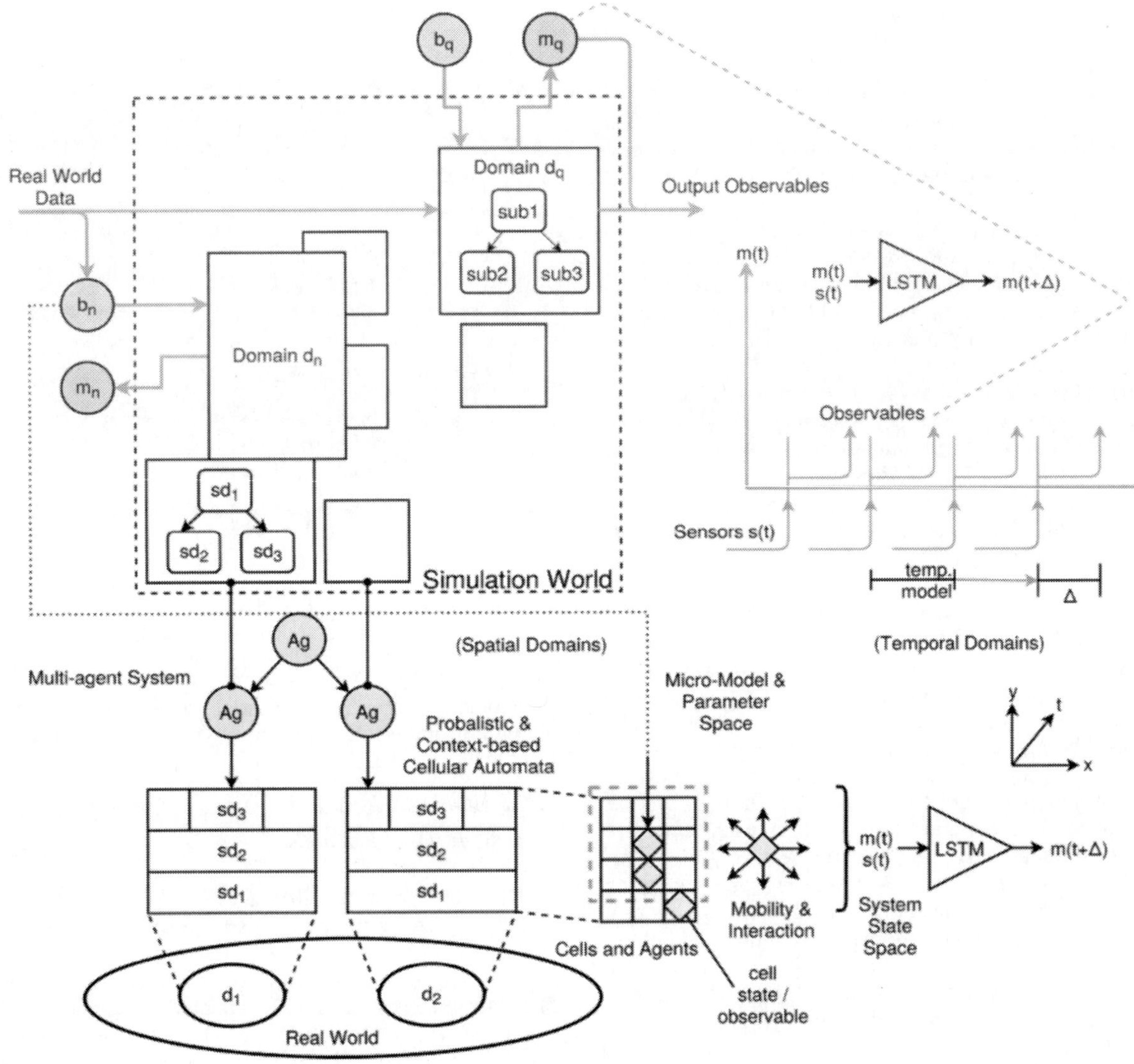


Figure 1. Hybrid simulation with domain-specific MAS-ABS combined with probabilistic CAs. Each CA (bottom) represents a simulation container with simple agents (diamonds) for a spatial domain $d_i$ controlled by a domain agent (circle). Each CA world is partitioned in logical domains $sd_j$, too (bottom, left). Spatial domains are connected by the domain controller agents (middle,left). The LSTM (bottom, right) is trained with simulation data.

The real-world data is collected remotely by computational agents, e.g., performing WEB scraping to get environmental state information.

The next section demonstrates the novel hierarchical simulation approach for a pandemic use-case. The methodology can also be applied to other fields like traffic flow prediction and optimisation, logistic flows, and long-term prediction with respect to migration and segregation effects (social networking).

## III. Use-Case: Pandemic Modelling and Prediction

We demonstrate the proposed hybrid and hierarchical simulation approach of real-world coupled MAS-CA simulation and longitudinal surrogate modelling for the forecasting of pandemic situations. Pure CA-based approaches were already applied to pandemic simulations [8]. This worst-use-case poses a highly unreliable and distorted measuring process, varying on longitudinal scale, and high dynamics based on micro-scale effects.

### *A. Simulation and Surrogate Modelling*

Preliminary experiments were performed to investigate the accuracy and generalisation of a domain-specific prediction model from real data with a time-series prediction of infection observables using an LSTM ANN architecture. The input data are weekly infection cases rates of COVID19 pandemic data base from [9], and the output of this model $m_\Delta(t)$ is the prediction of Δ week ahead infection cases rates with respect to spatial domains and population age domains.

Each spatial domain is trained with its own model. Models are finally exchanged between spatial domains to test generalisation capabilities. The input data was used for seed conditions of the simulation, too.

The simulation world consists of 38 domains of territorial units (TU) of Germany (shown in Fig. 2) with the simulation parameters: Spatial centre location, population statistics, and mobility interconnects between neighbouring TUs. The agent base model is SIRD (susceptible-infected-recovered-dead) population classification. Each spatial domain is represented by its own domain model and parameter set and is simulated independently by a domain agent associated with Lattice Gas Probabilistic and Context-based CA (LG-PCCA), i.e., each domain region is a container for statistical moving and interacting agents, defined by a set of cross-section parameters. Longitudinal day-night cycle simulation is performed. The domain agent is responsible for sensor data acquisition, monitoring, and inter-domain interaction. The CA is partitioned into logical domains, e.g., home, work, outside, school, and culture/sports areas. Sub-agents given by data structures holding parameter and state variables located at cells represent people. Mobility of individuals is given by random walk (gas model), directed diffusion (context model), a mean velocity, and neighbouring and sub-domain constraints. Interaction (infection) is given by a dynamic cross-section and accumulator model, i.e., the integral of mobility and interaction cross-section. Perception and movement of an agent is limited to neighbouring cells (Moore neighbourhood); an agent can change it place (cell) either my moving to a free neighbour cells or by agent-pair swapping. Agent can migrate between different CAs via the domain agents, i.e., domains interact with each other by crowd flows (holiday, travelling, and business).

The agent behaviour model covers a wide range of behaviour parameter, i.e., age domains (child, youth, middle, elder people, etc.), activity domains (children, scholars, students, workers, non-workers, retired people), parameter sets (social networking factor, risk, mobility rate, protection, ...), networks (family, temporary groups), infection test coverage and strategies.

Output observables are accumulated monitored infection cases counts (with age distribution?) on daily basis (simulation) and on weekly basis (rates, real-world data). Input sensor variables (for simulation) are population and density distribution, age distribution, start infection count, social networking parameters, social cluster densities, mobility, opening status of domestic and private facilities, social restrictions, lethality, mortality, and the infection reproduction factor adapting the agent cross section and accumulator thresholds. Simulation is synchronised with real-world statistical pandemic data (accumulated, 1 week period). Agent-based WEB Scraping and Mining is used to sense environmental state variables, e.g., closed stores or schools, contact limitations.

Population representation by agents in a CA world is controlled by a domain agent. A typical population-agent scale ranges from 1:1000 to 1:100 depending on population density; if infection probability is low (<0.01), a higher density is required.

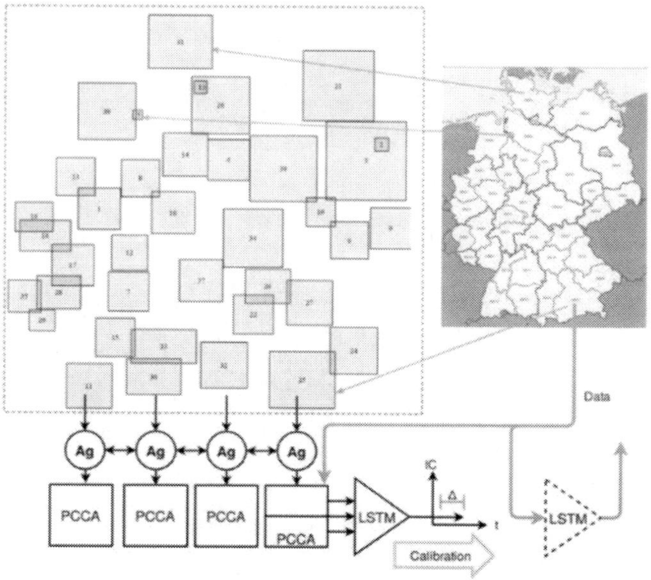


Figure 2. Simulation world partitioned into 38 TUs (NUTS level 2) mapped on 38 CA worlds (left), Cartesian coordinates, not ratio scaled. Size of CA grid is related to TU domain size and population density. Each CA produces data for surrogate modelling by an LSTM (bottom, right).

Model calibration is required for the simulation model (including time-scale calibration) from real to virtual world, and for the surrogate model from virtual to real world.

### B. *Preliminary Results*

#### *1) Real-Data Prediction*

Raw real-world data from national RKI data base [9] was chosen to perform preliminary tests for predictive time-series modelling and simulation and to demonstrate the impossibility to predict future developments from past data. The data consists of weekly updated pandemic COVID19 infection cases (positive tests), i.e., infection rates, partitioned horizontally in 5 year age ranges, and vertically in TUs. The accumulated absolute infection cases, i.e., the number of infected persons, cannot be measured accurately and is not used here (in contrast to simulation).

The input sensor variables for the LSTM predictor is the infection rate (IR) grouped in four age ranges $\langle IR(A_{00}\text{-}A_{09})$, $IR(A_{10}\text{-}A_{19})$, $IR(A_{20}\text{-}A_{59})$, $IR(A_{60}\text{-}A_{99})\rangle$. The output prediction variables (longitudinal extrapolation) are also the infection rates ($IR$), i.e., $\langle IR_{\Delta}(A_{00}\text{-}A_{09})$, $IR_{\Delta}(A_{10}\text{-}A_{19})$, $IR_{\Delta}(A_{20}\text{-}A_{59})$, $IR_{\Delta}(A_{60}\text{-}A_{99})\rangle$. The LSTM predictor has a layer configuration of [4,8,4] with 8 fully connected LSTM cells [10], a sigmoid transfer function, trained by single-sequence learning. Results of a playback experiment for one TU (Bremen) used to train and predict the infection rate development ($\Delta$=4 weeks) is shown in Fig. 3.

The entire data set was used for training and prediction (playback from start to end). A very high accuracy of prediction results were achieved (error below 10%).

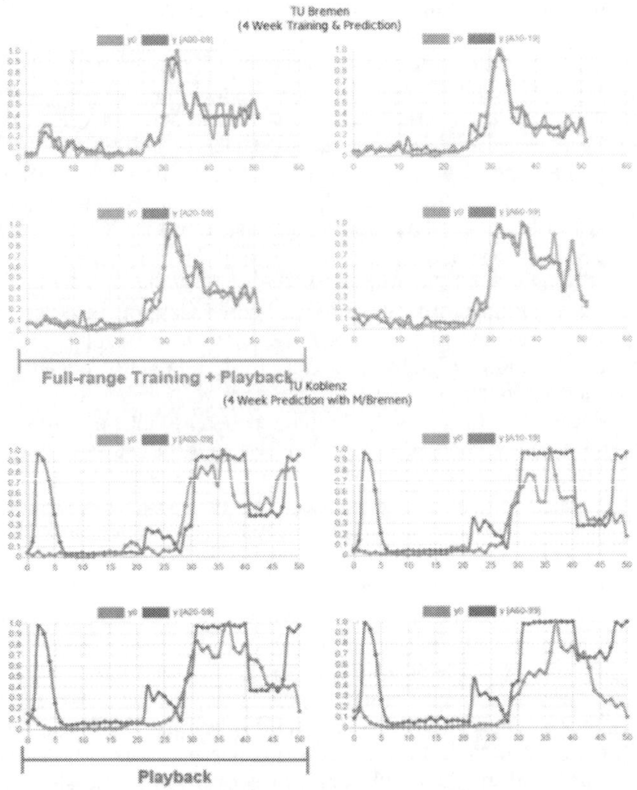


Figure 3. Playback of a domain-specific predictive system-level model derived from entire data series of longitudinal infection case rate development from real-world data (Top) Four week prediction ($\Delta$=4w) for TU Bremen with respect to four population age ranges (Bottom) Model trained with TU Bremen data and applied to data from TU Koblenz [x: week, y: normalised infection case rate numbers, y0: reference data , y: predicted]

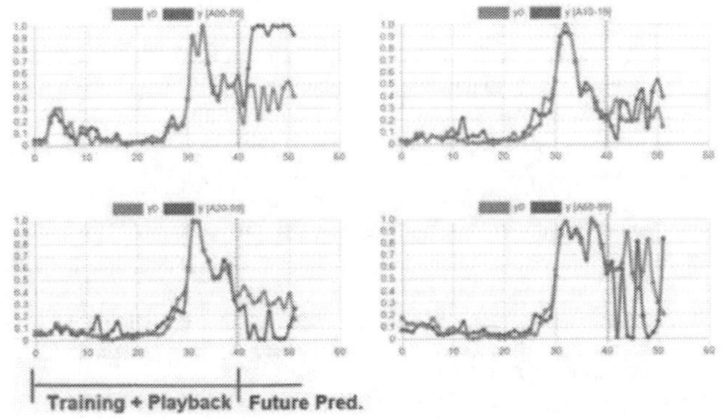


Figure 4. Future estimation of the same domain-specific predictive system-level modelling derived from the half of the data series (cut-off at week 40) of longitudinal infection case rate development from real-world data (Top) Four week prediction ($\Delta$=4w) for TU Bremen with respect to four population age ranges [x: week, y: normalised infection case rate numbers, y0: reference data , y: predicted]

But if a model trained for one domain is applied to data of another domain the prediction shows very high prediction errors and peaks, shown for the TU Koblenz. This result shows the requirement for domain-specific simulation and surrogate modelling, and that the surrogate prediction model learned some longitudinal data structure that is not related to any pandemic model and behaviour (black box pitfall)! But the aim of the predictive modelling of aggregate variables is future prediction. To illustrate the impossibility of long-term future prediction the experiment was repeated but with a training only using the first half data set, show in Fig. 4. The predictor function diverges quickly after the last trained point and tends to oscillate.

### 2) *Simulation and Prediction*

The simulation was performed with the probabilistic and contextual CA representing one artificial TU domain. The CA was spatially partitioned into 6 logical regions, shown in Fig. 5 (a): Home, outside, working area, shopping area, schools, and culture/sports. Agents that want to change the region always pass the centred outside region. Each region is defined by a mobility scaling factor. The agent movement is either randomised or directed. The simulation addresses day-night cycles.

All agents return to their root home position at night. Fractions of agents migrate to different regions at different time slots. In contrast to the real-world prediction, the normalised accumulated infection case number is the aggregated system state variable that is measured and predicted by the trained surrogate model. The sensor input variables is the infection count *IC* (full age distribution) with an auxiliary variable, the derivation: $\langle IC, \delta IC/\delta t \rangle$. The output prediction variable is again $IC_{\Delta}$. The LSTM model has a layer configuration of [2,7,7,1] with two × 7 fully connected LSTM cell layers [10] (each cell with `memoryToMemory`, `inputToOutput`, and `inputToDeep` gates control), a sigmoid transfer function, and was trained periodically with multi-sequence learning.

A high prediction accuracy for $\Delta$=4 (arb. units) was achieved in playback mode (i.e., full-range training and replay prediction), as shown in Fig. 5 (b). But in contrast to the highly distorted and temporally biased real-word data predictions (with useless results), future prediction (of a second infection raise) can be predicted with high accuracy just by using past date only (cut-off point is here 30), as shown in Figure 5 (c). To conclude, the surrogate modelling of the CA/MAS system poses a high degree of generalisation (on the longitudinal scale), in contrast to the same model trained on real-world data.

The seed of the simulation was a population of 600 agents with a share of 5% infected agents. The cell placement is randomised. Some simulation runs (with same seed parameters) did not show a pandemic development. Without the (dependent) auxiliary variable, the prediction model could not be trained (no training convergence).

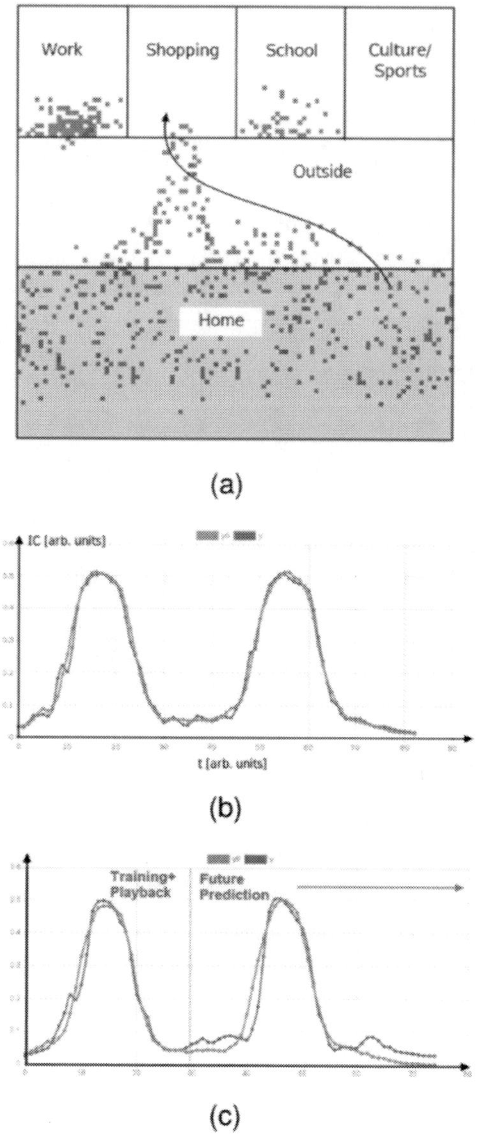


Figure 5. (a) CA simulation world with logical regions (b) Playback of predictive modelling of longitudinal infection cases development; full-range training (Δ=4 arb. units) from simulation data (c) Partial-range training and future prediction [x: time (arb. units), y: normalised infection case numbers, y0: reference data , y: predicted] Using the Template

In the real-data prediction case, there were already four correlated input variables (age range variables). There is still no longitudinal updated simulation (with real world data) and surrogate model calibration. The time scale is artificial and arbitrary.

## IV. Conclusion

The acquisition of real-world sensor data and the derivation of time-dependent system state observables can be a challenge. The measurement and the test sample distribution of real-world sensors are often distorted and biased, or sensor variables are nor accessible (on spatial and/or longitudinal scale). Pandemic situations are prominent examples. Simulations rely on accurate data for simulation world parametrisation and model calibration. Time-series prediction of system state variables is of high relevance for political and domestic decision making processes. We evaluated time-series prediction on real data from a RKI data base containing infection cases data rates of the COVID19 pandemic (54 weeks) using a LSTM neural network. Firstly, we showed a high prediction accuracy on the longitudinal axis (4 week prediction) in playback mode, but very low accuracy on spatial scale, i.e., by applying a trained model to another spatial domain, and for future predictions. Secondly, we concluded that the trained model do not base on any reasonable pandemic model and that the original RKI data base contains highly distorted and biased data (especially on longitudinal scale). In the next step we introduced a multi-domain hybrid and hierarchical agent-cellular automata simulation approach. The CA was partitioned into logical regions and agent mobility and interaction bases on a constrained lattice-gas model. The data collected from the simulation was again used for time-series prediction using a LSTM-ANN providing a surrogate model for the system state variable infection cases of the MAS-CA simulation. Again, a high accuracy for playback and forward predictions was achieved. But the simulation model cannot actually be applied to real-world data, and sensor calibration addressing longitudinal, measuring, and pandemic parameters have to be performed in future work to achieve a transfer to real-world data prediction. Finally, domain-specific variance must be improved and derived from real-world data. The surrogate modelling of the MAS-CA system poses a high degree of generalisation (on the longitudinal scale), in contrast to the same model trained on real-world data.

## References

[1] L. von Rueden, L., S. Mayer, R. Sifa, C. Bauckhage, J. Garckel, "Combining Machine Learning and Simulation to a Hybrid Modelling Approach: Current and Future Directions", IDA 2020, LNCS 12080, 2020.

[2] C. Angione, E. Silverman, E. Yaneske, "Using Machine Learning to Emulate Agent-Based Simulations", arXiv preprint arXiv:2005.02077. 2020.

[3] S. van der Hoog, "Surrogate Modelling in (and of) Agent-Based Models: A Prospectus", Comput. Ecom., vol. 53, 2019.

[4] F. Recknagel, "Applications of machine learning to ecological modelling," Ecological Modelling, vol. 146, 2001.

[5] V. C. Raykar et al., "Learning From Crowds," Journal of Machine Learning Research, vol. 11, 2010.

[6] S. Bosse, U. Engel, "Real-time Human-in-the-loop Simulation with Mobile Agents, Chat Bots, and Crowd Sensing for Smart Cities", Sensors (MDPI), 2019, doi: 10.3390/s19204356

[7] S. Saadatnejad, M. Oveisi, M. Hashemi, "LSTM-Based ECG Classification for Continuous Monitoring on Personal Wearable Devices", IEEE Journal Of Biomedical and Health Informatics, 2019.

[8] S. Ghosh, S. Bhattacharya, "Computational model on COVID-19 Pandemic using Probabilistic Cellular Automata", SN COMPUT. SCI. 2, 230, 2020

[9] Robert-Koch Institute, Germany, "Infection case data base", accessed on 19.3.2021, https://survstat.rki.de/Content/Query/Create.aspx

[10] Neataptic, https://github.com/wagenaartje/neataptic, last accessed 1.7.2021

# Emergence of a Multiple-Sourcing Strategy in a Buyer-Supplier Network: Effects of different Quantity-Quality and Quantity-Price Trade-Offs

Kristian Strmenik, Christian Mitsch, Friederike Wall, Gernot Mödritscher
*Department of Management Control and Strategic Management*
*University of Klagenfurt, Klagenfurt, Austria*
Email: {first.last}@aau.at

***Abstract*—In this paper, a buyer-supplier network is considered, which consists of a buyer and several suppliers who differ from each other in terms of quality and price. A buyer who puts its focus solely on quality pursues a different strategy than a price sensitive buyer, and, hence, allocates the procurement volume of a product in a different way among the suppliers, which in turn affects the supplier structure. Besides the buyer's strategic considerations, the suppliers also try to act strategically to maintain their competitiveness. We apply an agent-based simulation to analyze how different procurement volumes and levels of precision of the buyer's quality measurement system affect the supplier structure when (1) the suppliers' qualities and prices are modeled by generalized logistic functions and log-linear models, respectively, (2) the buyer uses a proportional volume allocation rule to allocate its procurement volume among the suppliers, and (3) the buyer learns its own quality-price preference via temporal difference learning. In order to express the buyer's quality-price preference, we apply an additive weighted sum model. The results show that, for low (high) procurement volumes, the buyer learns that sourcing from suppliers who pursue a high-quality (low-cost) leadership strategy leads to a more profitable supplier structure. But if the buyer's precision of quality measurement system decreases, these suppliers are not able to continue their position in the market and, therefore, lose market shares to suppliers who focus on a different competitive strategy.**

***Keywords*—Multiple-sourcing strategy; Buyer-supplier network; Volume allocation; Temporal difference learning.**

## I. INTRODUCTION

It is not uncommon for a firm to source goods and services from two or more suppliers at the same time. The sourcing strategy of a firm can be described by three essential criteria [3]: (1) a criterion for establishing a supplier base, (2) a criterion for selecting suppliers who receive an order from the firm, and (3) a criterion for allocating the quantity of goods among the suppliers. In this paper, we assume that a firm (hereafter referred to as the buyer) pursues a multiple-sourcing strategy, which is characterized by a proportional volume allocation rule. This means that each supplier receives at least a part of the total procurement volume. In addition, we assume that the criterion for allocating the procurement volume is only based on the supplier's product quality and the price that the supplier charges for the product. Moreover, the procurement volume needs to be allocated in a trustful way, so that the buyer's expectations and preferences regarding quality and price are met [2]. Within that, the preference whether quality or price is more important depends on different factors like, for example, the buyer's industry, the buyer's strategic positioning and business model, and the importance of the purchased product.

On the other hand, also the suppliers try to act strategically and position themselves well in the market to earn high rates of return, even if the industry structure is unfavourable. Following [10], the basis for this in the long-term is a competitive advantage of the supplier, which may either stem from differentiation or low cost. Both strategies require a fundamentally particular path, including the choice about the type of competitive advantage and the scope of the strategic target in which the supplier wants to achieve a competitive advantage. In a multiple-sourcing strategy the employed suppliers may differ from each other in terms of their objectives and competitive strategy, and, hence, the quality and price they are able to offer for a certain procurement volume.

The paper focuses on a possible quantity-quality trade-off, which might exist between the supplier's quality and the requested quantity. This trade-off indicates the responsiveness of quality to changes in volume and implies that with an increased volume the supplier is not able to maintain its level of quality, which will subsequently drop to a lower level. A quantity-quality trade-off might stem from technological reasons, for example, increasing the operating speed to produce more pieces or using less-skilled workers to meet the higher demand. Ultimately, this may result in a lower quality. Besides this trade-off, we assume that depending on the allocated procurement volume, suppliers may offer the buyer different price reductions.

The main objective of this paper is to investigate *how different procurement volumes affect the buyer's supplier structure when (1) the suppliers are heterogeneous with respect to the above-mentioned quantity-quality and quantity-price trade-offs, (2) the buyer pursues a multiple-sourcing strategy, and (3) the buyer learns its own quality-price preference based on its supplier environment.*

In certain situations, the observed quality of a product may not match the agreed quality because, for example, it might result from an imperfect buyer quality perception. Therefore, we extend our research question to *how the model reacts when imperfect quality is imperfectly measured by the buyer's quality measurement system.*

To answer our research questions, an agent-based simulation is set up, which captures a buyer and three heterogeneous (in terms of quality and price) suppliers. In particular, we describe the suppliers' qualities and prices by generalized logistic functions and log-linear models, respectively. To express the buyer's preference regarding quality and price, we apply an additive weighted sum model and, in order to model the buyer's multiple-sourcing strategy, a proportional volume allocation rule is used. Last but not least, we model the buyer's learning process via temporal difference learning.

The remainder of our paper is organized as follows. In Section 2, we review the literature regarding to sourcing strategies and volume allocations. In Section 3, we introduce our agent-based model, explain the model specifications, and introduce the buyer's learning method for learning its quality-price preference. The parameter settings for our simulation experiments are explained in Section 4. In Section 5, we present and discuss our results. Section 6 contains concluding remarks and suggests possible directions for future research.

## II. Related Research

Several studies have been conducted on the topic of volume allocation discussing the benefits of certain sourcing strategies and suggesting using different criteria in case of a multiple-sourcing strategy. [12] presents a model to optimize the allocation of volumes among suppliers by considering different cost factors. The authors conclude that, if the reliability of the suppliers is low, the buyer should consider a multiple-sourcing strategy. [3] proposes a supplier selection and volume allocation model where minimum order quantities and supplier capacities are considered. The authors find out that, if suppliers are incapacitated, the preferred strategy of the buyer is to source the product from multiple suppliers. However, the largest part of the required volume should be allocated to the least cost supplier and only marginal quantities to all other suppliers. [8] introduces a model of quality selection in an imperfectly competitive market considering quantity-quality trade-offs with constant values and studies its implications.In his findings, the author shows that the stronger the relationship between these two factors is, the more sales are shifted from the high to the low quality supplier [8]. [13] set up an agent-based simulation and take the assumption of [8] work to extend the literature on volume allocation, taking into account the impact of a non-linear trade-off between quantity and quality on the buyer's supplier structure. With their simulation experiment, they find out that, in cases where the buyer has to allocate large procurement volumes, a proportional volume allocation mechanism that only considers the suppliers' qualities leads to stronger oscillations of the supplier volumes. To mitigate this phenomenon, the buyer should form its expectations not only based on short-term perception, but on a more sophisticated method by allowing adaptive expectations. In addition, the authors are also considering additional indicators such as prices in order to stabilize the behaviour of the buyer's volume allocation.

## III. The Model

### A. Overview

We consider a buyer-supplier network, which is characterized by a buyer who is ordering the same procurement volume of a certain product in every time period and different suppliers who are offering the demanded product. Each supplier is characterized by a non-linear quantity-quality and quantity-price trade-off. Table I gives an overview of the before-mentioned trade-off relationships of suppliers, which we investigate in our model.

TABLE I
TRADE-OFF RELATIONSHIPS OF DIFFERENT SUPPLIER TYPES.

| competitive strategy | quantity-quality trade-off | quantity-price trade-off |
|---|---|---|
| quality leadership | high | low |
| 'stuck in the middle' | medium | medium |
| cost leadership | low | high |

Moreover, we take into account the possibility that the buyer puts more emphasis either on quality or on price, or to consider both as equally important while allocating the procurement volume among the suppliers. To get a relation between quantity and quality, we apply a generalized logistic function, which has an S-shaped form. This function type corresponds to our before-mentioned assumption that with an increase of the quantity, the supplier is not able to maintain its level of quality, which will subsequently drop to a lower quality level. S-shaped functions are very flexible and have essential properties so that they are often used, e.g., in neutral network learning methods as an activation function [9] or in biological growth models for animal sciences and forestry [6]. In our paper, we model the correlation between quantity and price with a log-linear model. A log-linear model can be used to describe, for example, the cost reduction in manufacturing, specifically, in areas with repetitive procedures such as production plants (e.g., [1]). Further we incorporate price reductions depending on the allocated procurement volume.

Finally, to express the buyer's preference regarding quality and price, we apply an additive weighted sum model, which is commonly used in multi-attribute decision making [4][15]. This type of model easily allows the buyer to put more weight either on quality or on price, or to consider both as equally important. The weight parameter in the additive weighted sum model is determined via temporal difference learning, a progressive learning process that comes from the area of reinforcement learning. With this type of learning, the buyer tries a variety of actions to find out, which of them seem to be the best. The big challenge of this learning approach is that the buyer has to exploit what it has already learned in order to receive high rewards, but it also has to explore in order to find better actions that may earn higher rewards in the future.

*B. Model specifications*

We suppose that the buyer initially, without placing an order, requests each supplier to submit an offer stating the quality and the price for the requested quantity. After receiving this initial information, the buyer allocates the procurement volume according to its quality-price preference among the suppliers. Following the delivery of the supplier volumes, the buyer imperfectly observes the quality of the suppliers and captures the price. In order to update the supplier volumes for the next order period, the buyer weights the observed quality and the captured price according to its quality-price preference. The sequence of events is sketched in Figure 1.

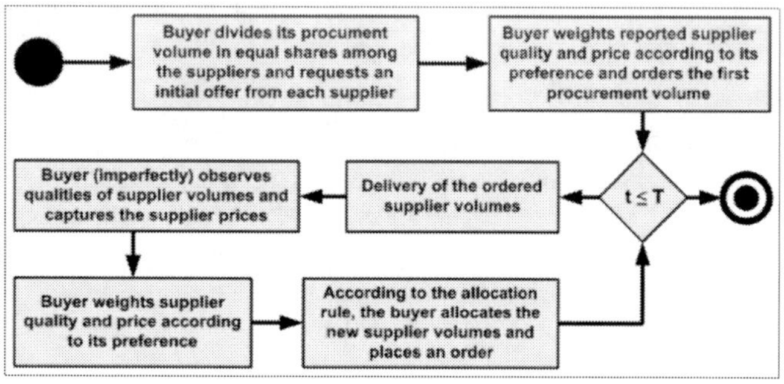


Figure 1. Sequence of events.

**Buyer's procurement volume**

We consider a buyer (abbreviated to $B$ in formulas) who plans to allocate a constant procurement volume $X \in \mathbb{R}^+$ of a certain product among multiple suppliers in each period $t \in \{1, ..., T\} \subset \mathbb{N}$ of the entire observation time $T$. The buyer selects $m \in \mathbb{N}$ suppliers (abbreviated to $S$ in formulas) for the delivery of the product, whereby the sum of the individual supplier volumes $x^S_{i,t} \in \mathbb{R}^+$ of $m$ suppliers defines the buyer's procurement volume

$$X = \sum_{i=1}^{m} x^S_{i,t} \, . \tag{1}$$

**Supplier quality**

Each supplier is characterized by a quality function, which is described by a generalized logistic function, sometimes called Richards [11] curve. This S-shaped curve characteristic matches with our assumption that an increase in volume leads to a loss of quality and vice versa. Hence, each supplier's quality function is determined by

$$q^S_{i,t}(x^S_{i,t}) = H_i - \frac{H_i - G_i}{1 + C_i \cdot e^{-k_i \cdot x^S_{i,t}}} \tag{2}$$

where $q^S_{i,t} \in (0,1)$ denotes the quality of the $i$'th supplier at time $t$. The quality parameters $(H_i, G_i, C_i, k_i) \in \mathbb{R}^4$ are set exogenously for each supplier at the very beginning of a simulation run. The parameter $G_i$ ($H_i$) refers to the lower (upper) asymptote of the quality curve, while $C_i$ is related to the quality in point $x^S_{i,t} = 0$, and $k_i$ represents the logistic growth rate (or, in a negative sense, the logistic shrinkage factor). The quality parameters $H_i$, $G_i$, $C_i$, and $k_i$ are purposefully designed so that the suppliers represent our 'typology' of suppliers. For the sake of simplicity, we suppose that all four parameters do not change over time.

**Supplier price**

We consider that each supplier sets a price $p^S_{i,t} \in \mathbb{R}^+$ for the quantity $x^S_{i,t}$ allocated by the buyer. Based on the aforementioned quantity-price trade-off, a monotonically decreasing price function is considered. Since we assume that doubling the quantity leads to a price reduction of a certain value, we use Wright's [16] log-linear model to describe the supplier price

$$p^S_{i,t}(x_{i,t}) = p^M \cdot (x^S_{i,t} + 1)^{\frac{log(1-L_i)}{log(2)}} \, . \tag{3}$$

While $p^M \in \mathbb{R}^+$ corresponds to the market price of one unit, $L_i \in (0,1)$ denotes the supplier's relative price reduction. In regard to the experience curve effect, $L$ reflects the proportion reduction in the unit cost with each doubling in the cumulative procurement volume (see, e.g., [1]). This means that with a doubling of the supplier volume, the supplier price deceases by $L_i \cdot 100\%$. Similar to the quality parameters, we also set the price parameters ($p^M$, $L_i$) exogenously at the very beginning of a simulation run.

**Buyer's quality measurement**

After the ordered supplier volumes are delivered, the buyer imperfectly observes the quality $q^B_{i,t} \in (0,1)$ of the suppliers according to

$$q^B_{i,t} = q^S_{i,t} + Q_{i,t} \qquad \text{with } Q_{i,t} \overset{i.i.d.}{\sim} N(0, \sigma^2) \, . \tag{4}$$

We assume that there is a discrepancy between the actual quality $q^S_{i,t}$ and the observed quality $q^B_{i,t}$ , since the observed quality is noise-afflicted captured in a normally distributed random variable $Q_{i,t}$ with mean 0 and standard deviation $\sigma \in \mathbb{R}^+$, which reflects the buyer's precision of quality measurement.

**Buyer's quality-price preference**

To express the buyer's preference regarding quality and price, we use the following additive weighted sum model

$$w_{i,t} = \alpha_t \cdot q^B_{i,t} + (1 - \alpha_t) \cdot \frac{p^M - p^S_{i,t}}{p^M} \tag{5}$$

where the individual weight of the $i$'th supplier is denoted by $w_{i,t} \in (0,1)$. The term $(p^M - p^S_{i,t})/p^M$ can be interpreted as a relative price saving on the part of the buyer. $\alpha_t \in [0,1]$ and $(1 - \alpha_t)$ indicate the buyer's quality weight and buyer's price weight, respectively. Note, in our agent-based model, the parameter $\alpha_t$ is learned by the buyer using temporal difference learning (see Section III-C). A high (low) $\alpha_t$ indicates that the buyer puts more emphasis on quality (price) rather than on price (quality). Ultimately, a high individual weight $w_{i,t}$ implies that the buyer is generally content with the quality and price of the supplier.

**Volume allocation**

The procurement volume is allocated proportionately to all $m$ suppliers depending on their individual weights. Thus, the buyer's volume allocation rule is given by

$$x^S_{i,t+1} = \frac{w_{i,t}}{\sum_{i=1}^{m} w_{i,t}} X \, . \quad (6)$$

Since the buyer might pursue different objectives regarding quality and price, a bigger share of the total procurement volume may be allocated to suppliers with a high individual weight.

**Offer submission**

At the beginning of a simulation run (hereafter abbreviated to $t_1$), we assume that the buyer splits the procurement volume in equal shares among the suppliers.

$$x^S_{i,t_1} = \frac{X}{m} \quad (7)$$

The suppliers are requested to submit an offer, stating quality $q^S_{i,t_1}$ and price $p^S_{i,t_1}$ for the requested supplier volume $x^S_{i,t_1}$. After the initial submission, the buyer orders its first delivery in consideration of (5) and (6). Whenever the supplier volumes are delivered (apart from $t_1$), the buyer observes the quality of each supplier according to (4). After the observe quality and the captured price have been determined, the buyer allocates the next procurement volume in accordance with (5) and (6). This procedure continues until $t > T$.

*C. Learning method*

In our agent-based model, the buyer has to specify the quality weight $\alpha_t$ in the additive weighted sum model (5). For this purpose, we use a temporal difference learning approach, which was invented by Sutton [14] because we suppose that the buyer does not have enough resources and, especially, no prior knowledge of its suppliers' structure to provide an adequate model of its multiple-sourcing environment.

**Action-value function**

The simplest temporal difference learning approach is given by the following update rule

$$V_{t+1}[\alpha_t] = (1 - \beta_t) * V_t[\alpha_t] + \beta_t * (\pi_t + \gamma * V_t[\alpha_{t+1}]) \quad (8)$$

where $V_t[\alpha_t] \in \mathbb{R}$ denotes the action-value function of action $\alpha_t \in A \subset [0,1]$ with reward $\pi_t \in \mathbb{R}$, learning rate $\beta_t \in [0,1]$, and discount factor $\gamma \in [0,1)$. In the TD(0) method, the action $\alpha_t$ is a value from the discrete action space $A$ that corresponds to all possible buyer's quality-price preferences and, besides that, the values of the action-value function are stored in a lookup table (labelled with square brackets) initialized to be zero for all actions, i.e., there is no information about the buyer's preference for quality and price when the simulation is started. Further, the action-value function can also be read as a long-term memory vector of length $|A|$ accumulating the discounted rewards over the time of a simulation run and, in the TD(0) algorithm, only one value of the action-value function is updated in each time step, while all other V-values remain unchanged.

**Buyer's profit**

The reward in the update rule (8) corresponds to the buyer's profit

$$\pi_t = \sum_{i=1}^{m} x^S_{i,t} \cdot min(q^B_{i,t}, q^S_{i,t}) \cdot p^R - x^S_{i,t} \cdot p^S_{i,t} \quad (9)$$

with retail price $p^R \in \mathbb{R}^+$. The buyer's profit, which is revenue minus costs depends only on how much the buyer produces in its firm because quality and price are functions of the delivered quantity $x^S_{i,t}$. For the sake of simplicity, we suppose that products of poor quality are sorted out.

**Learning rate and learning time**

A very key part in temporal difference learning is the speed of learning things. At the beginning of a simulation run, the learning rate $\beta_t$ should be so high that any initial random fluctuations have only a minor impact and, on the other hand, $\beta_t$ should decrease with time to assure that the buyer finds a local optimum of its action-value function [14]. Therefore, we use a variable learning rate $\beta_t$ that decreases over time. The time or, more precisely, the number of time steps during which the buyer learns the parameter $\alpha_t$ is called the learning time $T_L \leq T$.

**Action-selection policy**

After the buyer has calculated the action-value function $V_t[.]$, the buyer tries to select an action $\alpha_{t+1}$ from its action space $A$ in order to maximize the sum of its discounted rewards, which are received over time. Thus, the buyer is confronted with the trade-off between choosing the current action and choosing a varied action with the prospect of a higher reward in the future. An easy and common action-selection policy is the so-called $\epsilon$-greedy policy, which means that with probability $(1 - \epsilon_t)$ the action with the highest $V_t[.]$ is chosen, while with probability $\epsilon_t \in [0,1]$ a random action is selected [14].

$$\alpha_{t+1} = \begin{cases} \underset{\alpha \in A}{argmax} \; V_t[\alpha] & \text{with probability } (1 - \epsilon_t) \\ \sim Unif(A) & \text{with probability } \epsilon_t \end{cases} \quad (10)$$

Furthermore, in our model, $\epsilon_t$ is a decreasing function of the time with the two properties that, at the beginning of a simulation run, $\epsilon_{t_1}$ is one which indicates that the action-selection is total random (pure exploration) and, in the end, $\epsilon_{T_L}$ is zero (pure exploitation) and, thus with probability one, the final learned action $\alpha_{T_L}$ leads to the highest value of the action-value function learned during the simulation run.

**Number of time steps after learning**

After the buyer has learned which quality-price preference is a good choice, the buyer's supplier structure is analyzed. For this purpose, more time steps are simulated in which the parameter $\alpha_t$ is unchanged. In the case, the buyer's quality measurement system works perfectly, i.e., $\sigma = 0$, the buyer's supplier structure stabilizes within $T_S \in \mathbb{N}$ time steps after learning. Since we are also interested in how the model reacts when imperfectly quality is imperfectly measured by the buyer's quality measurement system, i.e., $\sigma > 0$, further $T_E \in \mathbb{N}$ time steps are required to evaluate the stochastic simulation outcomes. This results in a total number of $T_L + T_S + T_E$ time steps of which only the last $T_E$ time steps are used to analyze the buyer's supplier structure.

## IV. Parameter Settings

We conduct our simulation experiments in two steps: (1) we start with the 'perfect scenario' in which there is no discrepancy between the actual quality and the observed quality. (2) we investigate further scenarios, called 'imperfect scenarios', to find out how the buyer's supplier structure changes when imperfect quality is imperfectly measured by the buyer's quality measurement system.

TABLE II
PARAMETER SETTINGS.

| **Exogenous parameters** | **Values/Types** | | |
|---|---|---|---|
| Time steps to learn the parameter $\alpha_t$ | $T_L = 100$ | | |
| Time steps to stabilize the allocation | $T_S = 10$ | | |
| Time steps to evaluate the outcome | $T_E = 10$ | | |
| Number of sim. runs | $N = 1000$ | | |
| Number of suppliers | $m = 3$ | | |
| Market price | $p^M = 1$ | | |
| Retail price | $p^R = 1$ | | |
| Supplier type | Type 1 | Type 2 | Type 3 |
| Supremum of $q^S_{i,t}$ | $H_1 = 1.0$ | $H_2 = 0.8$ | $H_3 = 0.6$ |
| Infimum of $q^S_{i,t}$ | $G_1 = 0.0$ | $G_2 = 0.0$ | $G_3 = 0.0$ |
| $q^S_{i,t}(x^S_{i,t} = 0)$ (in %) | $C_1 = 99$ | $C_2 = 79$ | $C_3 = 59$ |
| Logistic growth rate | $k_1 = 0.23$ | $k_2 = 0.109$ | $k_3 = 0.068$ |
| Inflection point | $x_1^{IP} = 20$ | $x_2^{IP} = 40$ | $x_3^{IP} = 60$ |
| Relative price reduction | $L_1 = 0.05$ | $L_2 = 0.10$ | $L_3 = 0.15$ |
| Action space | $A = \{0.0, 0.1, ..., 1.0\}$ | | |
| Discount factor | $\gamma = 0$ | | |
| Procurement volume | $X \in \{1, 2, ..., 100\}$ | | |
| Buyer's precision of quality measurement | $\sigma \in \{0, 0.01, 0.02, ..., 0.10\}$ | | |

**Supplier types**

In our paper, we focus on a small buyer-supplier network and, therefore, we distinguish only between three different supplier types (hereafter type 1, type 2, and type 3), which represent fictitious companies pursuing different competitive strategies. Supplier type 1 captures a company, which pursues a high-quality leadership strategy and, thus, seeks to be unique regarding the high level of quality of its product it offers to the buyer and that the buyer rewards this with a premium price. Supplier type 3, on the other hand, captures a company, which pursues a low-cost leadership strategy where cost advantages are essential to gain a high return and long-term success. Supplier type 2 is considered to capture a company that failed to achieve one of the above-mentioned generic strategies and can be, to put it in the words of [10], labelled as 'stuck in the middle'. Similar to supplier type 1, also supplier type 2's quality deteriorates with a higher procurement volume and falls below the quality of supplier type 3.

**Supplier quality**

Figure 2 depicts the quality functions of our three supplier types (for the quality parameters see Table II). We set the quality parameters as follows: The quality parameter $H_i$ corresponds to the quality that can be guaranteed with small volumes, while $G_i$ is associated with the worst quality that can occur. In order to obtain the quality parameters $C_i$ and $k_i$, we define the following two constraints: Parameter $C_i$ refers to the quality, if nothing is produced, i.e., $C_i = -(q_i^S(0) - G_i)/(q_i^S(0) - H_i)$. For simplicity, we assume $q_i^S(0) = H_i - 0.01$. Parameter $k_i$ can be obtained by solving $\frac{d^2}{dx_i^2} q_i^S(x_i) = 0$ or easier through $q_i^S(x_i^{IP}) = (H_i - G_i)/2$, which reflects the inflection point $x_i^{IP}$ of the quality function, i.e., up to this point, the quantity-quality trade-off (which is nothing more than the first derivative of the quality function, i.e., $\frac{d}{dx_i} q_i^S(x_i)$) increases and, concurrently, the quality drops to half of its value. Both equations lead to the same solution, namely $k_i = ln(C_i)/x_i^{IP}$.

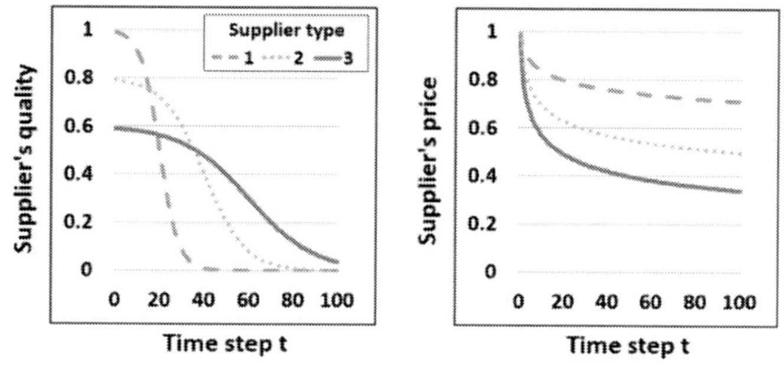


Figure 2. Suppliers' quality and price functions in our scenarios.

Incidentally, in the inflection point $x_i^{IP}$, the quantity-quality trade-off (hereafter abbreviated to $\tau_i^{IP}$) finds its maximum because the first derivative is bell shaped with a peak at $x_i^{IP}$. For the sake of simplicity, we set the inflection points $x_1^{IP} = 20$, $x_2^{IP} = 40$, and $x_3^{IP} = 60$ or rather their quantity-quality trade-offs $\tau_1^{IP} = -0.0575$, $\tau_2^{IP} = -0.0218$, and $\tau_3^{IP} = -0.0102$ for our scenarios (see Table II).

**Supplier price**

The suppliers do not only distinguish from each other in terms of the quality, but also in terms of the price they charge. In regard to the supplier price considered in our model, Figure 2 depicts the price functions for our three supplier types. As mentioned before, a supplier price curve results, for instance, from a combination of various effects of learning, volume, and specialization. Therefore, we set the suppliers' price parameters in such a way that supplier type 2 can offer the buyer a relative price reduction that is twice as high as that of type 1, while supplier type 3 can provide a relative price reduction that corresponds to the sum of supplier type 1 and 2. This way of proceeding is also applied to the quality functions where the inflection points of the quality functions are determined. Note that our price (quality) function has a non-linear quantity-price (-quality) trade-off and, hence, cannot be expressed by a constant exogenous parameter. For the sake of simplicity, we suppose that the price of supplier type 1/2/3 decreases by $5\%/10\%/15\%$ each time the volume is doubled.

**Action space**

Next, we discuss the choice of the discrete action space $A$. If the number of possible quality-price preferences is small, the buyer's supplier structure cannot be investigated thoroughly, and, on the other hand, if the size of the action space is chosen too large then learning is slowed. Since we guess that the buyer can only differentiate between a limited number of quality-price preferences, we vary the parameter $\alpha_t \in A$ between 0 and 1 in steps of 0.1. Consequently, the buyer has eleven possible quality-price preferences.

**Action-selection policy**

For the action-selection policy in our model, we apply a monotonically decreasing $\epsilon$-greedy policy (see Figure 3). To do this, we decide for a quadratic function ($\epsilon_t = at^2 + bt + c$).

$$\epsilon_t = -\frac{97}{970200} \cdot t^2 - \frac{1}{323400} \cdot t + \frac{9703}{9702} \qquad (11)$$

To determine $a$, $b$, and $c$, we use the boundary conditions $\epsilon_{t=1} = 1$, $\epsilon_{t=T_L} = 0$, and $\epsilon_{t=T_L/2} = 0.75$, where the learning time $T_L$ is set to 100. In order to achieve a higher level of exploration at the beginning than at the end, we set the third boundary condition to 0.75, which results in a degree of exploration of about $66\%$ during a simulation run. Note that the area under the $\epsilon_t$ curve represents the degree of exploration.

**Learning rate**

With respect to the aforementioned learning rate properties, we use a linear function ($\beta_t = a + bt$).

$$\beta_t = \frac{111}{110} - \frac{1}{110} \cdot t \qquad (12)$$

To solve $a$ and $b$, we apply the boundary conditions $\beta_{t=1} = 1$ and $\beta_{t=T_L} = 0.1$, where the learning rate at the end of the learning time is fixed to 0.1 and this value is small enough so that, in all scenarios, the action-value function converges to a local optimum.

**Discount factor**

Another exogenous learning parameter in temporal difference learning is the discounting factor $\gamma$. Since we limit our research to a manageable number of scenarios, we set $\gamma$ to zero, which means, that the buyer does not take future rewards into account.

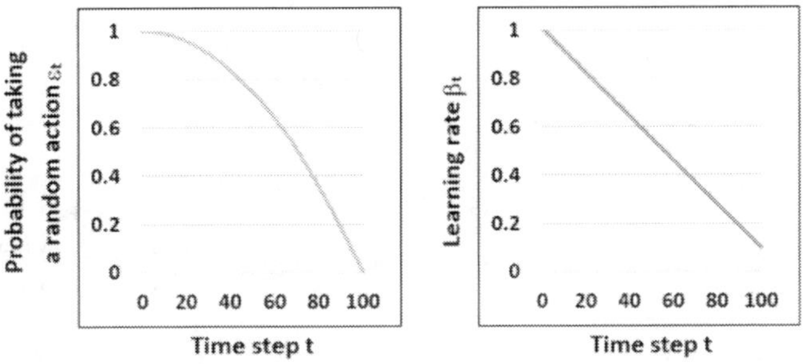


Figure 3. The left-hand-side graph shows the $\epsilon_t$-greedy policy and the right-hand-side graph depicts the learning rate $\beta_t$.

**Number of time steps and number of simulation runs**

In our simulation experiment, the number of time steps to learn the parameter $\alpha_t$ in one simulation run is determined, on the one hand, based on the size of the action space $A$ and, on the other hand, based on the degree of exploration. Our pre-generated simulations suggest a learning time of 100 to guarantee that the action-value function converges to a local optimum.

After the complexity of learning the parameter $\alpha_t$ has been determined by the cardinality of the action space and the degree of exploration, further $T_S$ time steps are run through until the buyer's volume allocation converges. According to our pre-generated simulations, 10 time steps are enough to stabilize the behavior of the buyer's volume allocation in each scenario, hence $T_S = 10$. After the buyer's volume allocation has stabilized, only the buyer's quality measurement system has an impact and, therefore, we simulate further 10 time steps to take the stochastic fluctuations into account, hence $T_E = 10$. Note that, in all our examined scenarios, only the last $T_E$ time steps are used to analyze the buyer's supplier structure.

Finally, we perform 1000 simulation runs for each scenario because, due to the coefficient of variance (ratio of standard deviation to the mean), 1000 simulation runs are sufficient to express the precision and repeatability of this simulation experiment.

**Procurement volume and buyer's precision of quality measurement system**

Besides the fixed exogenous parameters, we vary the procurement volume $X$ and the buyer's precision of quality measurement system $\sigma$, which are also set exogenously at the very beginning of a simulation run. In particular, we model the procurement volume between 1 and 100 in steps of 1, because up to about 100 the buyer's profit in the scenarios is positive, and, in addition, we study a number of different values of $\sigma$ ranging from 0 to 0.1 in steps of 0.01 in order to examine the effects of the buyer's suppler structure when the buyer's quality measurement system is not working perfect.

## V. Results and Discussion

In this section, we analyze the results of our agent-based simulation in two main steps: (1) we present the results of our perfect scenarios in which the quality is perfect measured by the buyer's quality measurement system. (2) we analyze the imperfect scenarios when there is a discrepancy between the actual quality and the observed quality, i.e., the buyer's quality measurement system works imperfectly.

In each scenario, we start by analyzing the quality-price preference parameter $\alpha_t$ that the buyer learns during its learning time. Then, we study the buyer's supplier structure by comparing the suppliers' volumes $x^S_{i,t}$ relative to each other, because this allows for an easy interpretation and comparison, and this is also the main objective of this paper.

### A. *Results of our perfect scenario with $\sigma = 0$*

**Buyer's quality-price preference**

We start by analyzing the buyer's quality-price preference $\alpha_t$ in our perfect scenario. Figure 4 depicts the means and standard deviations of $\alpha_t$ from 1000 simulation runs, whereby an extract for the means, standard deviations, and also the 95% percentiles of $\alpha_t$ from $X = 17$ to 23 is given in Table III. Interestingly, we identify a tipping point at around $X = 20$ where the buyer's preference changes from quality to price. Up to that tipping point, the buyer puts more emphasis on quality rather than on price and, from which onwards, the buyer's quality-price preference $\alpha_t$ gets lower, which means that the buyer prefers a supplier who charge a low price. In the tipping point, the quality-price preference is approximately 0.5, which implies that the buyer attaches equal emphasis on quality and price.

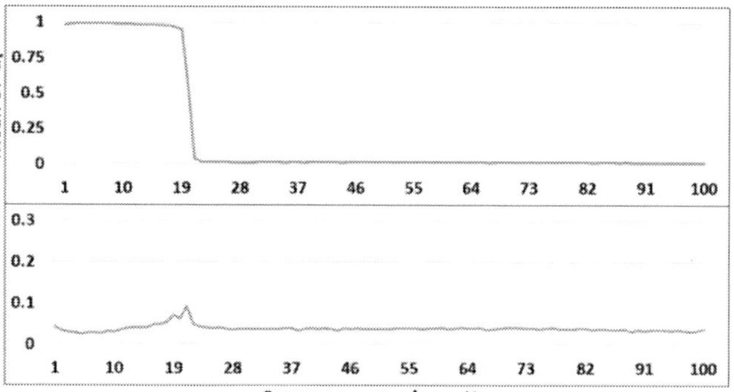


Figure 4. Means and standard deviations of the buyer's learned quality-price preferences $\alpha_t$ in our perfect scenario with $\sigma = 0$ from $X = 1$ to 100.

TABLE III
MEANS, STANDARD DEVIATIONS, AND THE 95% PERCENTILES OF THE BUYER'S QUALITY-PRICE PREFERENCES $\alpha_t$ IN OUR PERFECT SCENARIO WITH $\sigma = 0$ FROM $X = 17$ TO 23.

| $X$ | Mean of $\alpha_t$ | Std. dev. of $\alpha_t$ | 95% percentile of $\alpha_t$ |
|---|---|---|---|
| 17 | 0.98 | 0.05 | [0.9 − 1.0] |
| 18 | 0.97 | 0.05 | [0.8 − 1.0] |
| 19 | 0.95 | 0.07 | [0.8 − 1.0] |
| 20 | 0.52 | 0.06 | [0.4 − 0.6] |
| 21 | 0.04 | 0.09 | [0.0 − 0.3] |
| 22 | 0.02 | 0.05 | [0.0 − 0.2] |
| 23 | 0.02 | 0.04 | [0.0 − 0.1] |

In addition, it seems that the quality-price preference $\alpha_t$ slowly converges towards a value close to zero when the procurement volume increases. This would also be plausible because, if the procurement volume $X$ becomes larger, the qualities of all three suppliers drop to almost zero, while the suppliers' prices still differ from each other. In such a case, the buyer prefers a supplier who charge a low price.

**Buyer's supplier structure**

In the next step, we analyze the buyer's supplier structure. For this purpose, we compare the suppliers' volumes $x^S_{i,t}$ relative to each other. Figure 5 reports the means of $x^S_{i,t}$. In the tipping point $X = 20$, every supplier type gets approximately a third of the procurement volume (specifically, $x^S_{1,t} = 35.58\%$, $x^S_{2,t} = 33.82\%$, and $x^S_{3,t} = 30.60\%$). This volume allocation appears plausible as far as the buyer attaches equal emphasis on quality and price. To the left of the tipping point, i.e., $X < 20$, supplier type 1 receives about 42% and supplier type 3 about 25% of the procurement volume and, for $X > 20$, the buyer's supplier structure turns over so that the relative supplier volume of supplier type 1 (type 3) slowly converges towards 16% (49%) when the procurement volume increases (cf. Figure 5). Only supplier type 2 always receives about 34% of the procurement volume.

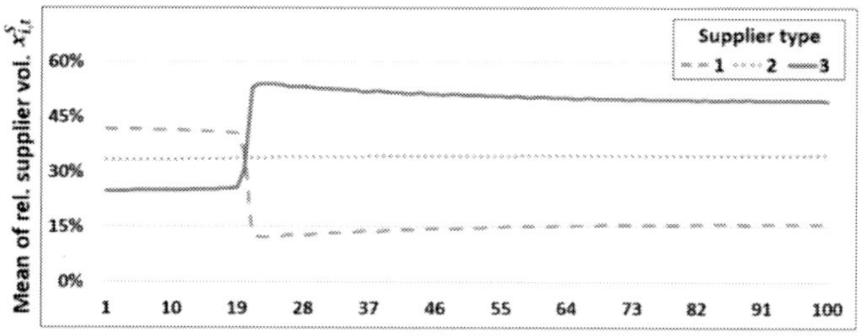


Figure 5. Means of the relative suppliers' volumes $x^S_{i,t}$ in our perfect scenario with $\sigma = 0$ from $X = 1$ to 100.

**Simulation results over time**

Conclusively, we investigate the quality-price preference and the supplier structure of the buyer for changes over time. In the first step, we look at the buyer's quality-price preference $\alpha_t$. Figure 6 represents the buyer's learned quality-price preferences $\alpha_t$ over time. For procurement volumes lower than the tipping point, $\alpha_t$ slowly grows towards one, while for $X > 20$, $\alpha_t$ slowly approaches zero. Note that the buyer's quality-price preference remains unchanged after learning.

In the next step, we look at the buyer's supplier structure and, especially, how does the buyer's supplier structure shape the way an equilibrium-state is reached over time. For this purpose, we depict the means of the relative suppliers' volumes $x^S_{i,t}$. Figure 7 shows how an equilibrium-state is achieved when the procurement volume is given by $X = 10$, $X = 20$ (the tipping point), and $X = 30$. For lower procurement volumes ($X < 20$), the buyer needs approximately 1/3 of

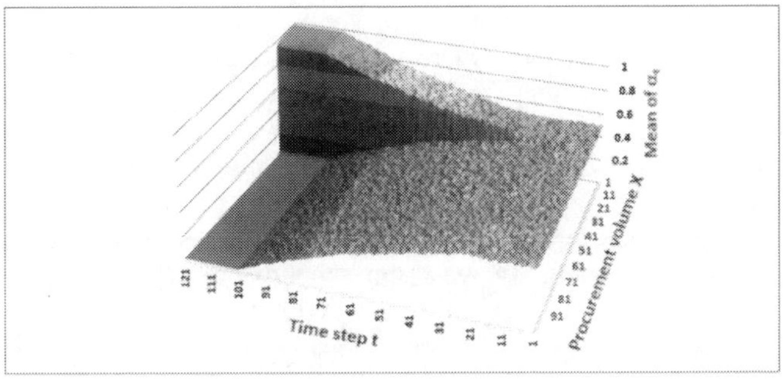


Figure 6. Means of the buyer's learned quality-price preferences $\alpha_t$ in our perfect scenario with $\sigma = 0$ from $X = 1$ to 100 and $t = 1$ to 120.

the learning time to separate the supplier types 1 and 3, while for larger procurement volumes ($X > 20$), the separation of suppliers proceeds much faster. In the tipping point, there is only a small separation, which means that all suppliers receive approximately the same proportion of the buyer's procurement volume.

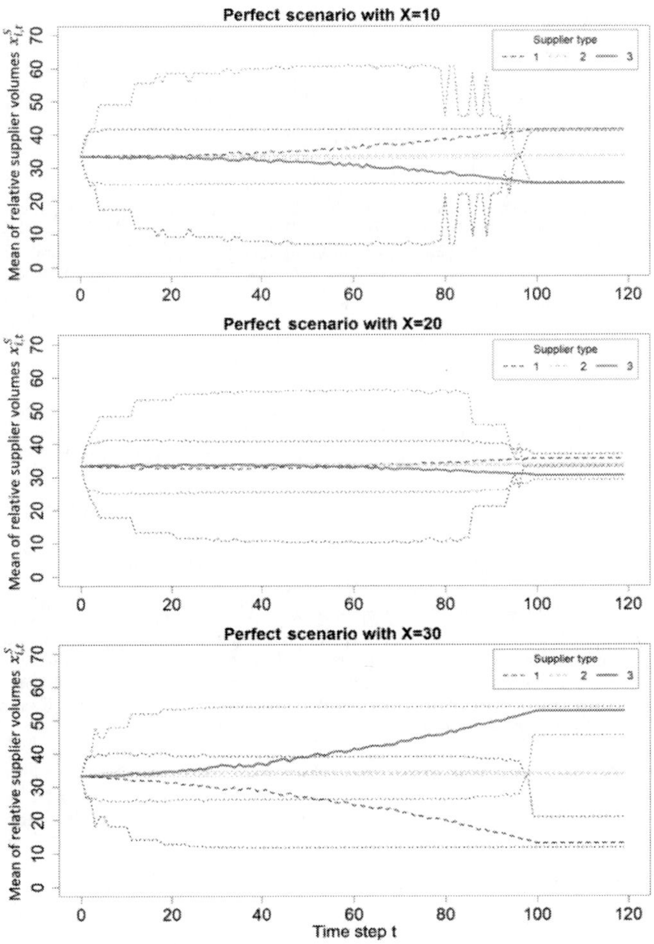


Figure 7. Means of the relative suppliers' volumes $x^S_{i,t}$ for selected procurement volumes with $\sigma = 0$ from $t = 1$ to 120. Means are represented by thick lines, while the 95% percentiles are displayed by thin lines.

## B. *Results of our imperfect scenarios with $\sigma > 0$*

For the so far presented results, a perfect level of precision of the buyer's quality measurement was considered. In this section, we investigate scenarios in which the precision of the buyer's quality measurement is affected by noise and, hence, the quality is imperfectly measured.

### Buyer's quality-price preference

Once again, we start with the buyer's quality-price preference. Figure 8 depicts the curve progressions of $\alpha_t$ from $\sigma = 0$ (minor differences on average between the actual quality and the observed quality) to $\sigma = 0.1$ (major differences).

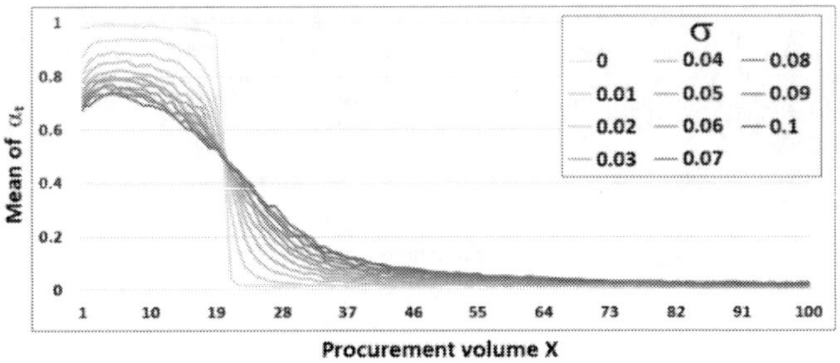


Figure 8. Means of the buyer's learned quality-price preferences $\alpha_t$, whereby $\sigma$ varies between 0 (light green) to 0.1 (dark green) from $X = 1$ to 100.

### Buyer's supplier structure

Next, we plot the means of the relative suppliers' volumes $x^S_{i,t}$ from $\sigma = 0$ to $\sigma = 0.1$ (see Figure 9). Based on the curve progressions in Figure 9, the buyer's supplier structure becomes more stable because the value difference around the tipping point becomes smaller. In the case of $\sigma = 0.1$, the buyer's supplier structure is smooth enough so that there is no longer a jumping behavior around $X = 20$.

In comparison to the perfect scenario (see Table IV), supplier type 1 receives about 3.4% less (3.9% more) procurement volume to the left (right) of the tipping point and, thus, supplier type 1 loses (gains) market shares. Oppositely, supplier type 3 obtains about 3.4% more (3.8% less) procurement volume to the left (right) of the tipping point and, hence, supplier type 3 gains (loses) a greater share of the market than the other two suppliers. Note that, again, supplier type 2 receives around 34% of the total procurement volume and, on average, supplier type 2 is able to continue its position in the market. Summarized, if the buyer's precision of quality

TABLE IV
MEANS OF THE RELATIVE SUPPLIERS' VOLUMES $x^S_{i,t}$ TO THE LEFT AND RIGHT OF THE TIPPING POINT $X = 20$ WITH $\sigma = 0$ AND $\sigma = 0.1$.

| | $X < 20$ | | | $X > 20$ | | |
|---|---|---|---|---|---|---|
| | $\sigma = 0$ | $\sigma = 0.1$ | Diff. | $\sigma = 0$ | $\sigma = 0.1$ | Diff. |
| $x^S_{1,t}$ | 41.3% | 37.9% | −3.4% | 14.8% | 18.7% | 3.9% |
| $x^S_{2,t}$ | 33.5% | 33.5% | 0.0% | 34.4% | 34.3% | −0.1% |
| $x^S_{3,t}$ | 25.2% | 28.6% | 3.4% | 50.8% | 47.0% | −3.8% |

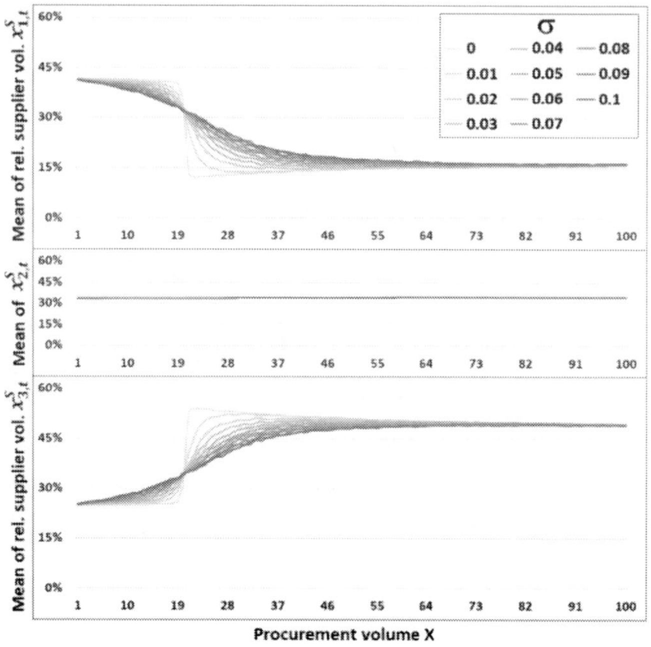


Figure 9. Means of the relative suppliers' volumes $x^S_{i,t}$ with $\sigma = 0$ to $0.1$ from $X = 1$ to $100$.

measurement system decreases, supplier type 1 benefits from large procurement volumes, whereas supplier type 3 profits from small procurement volumes.

## VI. CONCLUSIONS

In our paper, we analyze the effects of different procurement volumes and levels of precision of the buyer's quality measurement system on the buyer's supplier structure in a multiple-sourcing environment using an agent-based simulation.

The results of our simulation experiment show that, in case the buyer has to learn its own quality-price preference via temporal difference learning, the buyer puts more emphasis on quality than on price when a small procurement volume is allocated among the existing suppliers. On the other hand, the higher the procurement volume allocated to the suppliers, the more important the price that is offered to the buyer. In such a case, the buyer is considered to pursue a cost leadership strategy searching for sources of cost advantage including, for instance, economies of scale, proprietary technology, preferential access to raw materials, and other factors.

Interestingly, we identify a tipping point at which the buyer's preference behaviour abruptly changes from quality to price. Up to that tipping point, the buyer puts more emphasis on quality rather than on price and, from which onwards, the buyer prefers a supplier who charges a low price. In the tipping point, the buyer attaches equal emphasis on quality and price.

Furthermore, we find that the poorer the precision of the quality measurement system and the lower the total procurement volume, the less the buyer orders from suppliers who focus on a high-quality leadership strategy. As a consequence, these suppliers lose part of their market shares to other suppliers. Such noises in the buyer's quality measurement system are at the expense of these suppliers, however the noise stabilizes the buyer's supplier structure, so that there is no longer a jumping behavior. Moreover, we find that the buyer separates the different supplier types much faster when the procurement volume is large and the quality measurement system works perfectly.

Finally, there are some limitations in this research: (1) for the sake of simplicity, we assume that the buyer only employs a limited number of suppliers and, in particular, that the suppliers' parameters are constant over time, which may not adequately represent the true market situation in a multiple-sourcing environment. (2) the buyer only makes decisions based on the suppliers' quality and price in order to allocate the procurement volume among the suppliers. (3) the suppliers do not communicate between each other nor they have the possibility to outsource part of their volumes to other suppliers. We believe this model provides some useful insights into the sourcing behaviour of a buyer who allocates different procurement volumes to suppliers who pursue different competitive strategies.

## REFERENCES

[1] M. J. Anzanello, and F. S. Fogliatto, "Learning curve models and applications: Literature review and research directions," International Journal of Industrial Ergonomics, vol. 41, no. 5, pp. 573–583, 2011.
[2] J. Asker, and E. Cantillon, "Procurement when price and quality matter," The Rand journal of economics, vol. 41, no. 1, pp. 1–34, 2010.
[3] G. J. Burke, J. E. Carrillo, and A. J. Vakharia, "Single versus multiple supplier sourcing strategies," European journal of operational research, vol. 182, no. 1, pp. 95–112, 2007.
[4] R. L. Keeney, and H. Raiffa, "Decisions with multiple objectives: preferences and value trade-offs," Cambridge university press, 1993.
[5] S. E. Kimes, "The basics of yield management," Cornell Hotel and Restaurant Administration Quarterly, vol. 30, no. 3, pp. 14–19, 1989.
[6] P. R. Koya, and A. T. Goshu, "Generalized mathematical model for biological growths," Open Journal of Modelling and Simulation, 2013.
[7] M. Lin, Jr. H. C. Lucas, and G. Shmueli, "Research commentary–too big to fail: large samples and the p-value problem," Information Systems Research, vol. 24, no. 4, pp. 906–917, 2013.
[8] B. C. McCannon, "The quality-quantity trade-off," Eastern Economic Journal, vol. 34, no. 1, pp. 95–100, 2008.
[9] T. M. Mitchell, "Machine learning," 1st ed. New York, NY: McGraw-Hill Education, 1997.
[10] M. E. Porter, "The Competitive Advantage: Creating and sustaining superior performance," NY: Free Press, 1985.
[11] F. Richards, "A flexible growth function for empirical use," Journal of experimental Botany, vol. 10, no. 2, pp. 290–301, 1959.
[12] A. J. Ruiz-Torres, and F. Mahmoodi, "A supplier allocation model considering delivery failure, maintenance and supplier cycle costs," International Journal of Production Economics, vol. 103, no. 2, pp. 755–766, 2006.
[13] K. Strmenik, F. Wall, C. Mitsch, and G. Mödritscher, "Volume allocation in multi-sourcing: effects of the quantity-quality trade-off," Central European Journal of Operations Research, 2020.
[14] R. S. Sutton, "Learning to predict by the methods of temporal differences," Machine learning, vol. 3, no. 1, pp. 9–44, 1988.
[15] J. Wallenius, J. S. Dyer, P. C. Fishburn, R. E. Steuer, S. Zionts, and K. Deb, "Multiple criteria decision making, multiattribute utility theory: Recent accomplishments and what lies ahead," Management science, vol. 54, no. 7, pp. 1336–1349, 2008.
[16] T. P. Wright, "Factors affecting the cost of airplanes," Journal of the aeronautical sciences, vol. 3, no. 4, pp. 122–128, 1936.

# A Framework to Specify Agent-Based Models Using ODD* Protocol

Cédric Grueau
*Department of Systems and Informatics*
*EST Setúbal, Polytechnic Institute of Setúbal*
Setúbal, Portugal
0000-0003-3445-4070

Thyago Romagna Bendo
*Department of Systems and Informatics*
*EST Setúbal, Polytechnic Institute of Setúbal*
Setúbal, Portugal
0000-0003-2164-4270

Alan Gavioli
*Paraná Federal University Of Technology*
Medianeira, Brazil
0000-0002-5325-0754

João Junior Araújo
*Department of Computer Sciences*
*NOVA School of Science and Technology*
Caparica, Portugal
0000-0001-5914-1631

***Abstract*—The use of Agent-Based Models (ABM) is a popular approach to develop simulations in fields such as social sciences, geography and natural sciences. However, due to the complexity of the models, the sharing of models' specification becomes an arduous process, which makes it difficult to validate and replicate this type of model. To assist in this process, experts from the domain have developed the ODD (Overview, Design concepts, Details) protocol to help systematize ABM descriptions. However, because it is a protocol, the latitude allowed in the description of the models and the format in which these descriptions are made only address part of the problem. On the one hand, it may remain difficult to understand the description, and on the other hand, the access and processing of the ODD descriptions are still a manual task. To solve the problem, a framework, based on an ontology, was developed to allow traceability of ABM described with ODD. Concepts from other metadata initiatives, such as Dublin Core and Codemeta, were included to add important data to the ODD protocol. An application was developed to facilitate the access to the models, which allows the analysis of the data source of the model and the extraction of the protocol components. An API was also developed that gives access to ABM descriptions and promotes the processing of ABM descriptions. The application is ready for a series of tests to validate our approach, the usability of the application and the utility of the framework.**

***Index Terms*—ODD Protocol; ODD+D; ODD+2D; Linked Data; Agent-Based modelling.**

## I. INTRODUCTION

For the last two decades, individuals are in the center of research social and geographical systems research [1]. Networks and interactions of individual entities, called agents, contribute for the emergence of the system's behavior. Agent-based models (ABM) have become an efficient technique to simulate complex systems. The popularity of the field began to increase, leading to an increasing number of applications of ABM for Geographical Systems (see [2] or [3] for some examples).

After two decades of development and the creation of an enlarged user community, many challenges still need to be addressed in developing and advancing ABM applicable to geographical systems. Some of these challenges were first presented a decade ago in a publication by [4] and were recently revisited [5]. One of these challenges is Replication and Experiment. Replication of agent-based models is difficult to achieve due to multiple parameters, methods and contexts that pertain to a certain situation [5].

Another challenge is related with the vocabulary used by modellers and programmers to describe the concepts used in their model. The lack of standardization may lead to misunderstanding of the exchange of software metadata. [6] suggested a minimum standard of model description for good modelling practice, namely the provision of source code and an accessible natural language description, and argue for the development of a common standard.

However, as noted by [7], code is often only understandable by other modellers and even this can be problematic if it is badly written and poorly documented. It is only through such activities that we can replicate and experiment with agent-based models. Similar efforts with respect to reproducibility of results are also being called on in the geocomputation.

The ODD protocol [8] (Overview, Design concepts, and Details) was created to define a series of information that should accompany the description of each ABM. However, the first version of the protocol is limited by its ability to describe only one version of the model and does not have a direct relationship with the code for the model. These aspects were improved with the new versions of the protocol, ODD+D (ODD + Decision), with the latest version ODD + 2D (ODD + Decision + Data) having a considerably greater descriptive capacity [9]. In this paper, we will refer to OOD protocol and its different extensions by ODD*. Using ODD*, modellers should fulfill a series of fields to describe models' structure and data, simulations components and agents' rationale. Some questions to answer are provided by the protocol's authors in order to help modellers inform ABM descriptions. Modellers must organize this information into a document that will be used by other experts of the field to understand and replicate the model.

Despite the improvement brought by the odd* protocol, it still remains challenging for modelers to compare two ABM or to process quickly and safely an ABM description in order to reuse it. Ones will still need to manually collect descriptions, interpret them, compare them and adapt the code.

In section 2, we will see how researcher have been working on ODD* to improve models specification. Section 3 will describe our proposal and section 4 will present first results.

## II. Related Work

Different approaches have been followed to reduce the gap between modellers and the community of users interested in replicating, understanding and validating ABM. Early adopters of the ODD protocol have advocated that the more information about an ABM is given to the community, the more transparent the model is. This approach has evolved towards the development of repositories such as CoMSES [10], which is a network with the common goal of improving the way experts develop, share, and use computational modeling in the social and ecological sciences. However, suggestions of researchers [6] have headed towards a minimum standard of model description, namely the provision of source code and an accessible description. Yet, ABM specifications can be found in repositories of models and scientific articles, these specification only remain accessible by manual searches.

In [7], authors proposed an extension to the ODD protocol to build, document, and compare AMB for Coupled human and natural systems (CHANS). They included two new sections a "Model Verification and Validation" section and a "CHANS Characteristic Features" section. Authors also propose a technical development that facilitates CHANS- related agent-based modeling, including the online pseudo-code and preliminary library of reusable modules in Netlogo [11], a multi-agent programmable modeling environment. Authors presented a cross-site comparison in relation to CHANS models include reinforcing the need for standardized modules for CHANS ABMs. Yet, authors do not provide any suggestion on how to store and provide automatic comparisons of cross-sites ABM. Models stored in separate repositories are still hard to search for and compare.

The latest addition to ODD* is ODD+2D with a greater description of data used for the simulations. This new version implied a reorganization of the protocol's fields related to data, which highlighted a crucial aspect of ODD* protocol: the information to provide for the model description vary according to the version of ODD* the author is using to document his model. This point usually implies field removal or adaptation, damaging the development of a pattern on MBA documentation.

Despite efforts promoted to normalize ABMs' description Modelers still need better support for ABMs' specification, comparison and discovery. The development of a common standard remains thus limited to natural language. On the other hand, the analysis and comparison between models stored in such repositories remains a task that can only be performed by users. Different software repositories, software languages and scientific domains denote this information in different ways, which makes it difficult or impossible for tools to work across these different sources without losing valuable information along the way.

## III. Proposal

As stated before, the ODD* protocol is the most consistent proposition to describe ABM. It organizes information of an specific instance of an ABM in a document, according to a specific ODD version. As a document, the ABM description using ODD[a] should also be described with other metadata. Data about authors, date and keywords are essential for the management of models' specifications. On the other hand, computer code has been identified as a key element for the ABM replication and validation, we thus advocate that metadata about code should also be included in ODD* descriptions. We propose in these work to include these two components, document and code metadata, into models specifications described with ODD*. For the last decade different initiatives have led to the development of metadata sets that can describe both document and code. Dublin core [12] for documents and the CodeMeta Project [13], for computer code, are two initiative that are widely used to describe such data. For this work, we will take advantage of both. A subset of Dublin Core will be used to add data to identify and link ODD* specifications to authors and scientific papers. On the other hand, codeMeta metadata will allow to describe code versions and dependencies to facilitate software replication and code analysis.

To address some of the limitations and to enable better use and greater adoption of the ODD* protocol, we developed a framework to enhance the capacity of describing ABM provenance and provide a more flexible analysis and comparison of models. To prevent patterns on MBA documentation we propose a model for the ODD* based on an ontology. This will enable the analysis and reasoning on models components in order to compare models instances. The framework allows ABM users to better manage the version of the ODD* protocol associated with each model. It also allow to describe models authoring and computer code related to the implementation of simulations. Through the platform, MBA descriptions are stored as linked data that can easily be accessed and processed. The extended description is supported by an ontology called ODD* that can be extended according to new versions of the protocol that may be proposed. Figure 1 presents the architecture of the framework that will be detailed in Section III-B.

### A. Domain Model

To develop an ABM documentation model, it is important to provide support for all concepts existing in ODD*. At the present time there are four versions of protocols considered between ODD and ODD+2D. The differences between each versions consist in changes of fields' name, relocation of fields, and expansion of fields.

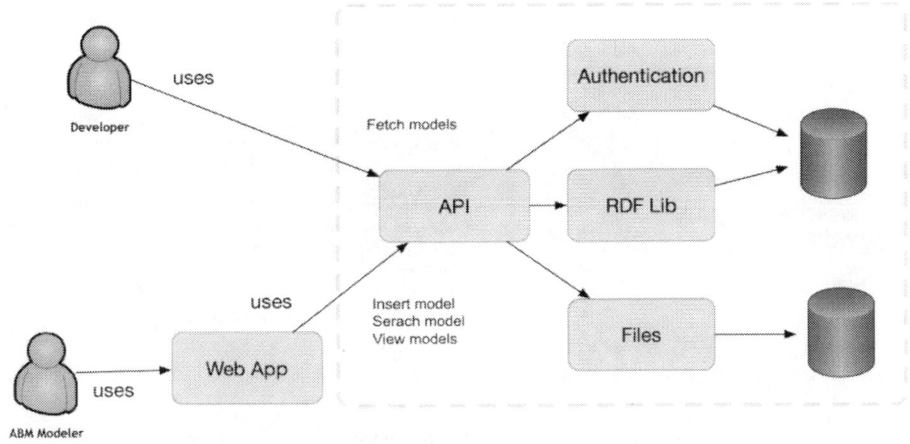


Fig. 1. Architecture of the framework

To provide a support for all the versions of ODD*, it was necessary to map all the concepts and constructs between versions. We used the descriptions of each versions presented in [8], [9], [14], [15]. The mapping process resulted in a feature model partially presented in Figure 2.

The feature model only describes concepts present in the ODD* protocol. Considering that the description of an ABM using the ODD protocol is a document, it is also relevant to provide metadata to describe this resource and provide provenance data. We chose to include a subset of the Dublin Metadata Element Set to achieve that. We added the following attributes from the Dublin Core schema for our domain model: Title; Creator; Contributor; Date; Subject; Language; Source; Rights; Publisher; Bibliographic Resource; and Identifier.

Another important concept included in the ODD* ontology is the the information regarding computer code. We incorporated the following fields from the CodeMeta schema to our model: URL; Maintainer; Version; Reference Publication; Programming Language; File Format; File Size; License; and Read Me.

The ontology which aggregates ODD* concepts, including selected fields from Dublin Core and CodeMeta, is presented in Figure 3.

It defines a structure of components that can be used and combined to build a description of an ABM, according to a certain version of the ODD protocol.

### B. ODD* as linked data

Linked Data is structured data linked to other data in order to create a larger set of data that can be used through semantic queries. It uses Web standards such as URIs, HTTP and RDF format to identify a resource object in the internet. The possibility to structure ODD* components as linked data offers the opportunity to define resources that can be accessed, analyzed and manipulated by both human and machines. For these reasons, we decided to represent and store ABMs as Linked Data.

### C. Framework

The framework is composed by a Web application that can be used by users to insert, search and visualize ABMs. A REST API manages the access to models repository that are store in a SQL Database after being transformed to RDF Format using the RDFLib Library. In the actual version of the application, some of the models' data are stored as files. This is the case for tabular data and images. Other application can also access models stored in the framework taking advantage of the API included in the framework.

The Web application provides access for users without any special requirement on the software use. This Web client encapsulate a didactic approach to explain to users how the model are organized and combined, according to ODD versions. It uses colors to explain the transition between protocol versions and facilitate models creation and visualization. The emphasis have been directed towards performance reading ease, allowing different screen sizes and navigation using keyboard keys.

To provide machine access, developers access the API, allowing access to models components according to the ontological model.

## IV. FIRST RESULTS

After the implementation of all components, we chose to test the usability of the Web application before any other aspect of the platform. We want to ensure that users are able to create and search for models using the Web application. The objective of the test are to verify how easy it is to create a new model, without errors, and store it using the Web application. We also want to understand if users could search, read and analyze a model stored in the platform. To evaluate the usability, a group of students from Computer Science and Software Engineer courses from bachelor and master degrees will be invited to use the application and execute two different tasks. A first group will be assigned the task to insert an ABM description and the second group will be assigned the task to retrieve information from a model already existing in the database. For the test,

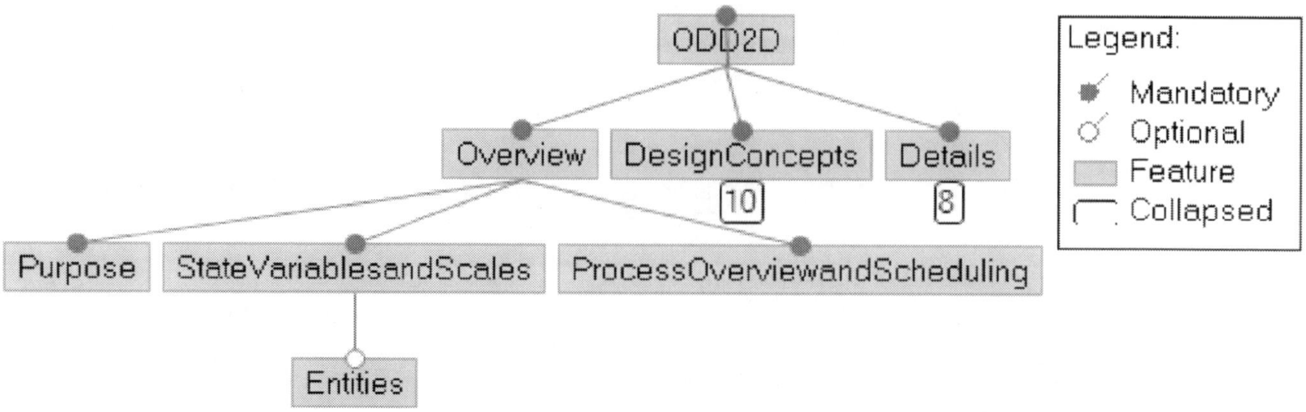


Fig. 2. Partial view of the feature model for ODD* protocol.

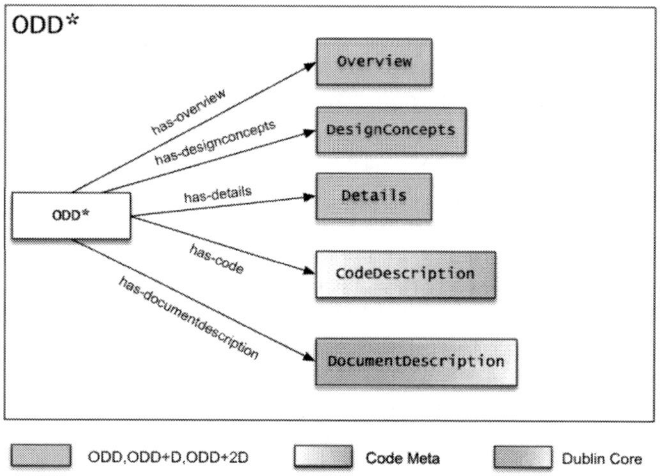


Fig. 3. Main concepts of ODD* Ontology.

we will use the ODD description of an ABM about Urgent Diffusion in Social Media, published by [16]. For both tests, the objectives of the experience will be clearly explained and some basic concepts about ABM will be introduced before start.

## V. Conclusions and Future Work

In this paper, we presented a project that aims at improving the documentation of ABM using the ODD* protocol. We introduced a framework, based on an ontology, to create and store ABM specifications available as Linked Data. This framework will contribute to enhance models provenance and manipulation to perform more complex tasks on those specifications. In addition, we presented a Web application that enables the creation, storage and retrieval of ABMs. The platform will be tasted to verify if the Web application can be used efficiently to analyze and understand ABMs based on their ODD descriptions. Future work will focus on testing the Web Application with experts from the domain in order to evaluate the utility of our approach. Tests will also be performed on the API in order to evaluate its usability by programmers.

## References

[1] M. Batty, *The New Science of Cities*. The MIT Press, 2013.
[2] A. J. Heppenstall, A. T. Crooks, L. M. See, and M. Batty, *Agent-based models of geographical systems*. 2012.
[3] J. Rocha, *Multi-agent Systems*. InTech, sep 2017.
[4] A. Crooks, C. Castle, and M. Batty, "Key challenges in agent-based modelling for geo-spatial simulation," *Computers, Environment and Urban Systems*, vol. 32, pp. 417–430, nov 2008.
[5] A. J. J. Heppenstall, A. Crooks, N. Malleson, E. Manley, J. Ge, and M. Batty, "Agent-based Models for Geographical Systems: A Review." 2019.
[6] B. Müller *et al.*, "Standardised and transparent model descriptions for agent-based models: Current status and prospects," *Environmental Modelling & Software*, vol. 55, pp. 156–163, may 2014.
[7] L. An, A. Zvoleff, J. Liu, and W. Axinn, "Agent-Based Modeling in Coupled Human and Natural Systems (CHANS): Lessons from a Comparative Analysis," *Annals of the Association of American Geographers*, vol. 104, pp. 723–745, jul 2014.
[8] V. Grimm *et al.*, "A standard protocol for describing individual-based and agent-based models," *Ecological Modelling*, vol. 198, pp. 115–126, sep 2006.
[9] A. Laatabi, N. Marilleau, T. Nguyen-Huu, H. Hbid, and M. A. Babram, "ODD+2D: An ODD based protocol for mapping data to empirical ABMs," *JASSS*, vol. 21, no. 2, 2018.
[10] "Comses network - abm." https://www.comses.net/, 2021. Accessed: 2021-01-29.
[11] "Netlogo." https://ccl.northwestern.edu/netlogo/, 2021. Accessed: 2021-01-29.
[12] D. Hillmann, "Using Dublin Core," 2008.
[13] "codemeta." https://codemeta.github.io/, 2021. Accessed: 2021-01-29.
[14] V. Grimm, U. Berger, D. L. DeAngelis, J. G. Polhill, J. Giske, and S. F. Railsback, "The ODD protocol: A review and first update," *Ecological Modelling*, vol. 221, pp. 2760–2768, nov 2010.
[15] B. Müller *et al.*, "Describing human decisions in agent-based models – odd + d, an extension of the odd protocol," *Environmental Modelling & Software*, vol. 48, pp. 37 – 48, 2013.
[16] W. Rand, J. Herrmann, B. Schein, and N. Vodopivec, "An agent-based model of urgent diffusion in social media," *Journal of Artificial Societies and Social Simulation*, vol. 18, no. 2, p. 1, 2015.

# Simulation of the Clinical Interactions Among COPD Patients and Healthcare Staff in the Emergency Department

1st Mohsen Hallaj Asghar
*Dept. of computer architecture and operating system Autonomous University of Barcelona*
*Barcelona, Spain*
*mohsenhallaj62@gmail.com*

2nd Alex Vicente Villalba
*Nursing School, Gimbernat University*
*Autonomous University of Barcelona*
Barcelona, Spain
alejandro.vicente@eug.es

3rd Alvaro Wong
*Dept. of computer architecture and operating system Autonomous University of Barcelona*
*Barcelona, Spain*
*alvaro.wong@uab.es*

4th Dolores Rexachs
*Dept. of computer architecture and operating system Autonomous University of Barcelona*
*Barcelona, Spain*
*dolores.rexachs@uab.es*

5th Emilio Luque
*Dept. of computer architecture and operating system Autonomous University of Barcelona*
*Barcelona, Spain*
*emilio.luque@uab.es*

***Abstract*—Chronic Obstructive Pulmonary Disease (COPD) has become a major and critical cause of death among the elderly with a history of acute pulmonary exacerbation. The aim of this research is twofold: on the one hand to create a conceptual and computational model of the evolution of COPD patients in treatment at the Emergency Department (ED) and, on the other hand, to model the process of evaluation, diagnosis and intervention, made by the ED nurses and doctors responsible for the treatment of COPD patients. The base of simulation we propose to use is the Probabilistic Finite-State Machines method, which applies the training method for the evolution of COPD patients. This method is in front of patient as an actions/treatment applied by healthcare personnel. In addition, the Delphi method applies expert method reasoning for the decision making process carried out by healthcare staff, in order to decide the treatment to be applied to the COPD patients.**

***Index Terms*—Simulation Model, COPD Patient, Pathologies, Emergency Department (ED), Emergency Medical Service (EMS)**

## I. INTRODUCTION

In recent decades, governments / academics have been developing applied technology for treating disease progression to control the prevalence of chronic diseases in order to improve public health and increase life expectancy in developed countries. COPD, with its inherent characteristics and gradual lifelong development, reduces independence, culminating in a high level of dependency on self-care activities in its later stage. The patient's low skill in controlling the disease to preserve their autonomy often leads to exacerbation's and subsequent readmissions, which are more common in older age groups. The world currently has a progressively ageing population. The number of the aged between 40-100+ is 2.87B. In Spain, the ageing process resulting from ever longer life spans has been particularly rapid, to the extent that the number of people aged over 65 has doubled in the space of less than 30 years [1].As populations age and live longer, chronic diseases become increasingly prevalent. Elderly persons with complex pathologies and conditions will require multiple sources of care to meet their healthcare needs. They will need to depend on healthcare decision systems that can adequately address and reliably serve their multiple needs. In this case, Emergency Decision Making (EDM) is an effective way to deal with any emergency situation, insomuch as it plays an alleviating role for the loss of attributes and lives caused by an emergency event. Unexpectedly, those responsible for environmental areas have many unplanned decisions and activities to carry out, which has recently been under the attention of governments and academics. When an environmental emergency occurs, EDM plays a key role in mitigating the loss of life and property facing two critical factors: lack of information and time pressure. EDM has become a remarkable topic in recent years. Normally people make decisions based on the potential value of losses and gains. Normally loss and gain properties in emergency situation distinguishing by reference point which the outcome is respect with attributes. In reference to Kahneman and Tversky, psychological behaviors of decision makers show risk-taking tendencies for profit and risk-taking tendencies for losses, meaning that people are more sensitive to losses that have equal profits [2]. To measure the amount of profit and loss, the S-value function is presented in landscape theory, as shown in Figure 1.

In addition, Kahneman and Tversky's law demonstrated value function where $x$ demonstrated the gains with the shape of $x \geq 0$ and losses with the shape of $x < 0$ also $\alpha$ and $\beta$ are the key point of the gains and losses which are respectively $0 \leq \alpha, \beta \leq 1$ (Equation 1). $\lambda$ is the risk parameter which represents the a characteristic. In this equation, the values of $\alpha, \beta$ and $\lambda$ are equal to 1 [2].

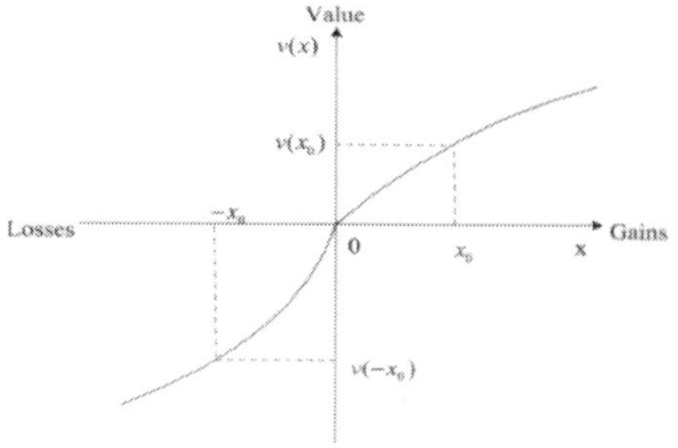


Fig. 1. S-shape diagram as value function according to Kahneman and versky's law.

$$v(x) = \begin{Bmatrix} x^{a}, & x \geq 0 \\ -\lambda(-x)^{\beta}, & x < 0 \end{Bmatrix} \quad (1)$$

In Spain, the elderly population is increasing rapidly. Simultaneously, the number of COPD patients will continue to rise. So, a large number of COPD patients refers to the medical wards. Reciprocally in EMS and ED, which are highly responsible for managing, caring for treating COPD patients, two major problems are being faced: the first is "resources", which are very limited in the field of therapy and the second is the "cost function", which requires more financial resources. The outcome of those challenges impact on COPD patients' needs as well as on the search for a higher quality of services (QoS). From our point of view, we need to consider two problems: the first is the need for correct time, witch limited in ED and Decision Making capability of the healthcare staff in charge of COPD patients. The second is the need for specific training to acquire these skills. Here is the exact point of problem dominating other services.

This research proposed research objectives in II, the regarding the COPD patients, Exacerbation the COPD. Section III presents the related work. Section IV introduces the decision making support system which is the main part of this article, in order to training nurses and student and help the healthcare personnel to take immediate decisions in front of the patient with high accuracy. The section V, deals with the simulation scenario in the emergency department and nursing activity in an emergency box (triage). Finally, in section VI, we present our conclusion and future work.

## II. Research Objectives

The objective of our research proposal is divided into the two important problems described below: 1) The Conceptual Model, which is concerned with the evolution of the COPD patient in the ED, defining several variables which are most relevant to our conceptual model, such as heart rate, blood pressure, skin color (Cyanosis), etc. These variables make up the condition of the COPD patient (cyanosis, accessory muscle, heart rate, oxygen saturation, pulmonary auscultation, x-ray, sputum, temperature, ECG and arterial blood gas).
2) The Computational Model, which is for the decision making carried out by the healthcare staff in training. The target is for training and/or improving the nurse/student's knowledge in a critical situation, such as in an emergency box, real patient analysis feedback from the simulator, improving the medical knowledge of a junior student, nurse or doctor without much experience in EMS in an ED [3]. For the development of the simulator, the Iterative Spiral Development Model (IDMS) will be followed [4]. Considering the importance for advanced training for healthcare staff working in emergency departments as well as the significance of COPD disease, we propose the design and implementation of a complex system where it would be possible to decide and virtually apply the selected treatment for COPD patients in the ED. This is carried out in two different ways: The first one interactive, for the healthcare staff in training (Area A in Figure 2). The second one involving an automatic decision- making process (an expert and experienced healthcare staff simulator), based on the cooperation of different sources of knowledge (Expert doctors and nurses' knowledge, scientific publications, medical guides) (Area B in Figure 2).

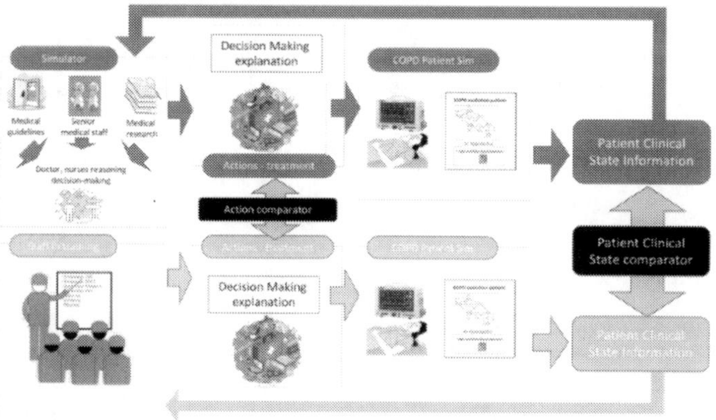


Fig. 2. Decision Making Support System.

## III. Related Work

Simulation can help us to quantify our model and what we design; we can evaluate our system numerically and it even enables us to reevaluate the system after we obtain feedback from of it. As we work with a conceptual model regarding the COPD patient, we have possibility of considering probabilities in all matters [5]. Clinical simulation is a participant-centered learning technique or method offering better curves than classical learning. Thus, the main limitation for its generalized application is the high cost derived from training in teaching methodology, infrastructure, and the excess time by participants in each clinical activity. On the other hand, computational simulation is a genre that aids student self-evaluation, providing feedback in real-time [3]. This method can carry out simulations at any time and place without a teacher on site, thanks to the possibility of sending messages throughout. The simulation will design for specific COPD patients and our research defines the other exacerbation pathologies which can cause and severity of the COPD pathology as an extensible system. COPD can occur as a result of two matters (Environmental and Genetical). The

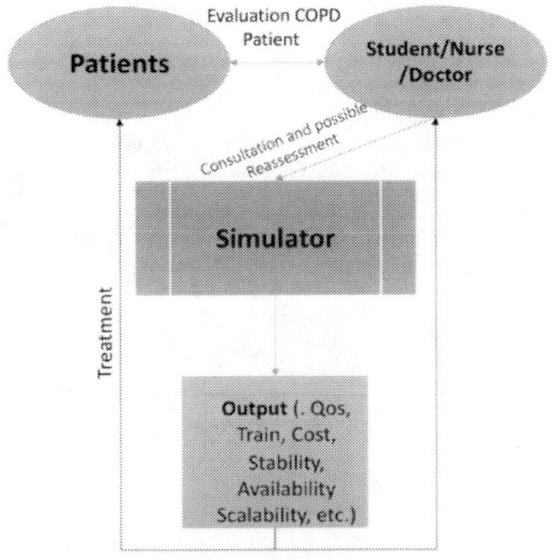


Fig. 3. Evaluation COPD Patient.

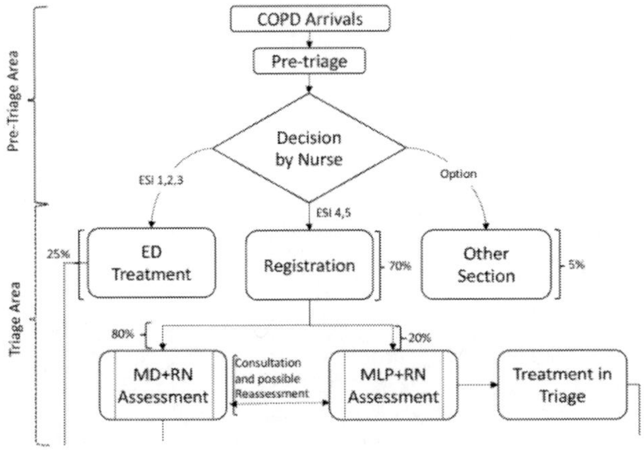


Fig. 4. Pre-Triage and Triage areas.

environmental factor include (defensive cell alternation, alternation anti protease and alternation in the cell that repair the lung). the environmental factor such as (smoking, air pollution and Lung irritants) are a pre-existing diseases background. Our intelligent system can be adopted to all these pathologies and the condition of the healthcare artificial system requirements and regarding the other pathologies as future research work. Figure 3 below shows the connectivity and hierarchy of the target research. The key point of the simulation can be the patient's evaluation, which captured and gathered by the nurse at the level of entry in the ED such as Heart Rate: (59, 60-99, 100), Breath Rate: (11, 12-19, 20) Oxygen Saturation: (80, 81-89, 90-95, 95), Temperature: (36-37.4, 37.5-37.9,38). This data departure to the simulator and user in front of the simulation system can learn and used in cooperation with a comprehensive data base, which regards the patient's various variables and can assist simulation to achieve better decision-taking for the COPD patient's treatment.

In short, a learning process which facilitates online training for both students and professionals is a unique idea which is intended to design a training simulator for students/professionals which can further enhance the learning curve. It also takes into account the fact that today we are living in a pandemic where capacity limitations, mobility, etc. are moving academic training towards a more digitized environment given that clinical simulation is affected by the difficulty of carrying it out.

## IV. Decision Making Support System in ED

The objective of the proposed" Decision-Making Support System" is to simulate the technical behavior of the experienced (highly-trained) healthcare staff of the Emergency Department (doctors/nurses), for the diagnosis and treatment of COPD patients. Our "Decision-Making Support System" is an Expert System (ES) designed with the abilities to reason and think like experienced healthcare staff, using rules, in the diagnosis and treatment of COPD patients. As an Expert System, in our" Decision-Making Support System" we can identify the following main components:

- Knowledge Base
- Inference Engine
- Explanation Facility

The Knowledge Base includes and integrates different sources of knowledge, as well as experience of doctors and nurses, COPD related scientific publications and COPD medical guides.

## V. Proposed Method and Simulation

This section introduces a new simulation scenario based on a proposed theory that can consider decision, triage area, simulation area and treatment area. Pre-triage and Triage areas are shown in Figure 4. Whenever the COPD patient arrives in the Pre-triage area, the duty of Triage Nurse (TN) is to classify the patient into one of five levels of the Emergency Severity Index (ESI), depending on pathology exacerbation [5]. The TN and Medical Doctor (MD) then fully reassess the treatment for the patient. In the simulation area, the base information to simulate will be the patient evaluation data taken on arrival at the ED.

This simulation has two critical aspects in relation to the training part and the expert part. Figure 5 shows the simulation area and the treatment area in the ED.

**Training Part**: the Triage Nurse (TN) has to classify the patient into one of five ESI levels, depending on the pathology's exacerbation [6]. In this section there can be active/interactive COPD patient simulator. This activity is based on the conceptual model formed by:

**Input:** patient condition / Actions – treatment.

**Output:** patient condition after Actions-treatment.

**Operation:** Evolution of the patient's condition.

**Expert Part:** We propose using a Rule Based Approach for modeling the patient's condition analysis and the decision process for the treatment to be applied, the reasoning for the decision making process of the healthcare staff, for deciding/elaborating the actions/treatment applied to the COPD patients. The simulation is based on the "Delphi method" for "integrating" the expert's knowledge. Whenever the user has

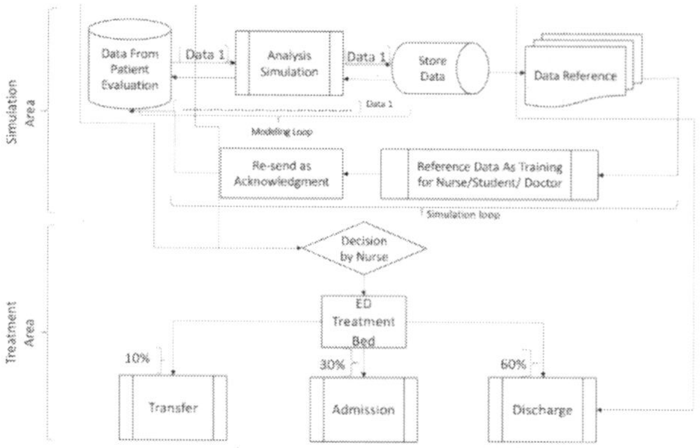


Fig. 5. Simulation and Treatment Area.

any doubt, they can use the data reference as a simulation loop. The data can be transferred as a pull notification. The Input variable of the simulation is the patient's clinical condition information and the output can be actions/ treatment, whose operation is based on the "Data base knowledge", processing the "Input" to generate the "Output".

## VI. Conclusion and Future Work

This research is based on the conceptual model (Qualitative) and the computational model (Quantitative) which explores the conditions for the implementation of simulating, based on COPD intervention. As initial work, and to guarantee the suggested model runs well, implementing a computational model in the near future. In addition to this, we would implement the conceptual model in order to generate a model as complex and as realistic as possible, in a long term professional period, we would use such a simulator to help and improve the quality of the medical services, in order to enhance student/nurse knowledge. This research could have an interesting potential in gathering/connecting some pathologies relevant to COPD and testing by healthcare professionals for stability, scalability and reliability of the system.

## Acknowledgment

This research has been supported by the Agencia Estatal de Investigacion (AEI), Spain and the Fondo Europeo de Desarrollo Regional (FEDER) UE, under contracts TIN2017-84875-P and PID2020-112496GB-I00 and partially funded by the Fundacion Escuelas Universitarias Gimbernat (EUG).

## References

[1] "Comunidad de madrid, canarias, illes balears, región de murcia and andalucía (statistics national institute) 28 october 2014." [Online]. Available: https://www.ine.es/prensa/np870.pdf

[2] D. Kahneman and A. Tversky, "Prospect Theory: An Analysis of Decision under Risk," *Econometrica*, vol. 47, no. 2, pp. 263–291, March 1979. [Online]. Available: https://ideas.repec.org/a/ecm/emetrp/v47y1979i2p263-91.html

[3] A. Vicente-Villalba, M. Antonin, D. Rexachs, and E. Luque, "A reactive "in silico" simulation for theoretical learning clinical skills and decision-making," vol. 1, pp. 3–7, 11/2019 2019. [Online]. Available: http://www.thinkmind.org/index.php?view=article&articleid=simul_2019_1_20_50013

[4] K. Becker, "Learning by doing, a comprehensive guide to simulations, computer games, and pedagogy in e-learning and other educational experiences, 2005. by clark aldrich." *The Canadian Journal of Learning and Technology*, vol. 31, pp. 105–108, 01 2005.

[5] M. Hallaj, A. Vicente-Villalba, A. Wong, D. Rexachs, and E. Luque, "Modelling and simulation of the copd patient and clinical staff in the emergency department (ed)," *Short Papers of the 9th Conference on Cloud Computing Conference, Big Data Emerging Topics, JCCBDET21*, pp. 59–62, 2021.

[6] E. MacDonald-Nethercott, S. Richter, A. Boyle, and I. Higginson, "What should be done to reduce emergency department crowding? – a delphi study," *Emergency Medicine Journal*, vol. 33, pp. 914.1–914, 12 2016.